SONG OF SONGS

Brazos Theological Commentary on the Bible

Series Editors

R. R. Reno, General Editor
Creighton University
Omaha, Nebraska

Robert W. Jenson
Center of Theological Inquiry
Princeton, New Jersey

Robert Louis Wilken
University of Virginia
Charlottesville, Virginia

Ephraim Radner
Wycliffe College
Toronto, Ontario

Michael Root
Lutheran Theological Southern Seminary
Columbia, South Carolina

George Sumner
Wycliffe College
Toronto, Ontario

SONG OF SONGS

PAUL J. GRIFFITHS

Brazos Press
a division of Baker Publishing Group
Grand Rapids, Michigan

© 2011 by Paul J. Griffiths

Published by Brazos Press
a division of Baker Publishing Group
P.O. Box 6287, Grand Rapids, MI 49516-6287
www.brazospress.com

Printed in the United States of America

Library of Congress Cataloging-in-Publication Data
Griffiths, Paul J.
    Song of Songs / Paul J. Griffiths.
       p.   cm. — (Brazos theological commentary on the Bible)
    Includes bibliographical references and index.
    ISBN 978-1-58743-135-7 (cloth)
    1. Bible. O. T. Song of Solomon—Commentaries. I. Title.
BS1485.53.G74 2011
223′.9077—dc22   2010040459

Unless otherwise indicated, scripture quotations are translated by the author from *Nova Vulgata Bibliorum Sacrorum Editio* (Rome: Libreria Editrice Vaticana, 1998).

11   12   13   14   15   16   17   7   6   5   4   3   2   1

I dedicate this book to my grandchildren,
Ralph Nayo and Tessa Nayo:
may they grow up to be good lovers

CONTENTS

SERIES PREFACE

Near the beginning of his treatise against Gnostic interpretations of the Bible, *Against the Heresies*, Irenaeus observes that Scripture is like a great mosaic depicting a handsome king. It is as if we were owners of a villa in Gaul who had ordered a mosaic from Rome. It arrives, and the beautifully colored tiles need to be taken out of their packaging and put into proper order according to the plan of the artist. The difficulty, of course, is that Scripture provides us with the individual pieces, but the order and sequence of various elements are not obvious. The Bible does not come with instructions that would allow interpreters to simply place verses, episodes, images, and parables in order as a worker might follow a schematic drawing in assembling the pieces to depict the handsome king. The mosaic must be puzzled out. This is precisely the work of scriptural interpretation.

Origen has his own image to express the difficulty of working out the proper approach to reading the Bible. When preparing to offer a commentary on the Psalms he tells of a tradition handed down to him by his Hebrew teacher:

> The Hebrew said that the whole divinely inspired Scripture may be likened, because of its obscurity, to many locked rooms in our house. By each room is placed a key, but not the one that corresponds to it, so that the keys are scattered about beside the rooms, none of them matching the room by which it is placed. It is a difficult task to find the keys and match them to the rooms that they can open. We therefore know the Scriptures that are obscure only by taking the points of departure for understanding them from another place because they have their interpretive principle scattered among them.[1]

1. Fragment from the preface to *Commentary on Psalms 1–25*, preserved in the *Philokalia* (trans. Joseph W. Trigg; London: Routledge, 1998), 70–71.

As is the case for Irenaeus, scriptural interpretation is not purely local. The key in Genesis may best fit the door of Isaiah, which in turn opens up the meaning of Matthew. The mosaic must be put together with an eye toward the overall plan.

Irenaeus, Origen, and the great cloud of premodern biblical interpreters assumed that puzzling out the mosaic of Scripture must be a communal project. The Bible is vast, heterogeneous, full of confusing passages and obscure words, and difficult to understand. Only a fool would imagine that he or she could work out solutions alone. The way forward must rely upon a tradition of reading that Irenaeus reports has been passed on as the rule or canon of truth that functions as a confession of faith. "Anyone," he says, "who keeps unchangeable in himself the rule of truth received through baptism will recognize the names and sayings and parables of the scriptures."[2] Modern scholars debate the content of the rule on which Irenaeus relies and commends, not the least because the terms and formulations Irenaeus himself uses shift and slide. Nonetheless, Irenaeus assumes that there is a body of apostolic doctrine sustained by a tradition of teaching in the church. This doctrine provides the clarifying principles that guide exegetical judgment toward a coherent overall reading of Scripture as a unified witness. Doctrine, then, is the schematic drawing that will allow the reader to organize the vast heterogeneity of the words, images, and stories of the Bible into a readable, coherent whole. It is the rule that guides us toward the proper matching of keys to doors.

If self-consciousness about the role of history in shaping human consciousness makes modern historical-critical study critical, then what makes modern study of the Bible modern is the consensus that classical Christian doctrine distorts interpretive understanding. Benjamin Jowett, the influential nineteenth-century English classical scholar, is representative. In his programmatic essay "On the Interpretation of Scripture," he exhorts the biblical reader to disengage from doctrine and break its hold over the interpretive imagination. "The simple words of that book," writes Jowett of the modern reader, "he tries to preserve absolutely pure from the refinements or distinctions of later times." The modern interpreter wishes to "clear away the remains of dogmas, systems, controversies, which are encrusted upon" the words of Scripture. The disciplines of close philological analysis "would enable us to separate the elements of doctrine and tradition with which the meaning of Scripture is encumbered in our own day."[3] The lens of understanding must be wiped clear of the hazy and distorting film of doctrine.

Postmodernity, in turn, has encouraged us to criticize the critics. Jowett imagined that when he wiped away doctrine he would encounter the biblical text in its purity and uncover what he called "the original spirit and intention of the authors."[4] We are not now so sanguine, and the postmodern mind thinks

---

2. *Against the Heretics* 9.4.
3. Benjamin Jowett, "On the Interpretation of Scripture," in *Essays and Reviews* (London: Parker, 1860), 338–39.
4. Ibid., 340.

interpretive frameworks inevitable. Nonetheless, we tend to remain modern in at least one sense. We read Athanasius and think him stage-managing the diversity of Scripture to support his positions against the Arians. We read Bernard of Clairvaux and assume that his monastic ideals structure his reading of the Song of Songs. In the wake of the Reformation, we can see how the doctrinal divisions of the time shaped biblical interpretation. Luther famously described the Epistle of James as a "strawy letter," for, as he said, "it has nothing of the nature of the Gospel about it."[5] In these and many other instances, often written in the heat of ecclesiastical controversy or out of the passion of ascetic commitment, we tend to think Jowett correct: doctrine is a distorting film on the lens of understanding.

However, is what we commonly think actually the case? Are readers naturally perceptive? Do we have an unblemished, reliable aptitude for the divine? Have we no need for disciplines of vision? Do our attention and judgment need to be trained, especially as we seek to read Scripture as the living word of God? According to Augustine, we all struggle to journey toward God, who is our rest and peace. Yet our vision is darkened and the fetters of worldly habit corrupt our judgment. We need training and instruction in order to cleanse our minds so that we might find our way toward God.[6] To this end, "the whole temporal dispensation was made by divine Providence for our salvation."[7] The covenant with Israel, the coming of Christ, the gathering of the nations into the church—all these things are gathered up into the rule of faith, and they guide the vision and form of the soul toward the end of fellowship with God. In Augustine's view, the reading of Scripture both contributes to and benefits from this divine pedagogy. With countless variations in both exegetical conclusions and theological frameworks, the same pedagogy of a doctrinally ruled reading of Scripture characterizes the broad sweep of the Christian tradition from Gregory the Great through Bernard and Bonaventure, continuing across Reformation differences in both John Calvin and Cornelius Lapide, Patrick Henry and Bishop Bossuet, and on to more recent figures such as Karl Barth and Hans Urs von Balthasar.

Is doctrine, then, not a moldering scrim of antique prejudice obscuring the Bible, but instead a clarifying agent, an enduring tradition of theological judgments that amplifies the living voice of Scripture? And what of the scholarly dispassion advocated by Jowett? Is a noncommitted reading, an interpretation unprejudiced, the way toward objectivity, or does it simply invite the languid intellectual apathy that stands aside to make room for the false truism and easy answers of the age?

This series of biblical commentaries was born out of the conviction that dogma clarifies rather than obscures. The Brazos Theological Commentary on the Bible advances upon the assumption that the Nicene tradition, in all its diversity and

---

5. *Luther's Works*, vol. 35 (ed. E. Theodore Bachmann; Philadelphia: Fortress, 1959), 362.
6. *On Christian Doctrine* 1.10.
7. *On Christian Doctrine* 1.35.

controversy, provides the proper basis for the interpretation of the Bible as Christian Scripture. God the Father Almighty, who sends his only begotten Son to die for us and for our salvation and who raises the crucified Son in the power of the Holy Spirit so that the baptized may be joined in one body—faith in *this* God with *this* vocation of love for the world is the lens through which to view the heterogeneity and particularity of the biblical texts. Doctrine, then, is not a moldering scrim of antique prejudice obscuring the meaning of the Bible. It is a crucial aspect of the divine pedagogy, a clarifying agent for our minds fogged by self-deceptions, a challenge to our languid intellectual apathy that will too often rest in false truisms and the easy spiritual nostrums of the present age rather than search more deeply and widely for the dispersed keys to the many doors of Scripture.

For this reason, the commentators in this series have not been chosen because of their historical or philological expertise. In the main, they are not biblical scholars in the conventional, modern sense of the term. Instead, the commentators were chosen because of their knowledge of and expertise in using the Christian doctrinal tradition. They are qualified by virtue of the doctrinal formation of their mental habits, for it is the conceit of this series of biblical commentaries that theological training in the Nicene tradition prepares one for biblical interpretation, and thus it is to theologians and not biblical scholars that we have turned. "War is too important," it has been said, "to leave to the generals."

We do hope, however, that readers do not draw the wrong impression. The Nicene tradition does not provide a set formula for the solution of exegetical problems. The great tradition of Christian doctrine was not transcribed, bound in folio, and issued in an official, critical edition. We have the Niceno-Constantinopolitan Creed, used for centuries in many traditions of Christian worship. We have ancient baptismal affirmations of faith. The Chalcedonian definition and the creeds and canons of other church councils have their places in official church documents. Yet the rule of faith cannot be limited to a specific set of words, sentences, and creeds. It is instead a pervasive habit of thought, the animating culture of the church in its intellectual aspect. As Augustine observed, commenting on Jeremiah 31:33, "The creed is learned by listening; it is written, not on stone tablets nor on any material, but on the heart."[8] This is why Irenaeus is able to appeal to the rule of faith more than a century before the first ecumenical council, and this is why we need not itemize the contents of the Nicene tradition in order to appeal to its potency and role in the work of interpretation.

Because doctrine is intrinsically fluid on the margins and most powerful as a habit of mind rather than a list of propositions, this commentary series cannot settle difficult questions of method and content at the outset. The editors of the series impose no particular method of doctrinal interpretation. We cannot say in advance how doctrine helps the Christian reader assemble the mosaic of Scripture. We have no clear answer to the question of whether exegesis guided by

8. *Sermon* 212.2.

doctrine is antithetical to or compatible with the now-old modern methods of historical-critical inquiry. Truth—historical, mathematical, or doctrinal—knows no contradiction. But method is a discipline of vision and judgment, and we cannot know in advance what aspects of historical-critical inquiry are functions of modernism that shape the soul to be at odds with Christian discipline. Still further, the editors do not hold the commentators to any particular hermeneutical theory that specifies how to define the plain sense of Scripture—or the role this plain sense should play in interpretation. Here the commentary series is tentative and exploratory.

Can we proceed in any other way? European and North American intellectual culture has been de-Christianized. The effect has not been a cessation of Christian activity. Theological work continues. Sermons are preached. Biblical scholars turn out monographs. Church leaders have meetings. But each dimension of a formerly unified Christian practice now tends to function independently. It is as if a weakened army had been fragmented, and various corps had retreated to isolated fortresses in order to survive. Theology has lost its competence in exegesis. Scripture scholars function with minimal theological training. Each decade finds new theories of preaching to cover the nakedness of seminary training that provides theology without exegesis and exegesis without theology.

Not the least of the causes of the fragmentation of Christian intellectual practice has been the divisions of the church. Since the Reformation, the role of the rule of faith in interpretation has been obscured by polemics and counterpolemics about *sola scriptura* and the necessity of a magisterial teaching authority. The Brazos Theological Commentary on the Bible series is deliberately ecumenical in scope, because the editors are convinced that early church fathers were correct: church doctrine does not compete with Scripture in a limited economy of epistemic authority. We wish to encourage unashamedly dogmatic interpretation of Scripture, confident that the concrete consequences of such a reading will cast far more light on the great divisive questions of the Reformation than either reengaging in old theological polemics or chasing the fantasy of a pure exegesis that will somehow adjudicate between competing theological positions. You shall know the truth of doctrine by its interpretive fruits, and therefore in hopes of contributing to the unity of the church, we have deliberately chosen a wide range of theologians whose commitment to doctrine will allow readers to see real interpretive consequences rather than the shadow boxing of theological concepts.

Brazos Theological Commentary on the Bible has no dog in the current translation fights, and we endorse a textual ecumenism that parallels our diversity of ecclesial backgrounds. We do not impose the thankfully modest inclusive-language agenda of the New Revised Standard Version, nor do we insist upon the glories of the Authorized Version, nor do we require our commentators to create a new translation. In our communal worship, in our private devotions, in our theological scholarship, we use a range of scriptural translations. Precisely as Scripture—a living, functioning text in the present life of faith—the Bible is not semantically fixed. Only a modernist, literalist hermeneutic could imagine that this modest fluidity is a liability. Philological precision and stability is a consequence of, not a basis for, exegesis. Judgments about the meaning of a text fix its literal sense, not the other way around. As a result, readers should expect an eclectic use of biblical translations, both across the different volumes of the series and within individual commentaries.

We cannot speak for contemporary biblical scholars, but as theologians we know that we have long been trained to defend our fortresses of theological concepts and formulations. And we have forgotten the skills of interpretation. Like stroke victims, we must rehabilitate our exegetical imaginations, and there are likely to be different strategies of recovery. Readers should expect this reconstructive—not reactionary—series to provide them with experiments in postcritical doctrinal interpretation, not commentaries written according to the settled principles of a well-functioning tradition. Some commentators will follow classical typological and allegorical readings from the premodern tradition; others will draw on contemporary historical study. Some will comment verse by verse; others will highlight passages, even single words that trigger theological analysis of Scripture. No reading strategies are proscribed, no interpretive methods foresworn. The central premise in this commentary series is that doctrine provides structure and cogency to scriptural interpretation. We trust in this premise with the hope that the Nicene tradition can guide us, however imperfectly, diversely, and haltingly, toward a reading of Scripture in which the right keys open the right doors.

R. R. Reno

AUTHOR'S PREFACE

My thanks are due for help with this project to John Cavadini, Nathan Eubank, Theodora Hawksley, Judith Heyhoe, Reinhard Hütter, Nanno Marinatos, Bruce Marshall, Walter Moberly, R. R. Reno, Miguel Romero, and Kavin Rowe.

ABBREVIATIONS

→   indicates a cross-reference to commentary on a Song passage
RSV   Revised Standard Version

Acts	Acts	Isa.	Isaiah
Amos	Amos	Jas.	James
Bar.	Baruch	Jdt.	Judith
1 Chr.	1 Chronicles	Jer.	Jeremiah
2 Chr.	2 Chronicles	Job	Job
Col.	Colossians	Joel	Joel
1 Cor.	1 Corinthians	John	John
2 Cor.	2 Corinthians	1 John	1 John
Dan.	Daniel	2 John	2 John
Deut.	Deuteronomy	3 John	3 John
Eccl.	Ecclesiastes	Jonah	Jonah
Eph.	Ephesians	Josh.	Joshua
Esth.	Esther	Jude	Jude
Exod.	Exodus	Judg.	Judges
Ezek.	Ezekiel	1 Kgs.	1 Kings
Ezra	Ezra	2 Kgs.	2 Kings
Gal.	Galatians	Lam.	Lamentations
Gen.	Genesis	Lev.	Leviticus
Hab.	Habakkuk	Luke	Luke
Hag.	Haggai	1 Macc.	1 Maccabees
Heb.	Hebrews	2 Macc.	2 Maccabees
Hos.	Hosea	Mal.	Malachi

Mark	Mark	Ruth	Ruth
Matt.	Matthew	1 Sam.	1 Samuel
Mic.	Micah	2 Sam.	2 Samuel
Nah.	Nahum	Sir.	Sirach
Neh.	Nehemiah	Song	Song of Songs
Num.	Numbers	1 Thess.	1 Thessalonians
Obad.	Obadiah	2 Thess.	2 Thessalonians
1 Pet.	1 Peter	1 Tim.	1 Timothy
2 Pet.	2 Peter	2 Tim.	2 Timothy
Phil.	Philippians	Titus	Titus
Phlm.	Philemon	Tob.	Tobit
Prov.	Proverbs	Wis.	Wisdom of Solomon
Ps.	Psalms	Zech.	Zechariah
Rev.	Revelation	Zeph.	Zephaniah
Rom.	Romans		

All is Solomon's Song.
I come to my garden, my sister, my bride.
Eat friend, drink and be drunk with love
And every moment I think I'm satisfied
Wakes me to desires I'm dreaming of.
In Solomon's blue curtain a cord of covenant,
A crimson thread until the crimson moment.

—Micheal O'Siadhail, *Love Life*

The Song is a wedding song for the bride and bridegroom: it is a spiritual marriage in which we must live with great purity because Christ has granted to the church and in spirit what his mother had in body: the grace of being both mother and virgin.

—Augustine, Sermon 138

What is love of God? It is the soul's yearning for the Creator, and turning to Him of her own accord, so that she shall cleave to His supernal light . . . and when she realizes the Almighty's infinite power and essential sublimity, she will bow down and prostrate herself before Him in fear, dread and awe, inspired by His power and greatness.

—Rabbi Bahya

For it [the Song] is not a melody that resounds abroad but the very music of the heart; not a trilling on the lips but an inward pulsing of delight; a harmony not of voices but of wills. It is a tune you will not hear in the streets; these notes do not sound where crowds assemble; only the singer hears it and the one to whom he sings—the lover and the beloved.

—Bernard of Clairvaux, Sermon 1

For those who do not know the Virgin, the face of Scripture is obscured.

—Philip of Harvengt, *In Cantica Canticorum*

Only tradition can tell the faithful how to love truly. But only the living God can confirm the quest. Perhaps that is why the seeker cries so longingly, "[Oh] let Him kiss me with the kisses of His mouth!"

—Michael Fishbane, *The Kiss of God*

What was said and done in the Old Testament was ordained and disposed by God with such consummate wisdom, that things past prefigured in a spiritual way those that were to come under the new dispensation of grace. Wherefore the exegete, just as he must search out and expound the literal meaning of the words . . . so also must he do likewise for the spiritual sense, provided it is clearly intended by God.

—Pius XII, *Divino Afflante Spiritu*

INTRODUCTION

Confecting the Song

In contemporary English Bibles, sandwiched between Ecclesiastes and Isaiah, is a short work called sometimes "Song of Songs" and sometimes "Song of Solomon." In this commentary I'll call it simply "(the) Song." This piece of scripture, like most, has a long and complicated history of composition, redaction, edition, translation, commentary, and liturgical use, much of which is no longer accessible to us. "Confection" is a useful summary term for this process: to confect is to make something sweet and beautiful by judicious mixing of ingredients; it may also imply a co-making, an act of making in cooperation with other makers. The confectioner makes sweetmeats; the Catholic priest, it used to be said (the usage is archaic but elegant), cooperates with God and the people of God in the confection of the sacrament of the Mass; and the people of the Lord cooperate with the Lord in the confection of the canon of scripture as a whole and in each of its parts. In the case of the Song the result is unusually sweet, and the confection went roughly as follows.

Long ago, perhaps some time after the return of the Jewish people from exile in Babylon midway through the first millennium before Christ, there began to take shape among the Jews a collection of Hebrew love songs. This collection belongs to the cultural and religious world of the ancient Near East—there are many parallels and echoes in the love poetry of the Egyptians and the Mesopotamians[1]—but it finds its specific location in the Hebrew-using, which is

1. Many modern commentaries on the Song include analyses of ancient love poetry. See especially Michael V. Fox, *The Song of Songs and the Ancient Egyptian Love Songs* (Madison: University of Wisconsin Press, 1985); Othmar Keel, *Das Hohelied*, Zürcher Bibelkommentare AT 18 (Zurich: Theologischer Verlag, 1986); Marvin H. Pope, *Song of Songs: A New Translation with Introduction and Commentary*, Anchor Bible 7C (Garden City, NY: Doubleday, 1977); John Bradley White, *A Study of the Language of Love in the Song of Songs and Ancient Egyptian Poetry* (Missoula, MT:

to say Jewish, part of that world. Gradually, by a long process of compilation and redaction whose details can no longer be known (which does not prevent scholars from attempting to know it), this collection of love songs came to be recognized by Jews as a single literary work associated with the name and reputation of Solomon, though never unambiguously said to be by him. By the time of the Maccabees, in the second century BC (and probably earlier), this Hebrew work was known by the title *Shir hashshirim 'asher lishlomoh* ("The Song of Songs which is Solomon's"), and under that title it was, after some argument, judged by Jews to belong to the Tanakh, the canon of scripture that is approximately equivalent to what Christians call the Old Testament.[2] By the second century AD, this Hebrew work was located firmly among the Writings (Ketubim) within the Tanakh, which is to say among those eleven works that do not belong to the Torah (the five books of Moses) or the Nebiim (the eight prophetic books). There the Hebrew Song remains to this day, a continuing fertile source of commentary and a constant object of study by Jews, as well as at various periods—though certainly not continuously—by Christians, and latterly by pagan scholars as well. But the Hebrew Song was not firmly and finally fixed as a text by Jews until, during the second half of the first millennium AD, the Masoretes (traditionists) supplied vowels in order to fix the pronunciation and meaning of a previously exclusively consonantal text, together with indications as to how the text should be sung and various devices (letter counts, among other things) intended to minimize scribally produced textual change. It is this Masoretic Text, an artifact a little more than a millennium old, that is the living text of the Song for contemporary Jews; it effectively displaced and largely extinguished Hebrew witnesses to earlier states of the Hebrew text,[3] and it is, with very minor modifications, what is printed in contemporary versions of the Hebrew text of the Tanakh and in contemporary Torah scrolls. It is also what is translated under the name "Song of Songs" (or "Song of Solomon") in most English Bibles since the seventeenth century.

Scholars Press, 1978); and Yair Zakovitch, *Das Hohelied*, trans. Dafna Mach (Freiburg im Breisgau: Herder, 2004).

2. "Approximately" because the books are enumerated and divided differently by Jews and Christians. Protestant Old Testaments enumerate thirty-nine books rather than the twenty-four of the Tanakh, but in fact include the same material divided differently; and Catholic and Orthodox Old Testaments enumerate forty-six books because they contain seven books not found in the Jewish and Protestant collections.

3. For discussion of the fragmentary Hebrew manuscripts of the Song found at Qumran, see Roland E. Murphy, *The Song of Songs: A Commentary on the Book of Canticles or the Song of Songs* (Minneapolis: Fortress, 1990), 8; Pope, *Song of Songs*, 21–22. The most useful resource for textual questions about the Song, and for easy reference to variations among the versions, is Giovanni Garbini, *Cantico dei cantici: Testo, traduzione, note e commento* (Brescia: Paideia, 1992). This contains, presented synoptically, the Masoretic Hebrew text (with comments on the Qumran fragments), Septuagint (with comments on other Greek versions, especially Aquila and Theodotion), Vetus Latina version(s), Vulgate, and Syriac.

There is also a Greek Song, provided by the energetic work of Jews and Christians in rendering into Greek states of the Hebrew text sometimes earlier than and often different from that fixed by the Masoretes. This work began in the second, or perhaps the first, century BC, when Jews produced a Greek version of the Song that is now ordinarily classified as belonging to the Septuagint, the Greek version of the entire Tanakh produced by Jews for Jews (but later taken up by Christians) over about two centuries beginning in the mid-third century before Christ.[4] That was only the first of several Greek versions: Origen, working at Alexandria in the third century AD, tabulated three others in addition to the one in the Septuagint,[5] and there may have been more. The earliest among these Greek versions of the Song is, therefore, the earliest complete surviving witness to the work by a long way; it was also the version most commonly used by Christian writers during the first three centuries; and it, like the Masoretic Hebrew text, is part of a living tradition with a long history of commentary and study and liturgical use: Orthodox Christians still treat it as their authoritative text, and commentary upon the Greek Song has been continuous since Origen.

And then there is a Latin Song. Here too, the story is not exactly straightforward. Latin versions of the Song began to be made (probably) in the second century AD, largely (and perhaps exclusively) from one or another of the Greek versions. There were several of these old Latin versions, collectively called *Vetus Latina*, but none of them now survives in anything other than quotations and references in Latin works composed by Christians between the second and fifth centuries AD and in liturgical tropes and formulas.[6] These earlier versions were displaced and largely extinguished by the Latin version made by Jerome, working in Bethlehem at the end of the fourth century. There, in 398, he produced a Latin text of 213 lines written *per cola et commata*, which is to say divided into sense-lines as a help for vocalized reading and understanding, but without other punctuation or division.[7] He called this work *Canticum Canticorum* ("Song of Songs") and

4. On the Septuagint version of the Song, see Jay Treat's translation in Albert Pietersma and Benjamin G. Wright, eds., *A New English Translation of the Septuagint and the Other Greek Translations Traditionally Included under That Title* (New York: Oxford University Press, 2007), 657–61, which enumerates about fifty differences between the Hebrew that may be speculated to have been read by those who produced the Septuagint version of the Song, and the Masoretic Text. The extent to which readers and hearers of the Septuagint were aware that they were reading or hearing a version is an interesting question; for discussion see Marguerite Harl, "La Septante et la pluralité textuelle des écritures: Le témoignage des pères grecs," in *Naissance de la méthode critique*, ed. Françoise Laplanche et al. (Paris: Cerf, 1992), 231–43.

5. Work toward a new critical edition of the surviving fragments of Origen's Hexapla is now under way. For preliminary details, see www.hexapla.org.

6. On the Vetus Latina texts of the Song, see Murphy, *Song of Songs*, 11; E. Ann Matter, *The Voice of My Beloved: The Song of Songs in Western Medieval Christianity* (Philadelphia: University of Pennsylvania Press, 1990), xxxiv–xxxv.

7. Jerome actually says, in his prologue *in libris Salomonis* (he means Proverbs, Ecclesiastes, and the Song), that the work of translating these three books took only three days in total (*Biblia Sacra iuxta Vulgatam Versionem*, 3rd ed., 957)—and since the Song is by a long way the shortest of

included it as part of the canon of scripture and as one of the Solomonic works along with Proverbs and Ecclesiastes—though he was not committed one way or another to Solomonic authorship of the Song. He had before him as he worked at least the following materials: (1) a Hebrew text, which was his primary point of reference and which he thought of himself as translating; (2) at least one of the Greek versions, and perhaps more; and (3) at least one, and probably several, of the Old Latin versions. Jerome's version became the standard—indeed, effectively the only—version used by Western Christian scholars between the fifth century and the sixteenth, which explains its coming to be called the Vulgate, the popular version. The Latin Song, like the rest of the Vulgate, did not pass through a thousand years of scribal transmission and liturgical use without change, and it never became as effectively frozen as did the Masoretic Text of the Hebrew Song: local and other kinds of variants developed, though most of them were fairly minor. But awareness of them on the part of the Catholic Church did mean that at various points attempts were made to edit, revise, and fix that text, a process that continues today.

There are many other Songs: Syriac, Coptic, Ethiopic, Chinese, English, German, French, and so on. But the three whose confection I've summarized above—Hebrew, Greek, Latin—are the ones most read, celebrated, chewed over, commented upon, preached about, and memorized by Christians.

For Christians, the process of confecting a scriptural book does not yield a single, authoritative original text from which all others are derived and upon which they are parasitic. There is, textually speaking, no real thing: there are only versions, all of them confected, some involving translation from one natural language into another and some not.[8] Affirming the possibility and desirability of translation, which Christians have almost always done, strongly supports this conclusion. If you think that when you're reading or hearing some version of the English Song you're reading or hearing scripture—and this is something Christians do think: when scripture is read in churches, in whatever language, its reading is ordinarily

---

the three, it seems fair to assume that it took him less than a day. This is quick work. But perhaps the three days he mentions is linked symbolically to the three books and is not meant as a simple descriptive statement about time taken.

8. In fact, all confections involve translation in a relaxed sense. Every natural language develops in intimate exchange with those around it: it is shaped by the borrowing and lending of words, syntax, and idioms (among other things). It is also the case that every text in any natural language has behind it, more or less distantly, a history of translation from texts in other natural languages. There is in fact no very easy way to individuate one natural language from another: this is a topic about as intractable as that of species individuation in biology. We may, for convenience and brevity, speak of the Hebrew original of the Song, for example. But that is no more than shorthand for a textual object confected in considerable part by translation. Consider, for example, the almost-indubitable resonances between the love lyrics of the Song and those of some Egyptian texts, on which see Fox, *Song of Songs and the Ancient Egyptian Love Songs*; Keel, *Das Hohelied*; and Zakovitch, *Das Hohelied*.

followed by the proclamation "the word of God" or "the word of the Lord"—then you must also think that the Lord speaks to you as effectively and fully by way of those words as he does to others by way of German or Hebrew or Latin words. Hearing the Song in English is not second best to hearing it in Hebrew: both are confected versions, and each is fully the word of the Lord.

What are they versions of? Among other things, of what the Lord says to his people. If scripture is the Lord's most explicit and complete verbal address to his people, then there is something that the Lord says to his people by way of scripture as a whole, and also by way of each of its proper parts, among which the Song is one. There is a complex verbal caress with which the Lord delights and instructs his people, a kiss that he places upon his people's lips—tropes especially apposite to the Song.[9] This particular caressing kiss can be given to us here below only by way of words in some natural language or other, and since the depth and passion of the kiss is unfathomable, no set of such words can exhaust it. The words in which each version consists are successive attempts on the part of the people at various times and in various places to respond to the Lord's verbal kiss: this is true of the anonymous poets and scribes who put together the various successive versions of the Hebrew text;[10] it is true of those who translated particular versions of that text into Greek and Latin and then subsequently into the languages of our times and places; and it is true too of those who have commented upon, preached about, or otherwise elucidated the words of the Song in any language. The confection of a scriptural book does not, therefore, end with the establishment of versions; those are its first yield, and they are inevitably and properly supplemented by commentary, which is confection's second yield, solicited by the first. Versions and commentary together are the people's return of the Lord's kiss (no kiss is given if one offered is not returned, as anyone knows who has kissed an unyielding pair of lips), and the exchange of verbal kisses will have no end here below. Versions and commentaries will, therefore, be endless.[11] This book is one among those returned kisses.

9. For an especially rich use of the trope of the kiss, with special reference to depictions of mystical death in Judaism, often by way of commentary on the Song, see Michael Fishbane, *The Kiss of God: Spiritual and Mystical Death in Judaism* (Seattle: University of Washington Press, 1994).

10. I am aware that there are many theories about how the Song came to be what it now is in its various versions, and that some of those theories consider it to be a unified literary text marked by the mind of a single human author, while others do not, thinking of it rather as a compilation of disparate song fragments. I incline to the latter view. But nothing hinges upon this so far as this commentary is concerned, and I place very little confidence in any particular view of the Song's literary prehistory, including my own.

11. Augustine expatiates in *De doctrina christiana* (Christian Teaching) 2.6.7–8 on the importance of scriptural obscurity, taking as his example Song 4:2, in which the beloved's teeth are likened to a flock of shorn sheep. It is, he says, a wonderful thing that the Holy Spirit has so arrayed the scriptures as to "satisfy hunger by its clearer parts and deter boredom by its more obscure ones" (*locis apertioribus fami occurreret, obscurioribus autem fastidia detergeret*); *Sant'Agostino: La Dottrina Christiana*, ed. and trans. Vincenzo Tarulli, Opere di Sant'Agostino 8 (Rome: Città Nuova, 1992), 64–66.

None of this means that all versions are equally good, equally effective at returning the Lord's kiss and thereby conforming the people's lips to the Lord's. But it is no simple matter to discriminate the good from the less so. This is because there are many variables in play: it is not only that one may be less faithful, less adequate, less beautiful than another; it is also that a kiss that elicits a response from some may fail to do so from others. Every teacher and preacher knows this: the same words, delivered in the same setting, by the same person, will be transformatively effective for some and lifeless failures for others. The Lord's people, whether synagogue or church, will, under his guidance, over time discriminate good versions of the Song from less good. Some versions die and some live; some enter deeply into the corporate and individual life of the Lord's people and some remain on the margins or fall dead-born from the press. Fortunately, those who offer a version or a commentary do not need to worry very much about this. They need only do their work thoughtfully, attentively, prayerfully, and with love.

Understanding scriptural books as confected versions in this way, none of which is identical with what the Lord says to his people, is at odds with two different widely held understandings of what scriptural books are, and it will highlight the distinctiveness of the view taken here (which is also the properly Christian view) to briefly explain the contrasts.

First, it is possible to think that a scriptural book consists essentially in a single set of words in some natural language and that any translation, paraphrase, gloss, or commentary upon this single set of words has authority or significance only to the extent of its intimacy with that single set. Some Jews, perhaps, think something like this about the set of Hebrew words that constitute the Masoretic Text of the Song; some Protestants, oddly, seem to think something like this about the set of English words that constitute the English Song found in the King James (Authorized) Version; maybe some Orthodox think this about the Greek Song of the Septuagint; and it is even possibly the case that some (misguided) Catholics think this about the words of the Latin Song in the Vulgate. And outside the spheres of Judaism and Christianity, it seems very likely that some Hindus think something like this about the Sanskrit phonemes of the Veda, and that most Muslims think this about the Arabic words of the Qur'an.[12] On this view, not everything is a version and not everything is confected: there is an originary natural-language text whose words are the Lord's very words, and nothing can approach it in authority. Those who think this are likely to be wary of translation, or at least to think of translations as expedients for the needy or incompetent, to be abandoned as soon as they can be done without.

Second, a historicist version of this single-inspired-text view identifies the authoritative text with the original (the autograph, the first spoken version, or

12. It is interesting to note that Christians and Buddhists (or at least the unconfused among their number) are united in not holding any such view, and (largely) in the reasons for not holding it: that is, their constant emphasis on the necessity of translating the sacred text. This differentiates Buddhism and Christianity from the other long-lived text-encumbered religious traditions.

something of that sort), devotes great effort to finding and establishing this original, and then (and therefore) treats all subsequent versions as secondary, derivative, and interesting only to the extent that they provide information helpful to the task of reconstructing and understanding the hypothesized original. It is true that the Greek and Latin Songs are derivatives of the Hebrew Song in the sense that without it they would not exist, while it could have existed—and for a while did—without them. But this has no implications for the desirability or interest of studying the Greek or Latin Song independently of the Hebrew. To think that it has is to confuse the two claims just mentioned: that x is a translation of y, and that the only interest x has is as a witness to y. Even without theological commitments or interests it should be easy enough to see that these two claims are easily separable. Suppose, for example, that x is a work with a long history of being read and commented upon—for example, Chapman's version of Homer or Dryden's of Virgil. Then, because it has itself prompted a history of reception and use, x warrants study in its own right, and not merely (or at all) for what it reveals about y. The stream of reading, writing, memorizing, thinking, and commenting that began with Virgil's composition of the *Aeneid* during the first century BC includes Dryden's Englishing of a version of the Latin during the last decade of the seventeenth century AD. Choosing to comment upon any one of the Latin *Aeneids* or Dryden's English *Aeneid* is not to choose between the most valuable version and a less valuable version: it is (or ought to be) to make a choice determined by the purposes of the commentary.

For most contemporary pagan (in the sense of neither-Jewish-nor-Christian) scholars, some version of the historicist view just given and criticized—though not usually expressed in quite this blunt way—informs the judgment that the real Song, the one that counts and the one that ought to be read and studied, is whatever contemporary scholarship takes to be the earliest state of the Hebrew text. A quick survey of recent scholarly commentary on the Song shows that almost all of it expounds the Masoretic Text; and almost all of it likewise makes a sharp distinction between the text and the history of its translation and interpretation. There is of course nothing wrong in expounding this text or, more generally, in paying attention to the Hebrew Song in any of its forms. For Jews, I should think, doing so is essential. But there is no reason, even for non- or antitheological historians, to adopt such a rigid demarcation of value between original text and everything prompted and solicited by that text; and there are positive reasons to reject such a view on the theological understanding of what a scriptural text is expounded above.

Christians, then, ought not think that a real or imagined original, whether of the Song or of any other scriptural text, is any more or less the word of the Lord than any chronologically subsequent version. But does some other kind of authority that the supposed original holds lead Christians to treat it differently than subsequent versions? There are some interesting questions here for Catholics, for whom there is an authoritative teaching tradition about these matters.

In 1943 Pope Pius XII issued an encyclical letter under the title *Divino Afflante Spiritu* (Inspired by the Spirit) in which he reviewed earlier papal teaching about the nature of scripture and how it should be interpreted and read by Catholics, and discussed then-recent advances in textual and historical knowledge relevant to scriptural interpretation. His purpose was to clarify the Catholic Church's mind on these matters and to make some recommendations. Relevant to the question of the authority of the versions is his urging of the study of the "ancient languages and original texts" (§14) in order that the "original text . . . which has more authority and greater weight than . . . even the very best version, whether ancient or modern" (§16) might be studied and expounded well.[13]

Four centuries earlier, the Catholic Church in council at Trent, had written: "The old Vulgate edition, tested by the church in long use over much time, should be retained as the authentic text in public reading, debate, preaching, and exposition."[14] These words have high authority for Catholics because Trent is, by Catholic reckoning, an ecumenical council; and of course Pius XII was aware of them. The Vulgate is a translation, not an original, because no part of the canon of scripture was composed in Latin. The council's words, therefore, provide a prima facie difficulty for Pius's claim that originals are weightier, which is to say more authoritative, than any translation.

Pius proceeds, as any Catholic thinker would, by making a distinction between two kinds of authenticity—or, as he also says, two kinds of authority. There is, he says (§21), critical authenticity (*authentia critica*) and juridical authenticity (*authentia iuridica*). The former belongs to the original texts in the original languages; and the latter belongs to the Vulgate because of its long use in the church. With Trent, Pius affirms that the Vulgate "may be deployed without danger of error in disputation, reading, and public discourse" (§21).

I read Pius's distinction between critical and juridical authority as establishing the grammar of a properly Catholic position on the authority of translations without specifying everything that flows from such a grammar. According to the grammar of the position Pius provides, two things must be said: (1) A translation—that is, a scriptural text rendered in any language other than that of its composition, whether by translation from that language or from some prior translation from that language—may (and in the case of the Vulgate does) possess full authority as the word of the Lord for the church's liturgical, homiletical, catechetical, and doctrine-developing purposes. (2) An original—that is, an untranslated text, a scriptural confection in the language of its composition—possesses authority greater than that of any translation for the purposes of critical scholarship. Those

13. Author's translation from Pius XII's *Divino Afflante Spiritu* (Latin at www.vatican.va/holy_father/pius_xii/encyclicals).

14. Author's translation from the second decree of the fourth session (April 1546) at Trent (Latin in Tanner 1990: 664).

purposes might include, though are certainly not limited to, reconstruction of the intentions of the author (if there was one); understanding the relation of the text to others contemporaneous with it, or nearly so; understanding the process of composition or compilation, and the sources used in that process. Both—that is, translations and originals, with their respective weights—are essential to the church's life. And the two kinds of authority are distinct, while related. Abandoning either option, whether by subsuming one into the other or by erasing one or the other, would be to move outside the grammar of a Catholic position on this matter. (I leave aside the question of the extent to which a properly Catholic position makes sense for non-Catholic Christians.) What remains in the sphere of speculative thought is the attempt to specify in a more detailed way the relations between the authority of translations and the authority of the original, or, to put the same matter differently, the relations between critical scholarship and preaching, teaching, and the formation of doctrine.[15]

The speculative position briefly developed above—that confection has been at play as much in the formation of originals as in that of translations—does not contradict Pius XII's distinction between original and translated texts. It affirms, as he does, the following claims: that translations can serve the church's teaching and preaching needs as well as the originals can; that translations are essential to the life of the church; and that attention to originals, in the limited sense of scriptural texts that are not translations, can provide answers to questions that attention to translations cannot provide. In making the more radical claim that, really, there are only versions, I intend to suggest that the lexicon, syntax, and history of one natural language, whether Hebrew, Aramaic, or Greek (the three "original" languages of scripture), together with the intentions and understandings of the authors and compilers of the works that now constitute the canon of scripture, cannot, in principle, exhaust or contain what the Lord says to his people by way of those works; and that proper to the work of the church in developing and extending its understanding of what the Lord says is the provision of translations, each of which is (potentially) a rendering of the word of the Lord as full and as

15. Subsequent magisterial teaching on the authority of the versions does not much develop Pius XII's position. The Second Vatican Council's Dogmatic Constitution on Revelation (*Dei Verbum*) has only a single paragraph on the versions (§22; Latin and English in Tanner 1990: 979), which are said to be made so that all the faithful might have easy access to scripture. This already implies that a version is indeed an instance of scripture, and by the time we reach §25, this is made explicit: the versions are indeed (instances of) the sacred text (Tanner 1990: 980–81). The work of the Pontifical Biblical Commission since the Second Vatican Council does not much advance the question, though the 1994 document "The Interpretation of the Bible in the Church" contains the following suggestive (and entirely accurate) claim: "Translating the Bible is already a work of exegesis" (from the text's conclusion; English at catholic-resources.org/ChurchDocs/PBC_Interp .htm). A translation is, then, the product of an exegetical act. From this can be quickly derived the conclusion that what is read and expounded in the church's public worship is the product of an exegetical act on the part of the church; and, if what is preached on and proclaimed is *Dei verbum*, then the word of the Lord is itself capable of being read and heard as the product of an exegetical act.

authoritative as that found in the originals. If that position is correct, among its implications is that exegetical attention paid to a translation is as important to the church's life as exegetical attention paid to an original. And there is a notable lack of the former in the work of the church's exegetes at the beginning of the third millennium.

⊹ ⊹ ⊹

If there are only confected versions of the Song, none in principle more intimate with what the Lord says than any other, then theological commentators must choose one among them to comment upon on grounds other than identifying the original or oldest text. They must, that is, choose a particular point in the stream of textual tradition that constitutes the Song and focus their work upon it. I choose one of the Latin Songs for my commentary—more exactly, the Latin text of the Song as printed in the second edition of *Nova Vulgata Bibliorum Sacrorum Editio*.[16]

Why the Latin Song at all, and why this particular version of it? The vast majority of Western commentators on the Song between the fifth century and the sixteenth (and a good many afterward) treated Jerome's Latin version. Jerome's Latin Song, rivaled only by one or other of his Latin renderings of the book of Psalms, attracted more commentary than any other scriptural book during those centuries;[17] and writing such commentaries was among the principal means used by Christian scholars during those centuries for the development of ecclesiological, mystical, and mariological theology. The vast body of Latin commentary provoked by Jerome's Latin Song is still largely untranslated into modern languages, although some parts of it have recently begun to be anthologized and studied,[18] and it seems

---

16. More exactly still, I have used for the text of the Song *Nova Vulgata Bibliorum Sacrorum Editio* (Rome: Libreria Editrice Vaticana, 1998), 915–21. This is a reprint edition of the second (revised) *editio typica* of the New Vulgate, issued in 1986.

17. On the commentary tradition, see Friedrich Ohly, *Hohelied-Studien: Grundzüge einer Geschichte der Hoheliedauslegung des Abendlandes bis um 1200* (Wiesbaden: Steiner, 1958); Helmut Riedlinger, *Der Makellosigkeit der Kirche in den lateinischen Hoheliedkommentaren des Mittelalters* (Münster: Aschendorff, 1958); and Anne-Marie Pelletier, *Lectures du Cantique des Cantiques: De l'enigme du sense aux figures de lecteur* (Rome: Editrice Pontificio Istituto Biblico, 1989). The last of these is a work of considerable theoretical interest in its own right.

18. For anthologies and studies of Latin commentary on the Song see Blaise Arminjon, *The Cantata of Love: A Verse-by-Verse Reading of the Song of Songs*, trans. Nelly Marans (San Francisco: Ignatius, 1988); Ann W. Astell, *The Song of Songs in the Middle Ages* (Ithaca, NY: Cornell University Press, 1990); Chrétien 2005; Russell J. de Simone, ed. and trans., *The Bride and Bridegroom of the Fathers: An Anthology of Patristic Interpretations of the Song of Songs*, Sussidi Patristici 10 (Rome: Istituto Patristico Augustinianum, 2000); Rachel Fulton, *From Judgment to Passion: Devotion to Christ and the Virgin Mary, 800–1200* (New York: Columbia University Press, 2002); Matter, *Voice of My Beloved*; Richard A. Norris Jr., ed. and trans., *The Song of Songs Interpreted by Early Christian and Medieval Commentators*, The Church's Bible (Grand Rapids: Eerdmans, 2003); Denys Turner, *Eros and Allegory: Medieval Exegesis of the Song of Songs* (Kalamazoo, MI: Cistercian, 1995); J. Robert Wright, ed., *Proverbs, Ecclesiastes, Song of Solomon*, Ancient Christian Commentaries, Old Testament 9 (Downers Grove, IL: InterVarsity, 2005).

likely that more will follow. Medievalists, theologians, and even, now, exegetes of scripture are increasingly interested in premodern scriptural commentary, and this interests me as well: in this commentary on the Song I will make use of, and sometimes explicitly engage, contributions from premodern commentators writing (in Latin) on Jerome's Latin Song. In order to be able to do so effectively, and in order for my comments to resonate effectively with theirs, to be a returned kiss like theirs, a moment in the history of response to the divine verbal kisses of the Song of the same kind as theirs, I must comment on a version lineally related to and intimate with the one they also commented on.

This means a Latin version, certainly. The New Vulgate is that; but it is not what Jerome set down in 398 in Bethlehem. It is, instead, the fruit of work set in motion by Pope Paul VI in 1965 and aimed at revision of the received Vulgate text of both Old and New Testaments, "so that the church might be enriched with a Latin edition which the progress of biblical studies demands, and which might be of special use in liturgical matters."[19] Those who worked on the revision of the received Vulgate text in the 1960s and 1970s made extensive changes to that text, but always with an eye (and ear) to what the Second Vatican Council's Constitution on the Liturgy called the "conventions and habits of Christian latinity together with liturgical use."[20] The New Vulgate's Song differs in verbal particulars and syntax from what Jerome set down in at least thirty places, and usually in the direction of assimilating the text toward what most interpreters take the Hebrew (or sometimes the Greek of the Septuagint) of the Song to mean. But it also preserves much of Jerome: perhaps 85 percent of the New Vulgate's Song is Jerome, verbatim. The New Vulgate is therefore sufficiently intimate with Jerome's version to make use of it easily compatible with constructive engagement with the premodern commentary tradition. It is also sufficiently close to the Hebrew version that underlies most contemporary English versions to make it useful for and usable by those familiar with those versions.

Another reason for using the New Vulgate's Song is liturgical. The Catholic Church has, since the end of the Second Vatican Council in 1965, devoted a good deal of attention to the theory and practice of preparing vernacular versions of its Latin liturgical books.[21] The New Vulgate has an important place in these discussions because it is now the version given in the authoritative Latin editions of the liturgical books—most importantly, the lectionary for Mass, both Sunday and

19. Author's translation from John Paul II's 1979 Apostolic Constitution *Scripturarum Thesaurus*, as given at *Nova Vulgata Bibliorum Sacrorum Editio*, 6; the words translated are John Paul's quotation of Paul VI's allocution of December 23, 1966, on the subject of the revision of the received Vulgate text.

20. From *Sacrosanctum Concilium* 91 (Tanner 1990: 836), with application there to the revision of the Psalter for use in the Daily Office.

21. A list of the forty or so magisterial texts on this matter promulgated between 1963 and 2001 may be had from *Liturgiam Authenticam* (Washington, DC: United States Conference of Catholic Bishops, 2001), 14–19.

daily, but also the books that contain the Liturgy of the Hours; and while this does not by itself mean that the scriptural parts of the revised vernacular versions of these books as they come into use during the second decade of the twenty-first century will be made directly from the New Vulgate, it does mean that the New Vulgate will be increasingly important as a shaping force behind new vernacular renderings of scripture for liturgical use in the Catholic world—which in turn means for the vast majority of the world's Christians.[22] A commentary on the Song as it appears in the New Vulgate may therefore take its place as a contribution to the reception of that version in at least the Catholic world, and may thereby also contribute to a renewed appreciation of the liturgical possibilities of the Song. There are, as yet, almost no commentaries on the New Vulgate's Song.

This decision about which version of the Song to expound, like all such decisions, is local, informed by particular interests that are not, and do not need to be, shared by all commentators on the Song. The church, understood broadly as the body of Christ, needs all the versions, and needs sustained textual attention to them all. Catholics have special interests in the Latin Song because of its deep significance for aspects of the European Christian tradition that were rejected by the Reformers but that have remained lively in the Catholic Church. Commentary on and liturgical use of the Song in late-medieval Europe was, for example, among the more important elements in the development in Christian understanding of and devotion to Mary that found their dogmatic formulations in 1854 (immaculate conception) and 1950 (assumption). Renewed attention to the Latin Song is, among other things, a way of understanding these developments more fully. But Orthodox Christians, Protestant Christians, and (certainly) Jews will and should have other interests in expounding the Song. I intend the commentary that follows, then, as a moment in the Catholic Christian reception and interpretation of the Song, a single note in a millennia-long symphony in which Jewish, Orthodox, and Protestant voices have essential parts to play even though they are not much sounded here.

Naming the Song's Voices

The Song has, on its surface, three voices, and all its words, with the exception of the title, come from the lips of one or another of them.[23] There is no narrative

---

22. New vernacular versions of the Catholic Church's liturgical books are on the way in many parts of the world, following with different degrees of faithfulness the principles set forth in *Liturgiam Authenticam* and its attendant documents, and attended by different levels of conflict about those principles. But the process is slow. In the English-speaking world, for instance, it is unlikely that these new vernacular versions will come into use before 2011 or 2012. The place of the New Vulgate in the production of vernacular liturgical books is described in *Liturgiam Authenticam* 24, 37, 41, 43; the interpretation and application of these principles is at the time of writing a topic of chronic and acute controversy in the English-speaking world.

23. Most premodern commentators find more than three voices in the Song. Origen, for example, in *Homeliae in canticum canticorum* (Homilies on the Song of Songs) 1.1 (Lawson 1956: 267–68),

voice: the Song is a lyric in direct speech. This is what provides it with its hallucinatory immediacy. You, the hearer, are plunged at once, as soon as the Song opens, into a series of passionate exchanges that appear to take place in an unmediated literary present.[24] It is certainly possible to hear the Song as an auditor only, preserving distance with the cynical smile of the worldly wise or the analytical sneer of the scholar. But that stance is not the one the Song's text calls you to. To hear it responsively, and with attention, is to be made breathless and to have your own loves reconfigured by what its lovers say.[25]

None of the voices in the Song is clearly named in its text, though each of them is identified with various titles and epithets and endearments. I call them, to begin with, the lover (a man), the beloved (a woman), and the daughters (a group of women). The speakers refer to one another most often by pronouns or by epithets; and their presence in the text, whether as speaker or addressee, ordinarily has to be inferred or, in cases of unclarity (there are many), guessed. It is often productive in such cases to consider different possibilities, and I do that sometimes in the comments that follow. Why should the Song or any scriptural text (or indeed any text at all) have just one meaning even when considered *ad litteram*?

The lover is identified by a number of titles and endearments. He is, most commonly, his beloved's "delightful man": she calls him this twenty-seven times. He is also her "king," though she never calls him this directly, rather twice (1:4, 12) describing him to others with this word. Once (5:16) she calls him her "lover." And five times (1:7; 3:1–4) she calls him "the man in whom my soul delights," using the same verb (*diligere*) that stands behind "delightful man" (*dilectus*). The daughters once, in the pivotal 5:1, address the lover and his beloved together as "lovers"; and in 5:9 they speak to the beloved about her "delightful man." Apart from those instances, no one other than the beloved ever calls the lover anything.

The lover speaks most of his lines directly to the beloved. He exchanges endearments with her in 1:8–2:15; the entirety of Song 4 is a hymn of praise by him of her, as is 7:2–10; and there are occasional other speeches from him to her (5:1–2;

---

finds four; and Bede, *In canticum canticorum* (On the Song), prologue (Latin in *Bedae Venerabilis Opera II.2b*, ed. D. Hurst, Corpus Christianorum Series Latina 119B [Brepols: Turnhout, 1983], 185–89), finds five and differentiates them further according to addressee, yielding a rather complex picture. There are many intermediate positions. I do not judge these analyses wrong; in some cases they are produced by textual differences, but for the most part the more complex enumerations of the Song's speaking characters come not from the surface features of the text (shifts in voice, mood, gender, number, and so forth), but rather from the retrojection of elements of a particular theological reading of the Song into the analysis of the Song's voices. That is not a method I follow here, though there is much to be learned from it.

24. On the question of how the Song works, literarily speaking—how it places the hearer into itself and what it does to the hearer by way of its literary form—see J. Cheryl Exum, *Song of Songs: A Commentary* (Louisville: Westminster John Knox, 2005), 1–12.

25. David J. A. Clines recognizes this, with clarity; see "Why Is There a Song of Songs and What Does It Do to You If You Read?" in his *Interested Parties: The Ideology of Writers and Readers of the Hebrew Bible* (Sheffield: Sheffield Academic Press, 1995), 94–121. Unfortunately, his recognition of it is deeply infected with a moral self-righteousness.

6:4–9; 8:5). In addition, he speaks directly to the daughters three times (2:7; 3:5; 8:4) and possibly a fourth (3:7–11). And there are two possible soliloquies (6:11–12; 8:11–13), though both of these are capable of other readings. About 45 percent of the Song's words are reasonably identified as the lover's.

We learn nothing from the lover's speeches about himself, except the flavor and range and intensity of his delight in and love for the beloved, and that he can adjure or command the daughters, which he does thrice (2:7; 3:5; 8:4). A little more can be gleaned from what the beloved says to or about him. He "grazes" (1:7), for example, and is thereby associated with "shepherds" (1:8). But the language is suggestive and associative rather than precise. Is the grazing metaphorical? Does he graze sheep or goats? Nothing is clear. And in reading most of what she says to or about him we do not learn about him but rather about the fire of her passion for him. We learn a great deal, for example, about how she thinks of him and his body. We learn too that she can call him her "king," but not whether she means this sexually or politically or metaphorically or some combination of all these.

As to the beloved: she is, on his lips, "beloved" (many times), "most beautiful of women" (1:8), "delightful woman" (2:7; 3:5; 8:4), "dove" (2:10, 14; 5:2; 6:9), "lovely one" (1:5; 2:10), "bride" (4:8–12; 5:1), "sister" (4:9–12; 5:1–2), "stainless one" (5:2), "Sulamite" (7:1), and "prince's daughter" (7:2). The daughters replicate some of this, also calling her "most beautiful of women" (5:9; 6:1) and "beloved" (5:2). This is a more elaborate and differentiated range of epithets and endearments than those given to him. She, the beloved, like him, the lover, neither speaks a name nor is addressed by one.

The beloved speaks most of her lines directly to the lover, as he does to her; but she also speaks to the daughters (1:5–6; 5:8, 10–16; 6:2–3) and twice, or perhaps three times, in soliloquy, which may also be dream (3:1–4; 5:2, 3–7). Her share of the Song's words is very slightly more than that of the lover, accounting for about 47 percent of the whole. That leaves about 8 percent for the daughters.

The beloved says a little more about herself than does the lover about himself, though what she says is in highly colored and apparently metaphorical terms. She says that she is "black but lovely" (1:5) and that her "mother's sons" (1:6) have been angry with her and have set her as guard over the vineyards, a duty at which she has failed (1:5–6). She has spent time with the king "on his couch" (1:12), and she and the lover have a shared bed, which she calls "flowerful" (1:16). He has embraced her intimately (2:6; 8:3) and has had sex with her (the most probable reading of the verses centering on 5:1), but when he comes to her bedroom she is reluctant to get up and open her door and herself to him (5:3). She wanders the city in search of him when he is not there (3:2–4; 5:6–7); and she is eager to take him "into my mother's house" (8:2; cf. 3:4), so that she can make love to him there. She takes the epithet "Sulamite" to herself (7:1).

The third voice is a chorus, the "daughters of Jerusalem," mentioned and apostrophized frequently (1:5; 2:7; 3:5, 10; 5:8, 16; 8:4), also called "daughters of Zion" (3:11), and given five or perhaps six speeches (3:6; 5:1, 9; 6:1, 10; 8:5).

They may also be identical with the "young girls" (1:3) who "have delighted" in the lover; but this is not clear. What the daughters say reveals nothing about who they are; they speak usually interrogatively (3:6; 5:9; 6:1, 10; 8:5). The daughters have several functions in the Song. First, they prompt speeches that could not plausibly be made if the work contained only the lover and the beloved as speakers; this is why they usually speak interrogatively. Second, they are intermediaries between the world of the couple and the world of the audience external to the Song—that is, the world of you and me. When they speak, the hothouse, closed world of the lovers' exchanges, a world that includes only two people, opens out, and it is a relief to the hearer that it does.[26] The daughters' questions are often and naturally taken by the Song's hearers to be theirs. The effect of what they say upon the Song's audience is in many ways like that of a Shakespearean soliloquy, spoken principally for the benefit of the audience.

There are a few personal proper nouns used in the Song, of which the most prominent is "Solomon." He is mentioned in the book's title ("Solomon's Song of Songs"), in the beloved's likening of herself to "Solomon's skins" (1:5), thrice in verses about his "bed" and his "litter" (3:7–11, probably spoken by the lover), and twice in the enigmatic verses about his "vineyard" (8:11–12, perhaps spoken by the lover). The Song's text, heard literally, does not make it clear either that Solomon is the lover in the Song (the attentive hearer, on the basis of the text alone, is given no strong reason to think so) or that he is the author of the book. That the book presents itself as having some association with him is clear, but the nature of that association is left entirely unclear: the words used in the title are equally compatible with the judgment that Solomon wrote the book, that he commissioned it, liked it, endorsed it, had it read at court, gave it as a love offering to some woman, and no doubt many other things as well. Solomon is called "king," and so this may dispose the reader to think that when the beloved calls her lover that, without adding the name "Solomon," she is really identifying the two. But there is much that speaks against this on the surface of the text, not least that she associates her lover with shepherding as well as ruling. Solomon is a figure of grandeur in the Song, certainly, most obviously in 3:6–11, where the lover (probably: there is no clear sign as to who speaks these words) describes the retinue accompanying Solomon's litter as it approaches through the desert. But in spite of the grandeur, he remains marginal to a literal reading of the Song.

"Pharaoh" (1:9) and "David" (4:4) are mentioned too, but each only as part of an extended trope or as an illustrative reference. They are not players in the drama. No other personal names are used, and so there are no other characters: the beloved, her lover, the daughters of Jerusalem, and a shadowy Solomon at the margins of the text exhaust the cast of characters. The most striking absence

---

26. I draw here upon the analysis in Exum, *Song of Songs*, 100–102, of the function of the daughters in the Song.

is the Lord: neither his name nor any epithet ordinarily applied to him is found in the Song.

The Lord is not named in the Song; neither is Jesus, neither is Mary, and neither is the church. Even the people of Israel are scarcely there, making an explicit entry only because of the naming of places in which they live. But it is the unanimous witness of Jewish and Christian commentators before the modern period (and to a considerable extent after it) that the unnamed characters of the Song are figures, which is to say that in addition to being themselves they point to and participate in and reveal, in part, others: the people of Israel, the church, the individual beloved by the Lord, Mary, she whom the Lord has most desired and with whom he has entered into the greatest intimacy. The romance and desire of the Song, on these views, are not only, and perhaps not at all, about two unnamed lovers; they are also, and perhaps principally, and perhaps even only, about the desire of the Lord for his Israel, for his church, for Mary, and for you and me.

Such views permit, and even require, those who read the Song under the guidance of them to see things both in the Song and in the canon to which it belongs that would not otherwise be apparent. All reading works like this: every work of literature is read under the tutelage of assumptions about what it may mean arrived at in part independently of reading it; and then, in a feedback loop, the particulars of the work read question, deepen, and alter the assumptions brought to the act of reading it. In the case of classics (Homer, Virgil, Dante, Shakespeare, Goethe), this process lasts a long time and is subtle. The classic is read and reread and as a result becomes ingredient to works composed later—they gloss it, comment upon it, use its characters, motifs, tropes, and themes, ingest and excrete it, bow in homage before it, and so on. The classic is also given new interpretations as its readers read it in new contexts and under new pressures. And the classic itself—its words—is one among the powers that alter the configuration and trajectory of the culture to which it belongs. All this is true of scriptural works as well, and in some ways more intensely so. The Song, as both scriptural work and classic, has provided a template for thought and writing about what it is like to be the Lord's beloved and, therefore, about who the Lord's ideal beloveds are. Those thoughts and writings then form part of the Song's burden: just as Dante's depiction and use of Virgil enters into readings of the *Aeneid* subsequent to Dante and contributes in that way to the *Aeneid*'s burden, so medieval Christian readings of the Song's beloved as if she were Mary form part of the weight now borne by the Song's words.

Four principal candidates have emerged among Jews and Christians as answers to the question of who the Song's human beloved figures. Sometimes, even often, these answers have been given in a flatfooted allegorical way, as if, once the beloved figured by the Song has been identified, the human beloved of the Song—the woman who figures but is not herself figured, this human woman panting for her lover, opening her door and her body to him, praising the beauties of his body, recalling the delights of his kisses, lamenting his absence, imagining his presence—can be left aside, having performed her figuring function and then having nothing left to do. This way of reading dissolves the figuring into the figured and leads all too easily into a dissolution of the text's surface, and even of its very words, into some deeper or higher meaning. On this allegorical view, the human beloved and the eroticism of the text vanishes, is neutered and absorbed. Better, certainly more fully Christian, is to read in such a way as to preserve both the text's figures and what they figure.

The first thought about whom the beloved figures is that she figures the people of Israel, the Lord's chosen people whom he loves with a passion. The relations between this people and their Lord are often set forth in scripture as those between spouses or lovers (Hos. 1–3; Isa. 50:1; 54:4–8; Jer. 2–3; Ezek. 16), and the Song can therefore reasonably be taken as another instance of the same kind, unusual perhaps in the intensity and explicitness of its imagery, as well as in its consistency in refusing to name the Lord as the lover or Israel as the beloved, but still far from unique in kind. On this reading, a fuller understanding of the desire of the Lord for the people and the people for the Lord can be had by attending to the history of the Jewish people.

The second thought is that the beloved figures the church, the community of those who have been incorporated into Christ by baptism and who confess his lordship explicitly.[27] This view, naturally, is not one offered by Jews; it is the Christian gloss upon the first interpretation and can stand together with it without replacing it. On this way of taking it, the Lord's beloved is a doppelgänger whose doubleness has often been conflicted, but that need not necessarily be so. On this reading, a fuller understanding of the divine love affair with the people can be had by attending to the history of the church.

These first two thoughts may, but need not, contradict one another. Whether they do depends on the narrowness with which "church" or "people of Israel" is construed. On a wide construal, like that adopted by Nicholas of Lyra in the fourteenth century in his commentary on the Song, each term denotes the *una fides modernorum et antiquorum* ("the one faith held by moderns and ancients").[28] For him, both Jews and Christians are church because they share the same faith, though he takes the latter to have a more intimate relation with the Lord than the former. On a narrow construal, according to which church is defined, for

27. The identification of the Song's beloved with the church is sufficiently standard by Augustine's time that he can refer to it in his early-fifth-century *De baptismo contra donatistas* (On Baptism, against the Donatists; Latin at augustinus.it/latino/sul_battesimo/index2.htm; Latin and Italian in *Sant'Agostino: Polemica con i Donatisti*, ed. and trans. Antonio Lombardi, Opere di Sant'Agostino 15/1 [Rome: Città Nuova, 1998]) 5.27.38, offhandedly as though it is obvious, as in his comment that it is the church's soul, *perfecta et sine macula et ruga* (quoting or echoing Eph. 5:27), that the king has brought into his storerooms (Song 1:4).

28. Nicholas of Lyra, *Postilla super Cantica Canticorum* (Latin and English in *The Postilla of Nicholas of Lyra on the Song of Songs*, ed. and trans. James George Kiecker [Milwaukee: Marquette University Press, 1998], 32).

example, as in the preceding paragraph, things are a little more complex. But even here, there is no necessary incompatibility: it could be said—I would say—that the Song's beloved figures both the people of Israel and the church and that the embraces given and returned between the Lord and both beloveds continue to this moment. I will often use the term "Israel-church" in the commentary that follows as an expression of this view.

The course of the love affair between the Lord and his Israel-church has not been smooth, and this too is figured in the Song. She is separated from him and suffers because of it (3:1–3; 5:6–7); she remembers his lovemaking and hopes for it again, but throughout most of the Song she is not experiencing it directly; and she is frustrated because she cannot publicly express her devotion to and love for him (8:1–2). Similarly, the histories of the Jewish people and the Christian church with the Lord have been and continue to be disfigured by denial, betrayal, absence, suffering, and unfulfilled longing. These two views of the beloved, as people of Israel and church, need not contradict one another.

The third view of the figure of the beloved, again offered only by Christians, is that she figures Mary, the virgin mother of the Lord. This understanding of the beloved is most often based upon a rule of interpretation of which the following is a good example:

> The glorious Virgin Mary represents the type of the church, which exists as virgin and mother, for she is proclaimed as mother because she, fertile through the Holy Spirit, daily brings forth children through baptism. But she is said to be virgin because, serving inviolate the purity of faith, she is not corrupted by vicious heresy. Thus Mary was mother in giving birth to Christ, and, remaining closed even after giving birth, she was virgin. Therefore all that is written of the church is suitably ascribed to her as well.[29]

A series of parallels is here drawn between the church and Mary, and the rule derived from them is that anything said of the church can also be said of Mary. This third understanding of who the Song's beloved figures is therefore not incompatible with the first two: indeed, it presents itself as an outworking of the second, which is itself an outworking of the first. There are some difficulties in the rule of interpretation as baldly stated in the last sentence of the quotation just given. Does it mean, for example, that the church's constant need for repentance, purification, and renewal also belongs to Mary? There is also the further question of whether the rule of interpretation works in the other direction, which would be to say that everything written of Mary can also be written of the church. Here, I suspect, there are even more difficulties. Is it possible to say, for instance, that the church conceives Jesus in its womb or is married to Joseph? But whatever

---

29. Honorius Augustodunensis, *Sigillum Beatae Mariae* (Seal of Blessed Mary) (English in *The Seal of Blessed Mary*, trans. Amelia Carr [Toronto: Peregrine, 1991], 53, amended on the basis of *Patrologia Latina* 172.499).

the proper conclusion is about these difficulties, it remains true that the Marian thread is woven deeply into the fabric of Christian interpretation of the Song and forms part of the Song's burden.

A representative statement of the Marian approach to the Song is the following, from Alan of Lille, writing probably in the second half of the twelfth century:

> And just as a spark is struck from a stone or honey extracted with a fragile reed; and inasmuch as the tongues of men and angels sing in praise of the Virgin, so too is her praise drawn forth from every creature capable of speech and in all of Scripture the great worth of this mother is told. And so, although the song of love, Solomon's wedding song, refers particularly and according to its spiritual sense to the Church, in its most particular and spiritual reference it signifies the most glorious Virgin: this, with divine help, we will explain as far as will be within our power.[30]

The fourth thought about who is figured by the Song's beloved is that it is the individual human soul or, better, the individual human person. The Latin tradition has been encouraged in this interpretation by *anima*, the Latin word usually translated "soul," being feminine in gender, which is an important matter when considering the appropriateness of this line of interpretation. Commentators on the Song in the Latin tradition often move happily back and forth among *ecclesia* ("church"), *anima* ("soul"), and *Maria* ("Mary") when discussing the resonances and depths of the Song's beloved, and are encouraged in doing so by the fact that each word is feminine in gender, as the Song's beloved also is. This fourth thought, therefore, does not need to displace or be seen in tension with the first three. Reading the Song's beloved as figure for the church led the church before long to consider her also as figure for Mary because Mary is the church *in nuce*, as well as the church's mother. The church too is the collectivity of Christians, and so what is said of her can in significant part also be said of each individual Christian: the church's acceptance of the gift of Christ and her yearning for fuller union with Christ and fuller understanding of the gift given are acts and attitudes and desires in which the individual Christian also participates.

And in similar fashion, Mary's acceptance of the gift of Christ figures with a peculiar intensity the acceptance of the church and of the individual Christian. This is not to say that there can be a simple exchange of predicates among Mary, church, and individual Christian: Mary does become pregnant with Jesus, and I do not; the church has the power to mediate the Lord's forgiveness of sins, and I do not; I can receive baptism and be received into heaven (should that happen) after the death and destruction of my body, neither of which is possible for Mary; and I can reject the Lord and thereby succeed in moving myself toward the nothingness of damnation, perhaps even accomplishing that nothingness, which

---

30. Alan of Lille, *In Cantica Canticorum elucidatio* (Elucidation of the Song), prologue (Latin in *Patrologia Latina* 210.51–110, trans. Denys Turner, *Eros and Allegory: Medieval Exegesis of the Song of Songs* [Kalamazoo, MI: Cistercian, 1995], 294).

neither Mary nor the church can do. But even though not every aspect of Mary's acceptance of the gift is mirrored by the church's or mine, and not every aspect of mine is mirrored by hers or the church's, and not every aspect of the church's is mirrored by mine or hers, it remains the case that the church's reading of the Song weaves these three figurings together, often in such a way as to show their mutually illuminating character, and sometimes (not as often as I would like) without dissolving the figure into the figured. To signal the intimacy between the Song's beloved's figuring of Mary and church, I will sometimes use the compound expression "Mary-church" in the commentary that follows.

The Song's lover, also not named or otherwise explicitly identified in the Song, has most often been taken to figure the Lord, the God of Abraham and Isaac and Jacob and Mary and Jesus and the church. This figuration I wholeheartedly accept in the commentary that follows. Jewish and Christian commentators are at one in offering it. It provides, of course, some interpretive challenges, not least because the lover in the Song needs and wants his beloved as much as she needs and wants him, and this can easily be taken to call into question one or another theological understanding of the Lord's nature and the relations he bears to his Israel-church and his Mary-church. I will discuss some of these issues in the commentary, but for now it will suffice to say that I do indeed take the lover to figure the Lord, and will sometimes call him "lover-Lord" to signal that fact. Recall, however, that this is figural rather than allegorical exegesis. The Song's lover, with his "ringlets like palm fronds / raven-black" and his "eyes ... like doves'" (5:11–12), remains who he is.

✠ ✠ ✠

You may worry that this naming of the Song's characters goes altogether too far. Why not read the text just as a series of lyrics about love and desire? Well, of course that is possible. But to do that would not be to read the Song as a scriptural book; neither would it be to take seriously the weight of the Song's readings by Jews and Christians over two thousand years. I will offer a reading that tries to do both these things.

An English Version of the Song

What follows is an Englishing of the Latin Song, which is to say of the Latin version printed in the New Vulgate. Every translation of a much-translated work like the Song must echo earlier ones, and I have consulted and benefited from many other English versions made from a variety of languages.[31]

31. I first became familiar with the Song in the cadences of the King James (Authorized) Version and so no doubt those sonorosities linger in my words even though I've tried hard to expunge

In translating the Latin I observe a few conventions that it will be helpful to note before reading the translation.

First, I follow the New Vulgate's chapter and verse divisions in the Song without exception, which are for the most part identical with those found in contemporary English Bibles. The sole exceptions are that the phrases that open 5:1 in the New Vulgate belong to 4:16 in most contemporary English versions; and that 7:1 in the New Vulgate is 6:13 in most contemporary English versions, which means that it is necessary to subtract one from the New Vulgate verse numbers of Song 7 to arrive at the corresponding verse in a contemporary English version. I also follow New Vulgate chapter and verse divisions elsewhere in scripture, but where they differ from contemporary English versification, I include the Revised Standard Version equivalent.

Second, I do not follow the New Vulgate's punctuation, which is heavy. Generally, I punctuate more sparingly. This punctuational parsimony rarely contradicts what is suggested by the New Vulgate's heavier punctuation. It does, however—and this is an important reason for it—give the English a breathless, tensive, and (I hope suggestively) incomplete sense. This is entirely in accord with the Latin.

Third, I've taken care in the translation to avoid both the semantic thinning that comes from rendering different Latin words with a single English word and the semantic thickening that comes from rendering a single Latin word with a variety of English ones. So, for example, all and only members of the *diligere* complex (finite verbal forms, participles, and the nominal *dilectio*, principally) in Latin are rendered with terms from the "delight" complex in English; all and only members of the *amor* complex (verbal and nominal forms, including *amicus/a* and *amor*) are rendered by terms from the "love" complex in English; and *caritas*, which occurs only twice (2:4; 8:7), always as "loving-kindness." I take the same approach with the Song's rich vocabulary of herbs, spices, flowers, fruits, animals, and body parts. You can be sure, then, that when an English term occurs more than once, it is reflecting the same Latin word in each case. This semitransparency is

them. As to English versions made from one or another of the Latin songs, see especially Norris, *Song of Songs*; Matter, *Voice of My Beloved*, xvi–xxiii; and the original Douay-Rheims version of the Old Testament, first published in 1609–10, and in its eighteenth-century revision (which was sufficiently drastic as to make it effectively a different text). I've also found the French version in Claudel's 1948 *Cantique* very illuminating—even though, as the *nihil obstat* says, his work was "donné non comme une explication théologique ou exégétique, mais comme une poëme"; more poets should provide exegesis of scriptural texts if the quality and intellectual interest of Claudel's work is anything to go by. All the versions I've just mentioned were made from one edition/redaction or another of Jerome's Latin. I've found useful the literal rendering of the Septuagint version made by Jay Treat in Pietersma and Wright, *New English Translation of the Septuagint*, 662–66. And among the many English versions made from Hebrew, the Revised Standard Version and New Revised Standard Version have been constantly at my side, as have the versions in Richard S. Hess, *Song of Songs* (Grand Rapids: Baker, 2005); Matter, *Voice of My Beloved*; Christopher W. Mitchell, *The Song of Songs* (St. Louis: Concordia, 2003); Murphy, *Song of Songs*; Pope, *Song of Songs*; and Wright, *Proverbs, Ecclesiastes, Song of Solomon*.

important because the Song, more than most other scriptural books, has prompted commentary minutely attentive to verbal particularity. Precise verbal echoes and repetition of trope-patterns matter deeply to premodern commentators, and my commentary also attends to them; although I am writing (and largely thinking) in English, the echo and trope comments I make are effectively about the Latin text of the New Vulgate, both of the Song and of the corpus of scripture as a whole. And in order for it to be possible to do that in English, a translation of the kind mentioned is essential.

Fourth, I provide no information in the translation about who is speaking to whom other than that given on the surface of the text. Often, the gender of the addressee is explicitly indicated in the Latin text. For instance, in 1:7 someone male is addressed as the "man in whom my soul delights"; in 1:8 someone female is addressed as "most beautiful of women"; and then in 1:13 the "delightful man" is addressed again. But it is rare that the Latin text unambiguously indicates, with gender-specific pronouns or nouns, who is speaking; and it is often quite unclear just where a speech made to one addressee ends and one made to another (or by another speaker) begins. I discuss these matters in the commentary, but my translation provides neither more nor less than what is in the Latin text, which should permit you to make your own decisions about the matter. The only instance in which my English does not make gender clear on its face is that of the terms "lover," which always renders the masculine *amicus*, and "beloved," which always renders the feminine *amica*. The "lover," that is to say, is always him; the "beloved" is always her.

The running translation that immediately follows is given without verse numbers or notes and with breaks only where it seems to me that there is (probably) a change of voice or a significant shift of theme and focus. All of this translation will be given again, piecemeal, in the commentary that follows; the point of providing it here is to give you an opportunity to read the Song through once, naked—and to be appropriately puzzled.

Solomon's Song of Songs

Let me be kissed with your mouth's kiss
for your loves are better than wine
fragrant with your best ointments.
Your name is oil poured out
and so the young girls have delighted in you.
Drag me after you—let us run!
May the king lead me into his cellars
so that we might exult and rejoice in you.
Mindful of your loves above wine
they have rightly delighted in you.

I am black but lovely
O daughters of Jerusalem

like Kedar's tents
like Solomon's skins—
do not think me swarthy
for the sun has darkened me.
My mother's sons were angry with me
they placed me as guard of the vineyards
but my vineyard I did not guard.
O man in whom my soul delights
show me where you graze
and where you rest at noon
so that I might not begin to wander
after the flocks of your companions.

If you do not know
O most beautiful of women
then go out and depart
after the flocks' traces
and graze your young goats
close by the shepherds' tents.
To a mare among Pharaoh's chariots
I have likened you, O my beloved.
Your cheeks are beautiful with earrings
your neck with necklaces—
we shall make earrings for you
silver-chased.

While the king was on his couch
my spikenard gave off its scent.
A sachet of myrrh is my delightful man for me
he lingers between my breasts;
a henna cluster is my delightful man for me
in the vineyards of Engaddi.

O my beloved—
see how beautiful you are
see how beautiful you are
your dove-eyes.

O my delightful man—
see how beautiful you are
and splendid!
Our flowerful bed—
our cedar-beamed house—
our cypress-paneled ceilings.
I am a field-flower
and a valley-lily—

like a lily among thorns
is my beloved among daughters—
like an apple among forest trees
is my delightful man among sons.
I sat under his shade—that of the man I desired—
and his fruit was sweet to my throat.
He led me into his wine cellar
loving-kindness was his banner above me.
Sustain me with raisin cakes
fill me with apples
for I languish with love.
His left hand under my head
his right embraces me.
O daughters of Jerusalem—I adjure you
by the does and hinds of the fields
not to enliven or awaken this delightful woman
until she wishes.

The voice of my delightful man—
look—he comes
leaping among the mountains,
skipping over the hills
like a doe or fawn among harts.
He is the very one who stands behind our wall
looking through the windows
gazing through the lattices.
And my delightful man speaks to me—

"Get up, O my beloved,
my dove, my lovely one, and come—
for already winter has gone away
the rain has departed and withdrawn
flowers have appeared in the land
the time of pruning has arrived
the turtledove's voice is heard in our land
the fig tree has put out its figs
and the flowering vineyards have given off their scent.
Get up, O my beloved,
my comely one, and come,
my dove—
in the chinks of the rock
in the precipitous cave
expose your face to me
let your voice sound in my ears
for your voice is sweet
and your face splendid.
Catch for us the foxes—the little foxes—

who destroy the vineyards
as our vineyards are flowering."

My delightful man is for me and I am for him
the one who grazes among lilies—
until the day breathes
and the shadows flee.
Turn back, O my delightful man,
be like a doe or fawn among harts
on Bether's mountains.

In my bed—night by night—
I sought him—the man in whom my soul delights.
I sought and did not find him.
I will get up and walk around the city
through the streets and the squares
I will seek the man in whom my soul delights.
I sought and did not find him.
The watchmen found me
they who walk around the city.
"Have you seen the man in whom my soul delights?"
Soon after I had passed them by
I found the man in whom my soul delights.
I held him and would not let him go
until I could lead him into my mother's house
into the bedroom of my genetrix.
O daughters of Jerusalem—I adjure you
by the does and hinds of the fields
not to enliven or awaken this delightful woman
until she wishes.

What is this ascending through the desert
like a wisp of smoke
spiced with frankincense and myrrh
and all the perfumer's powders?

See Solomon's bed—
sixty strong men surround it
from Israel's strongest
each holding a sword
supremely skilled in war
each one's weapon on his thigh
against the terrors of the night.
King Solomon made himself a litter
from Lebanese trees—
its pillars he made of silver

its seat of gold
its step of purple
its middle ebony-inlaid.
O daughters of Jerusalem
O daughters of Zion
go out and see King Solomon
diademed as his mother crowned him
on the day of his wedding
on the day of his heart's joy.

How beautiful you are, O my beloved
how beautiful you are—
your dove-eyes
through your veil;
your hair like a flock of nanny goats
coming down from Mount Gilead;
your teeth like a flock of shorn sheep
ascending from the bath
each pregnant with twins
not a sterile one among them;
your lips like a scarlet thread
and your speech sweet;
your cheeks like a fragment of pomegranate
through your veil;
your neck like David's tower
built with battlements
hung with a thousand shields
with all the armor of the strong;
your two breasts like two fawns
doe-born twins
grazing among lilies.
Until the day breathes
and the shadows flee
I shall go to the mountain of myrrh
and to the hill of frankincense.
O my beloved—you are completely beautiful
and there is no stain in you.

O bride—come from Lebanon,
come from Lebanon,
come in—
look from the summit of Amana
from the peaks of Sanir and Hermon
from lions' lairs
from leopards' mountains.
O my sister-bride—you have wounded my heart
you have wounded my heart with one of your eyes

with one of the necklaces of your torque.
O my sister-bride—how beautiful are your loves
your loves are better than wine
and the scent of your ointments is above all spices.
O bride—your lips drip honeycomb
honey and milk are under your tongue
the scent of your clothes is like that of Lebanon.
A closed garden is my sister-bride
a closed garden
a sealed spring.
Your shoots are a paradise of pomegranates
with the best fruits—
henna with spikenard
spikenard and saffron
sweet calamus and cinnamon
with all the incense-bearing trees—
myrrh and aloe
with all the prime ointments.
The spring of the gardens is a well of living waters
streaming forcefully from Lebanon.
North wind get up—
south wind come—
blow through my garden—
let its spices stream!

Let my delightful man come into his garden
and let him eat his best fruits.
O my sister-bride—I have come into my garden
I have harvested my myrrh with my spices
I have eaten honeycomb with honey
I have drunk wine with my milk

O lovers—eat and drink—
O dearest ones—be drunk!

I sleep with wakeful heart—
the voice of my delightful man who is knocking—
"Open to me, O my sister, my beloved
my dove, my stainless one—
for my head is full of dew
and my ringlets of the moisture of the night."

I have stripped off my tunic—
how can I put it on?
I have washed my feet—
how can I make them dirty?

My delightful man put his hand through the chink
and my belly trembled.
I got up so that I might open to my delightful man
my hands dripping with myrrh
my fingers full of choicest myrrh
above the bolt's handle.
I opened to my delightful man,
but he had turned aside and gone away.
My soul melted because he had left.
I sought and did not find him
I called and he did not respond.
The guards found me,
those who walk around the city
those who care for the ramparts—
they beat me and wounded me
and took my cloak from me.

O daughters of Jerusalem—I adjure you
if you should find my delightful man
what should you say to him?
That I languish with love.

O most beautiful of women
how is your delightful man better than others
how is he better than others
that you so adjure us?

My delightful man is dazzling and ruddy
distinguished among thousands—
his head is of the best gold
ringlets like palm fronds
raven-black;
his eyes are like doves'
above rivers of water
milk-washed
beside completely full streams;
his cheeks are like seedbeds of spices
ointment piled up;
his lips are lilies
dripping prime myrrh;
his hands are lathe-turned gold
violet-full;
his belly is ivory
sapphire-adorned;
his legs are marble pillars
founded upon golden pedestals;

his comeliness is like Lebanon's
he is set apart like a cedar;
his throat is supremely smooth
and completely desirable.
Such is my delightful man—that very one is my lover
O daughters of Jerusalem.

O most beautiful of women
where has your delightful man departed?
Where has he turned aside?
Shall we seek him with you?

My delightful man has gone down into his garden
to a seedbed of spices
to graze in the gardens
to gather lilies.
I am for my delightful man and my delightful man is for me—
the one who grazes among lilies

O my beloved—you are beautiful like Tirzah
splendid like Jerusalem
terrible like an ordered rank from the camps.
Turn your eyes away from me
for they disturb me.
Your hair like a flock of nanny goats
coming down from Gilead;
your teeth like a flock of sheep
ascending from the bath
each pregnant with twins
not a sterile one among them;
your cheeks like a fragment of pomegranate
through your veil.

Sixty queens
eighty concubines
young girls beyond number—
but the dove—my perfect one—is the only one
her mother's only one
set apart by her genetrix.
The daughters saw her and proclaimed her supremely blessed
the queens and concubines also praised her.

Who is she who comes out
like the dawn rising
beautiful like the moon
set apart like the sun
terrible like an ordered rank from the camps?

I went down into the nut garden
to see the fruit trees in the valleys
to look closely at whether the vineyards had flowered
whether the pomegranates had budded.
My mind did not notice
when it placed me in the four-horse chariots of the prince of my people.

Return—return—O Sulamite
return—return—so that we might contemplate you.

What will you look at in the Sulamite
when she dances between two choruses?

O prince's daughter—
how beautiful your sandaled feet;
the curves of your thighs like necklaces
formed by craftsmen's hands;
your vulva like a lathe-turned bowl
never needing to be mixed with wine;
your belly like a heap of wheat
fortified by lilies;
your two breasts like two fawns
doe-born twins;
your neck like an ivory tower;
your eyes like fishpools in Heshbon
in the gate of Bathrabbim;
your nose like the tower of Lebanon
facing Damascus;
your head like Carmel
its tresses like purple
the king captured by your ringlets.
How beautiful you are
and how splendid
O my dearest
in your pleasures!

Your height like a palm tree's
your breasts its clusters.
I said—I will ascend the palm tree
and seize its fruit
and your breasts will be like clusters on the vine
and the scent of your mouth like apples.
Your throat is like the best wine—
worthy to be sipped by my delightful man
ruminated by his lips and teeth.
I am for my delightful man

and his appetite is for me.
Come, my delightful man—
let us go out into the meadow
let us linger in the villages
let us hasten early to the vines
to see whether they have flowered
whether the flowers have opened
whether the pomegranates have flowered—
there I will give you my loves.
The mandrakes give off their scent—
all the best of the fruit trees in our gates
new and old
I have saved for you, O my delightful man.

Who can give you to me as my brother
sucking my mother's breasts
so that I might find you outside and kiss you
and no one would despise me?
I will seize you and lead you into my mother's house—
there you will teach me
and I will give you a cup of flavored wine
with the pressed juice of my pomegranates.

His left hand is under my head
his right embraces me.

O daughters of Jerusalem—I adjure you
not to enliven or awaken this delightful woman
until she wishes.

Who is this woman ascending from the desert
leaning on her delightful man?

Under an apple tree I enlivened you
there your mother gave you birth
there your genetrix gave you birth.

Place me like a seal on your heart
like a seal on your arm
because delight is as strong as death
and zealous desire as hard as hell
whose lights are lights of fire and divine flames.
Many waters have not been able to extinguish loving-kindness
neither have floods been able to overwhelm it
if someone should give all the substance of his house for delight
they would despise him as if he were nothing.

Our sister is little
and without breasts—
what shall we do for our sister
on the day she is spoken for?
If she is a rampart
we should build silver battlements upon it;
if she is a door
we should buttress it with planks of cedar.
I am a rampart
and my breasts are like a tower;
and so I have become before him
like one who arrives at peace.

Solomon had a vineyard
in Baalhamon;
he handed it over to guards.
A man brings for its fruit
one thousand pieces of silver.
My vineyard is before me—
one thousand for you—O Solomon—
and two hundred for those who guard its fruit.

The woman who inhabits the gardens—
lovers are listening—
make me hear your voice.
Escape, O my delightful man—
be like the does
and like the fawns among the harts
upon the spice mountains.

A Commentary on the Song

The following commentary divides the Song into small parts, most of which extend to no more than two sentences, and some of which are only a phrase in length. My treatment of each part contains the following elements, variously combined and in various proportions.

First, a translation of the text, made from the Latin of the New Vulgate, as already discussed.

Second, an analysis of the text's surface features, coupled with a discussion of significant echoes of these features elsewhere in the Song and elsewhere in the canon of scripture. By "surface features" I mean those things evident at once to any ordinarily literate reader, including (at least) lexicon and syntax; speaker and addressee (often a difficult matter and one capable of generating several possibilities); diction, tropes, and themes; puzzles, ambiguities, incomprehensibilities, surprises.

The initial discussion of these surface features refers only to the lines under immediate discussion, but it then moves to the place of these lines in the Song as a whole, and especially to the resonances of the tropes and themes of the part of the Song under discussion to the Song as a whole. Where else in the Song is this vocabulary used or does this trope occur? Is this speech paralleled or reflected elsewhere in the Song? And so on. The first broader context for the explanation of a part is the whole of which it is a part, and so the first interpretive context for a line or word or speech of the Song is the Song as a whole. There are considerable pleasures and interesting puzzles at every stage of this first level of interpretation, and it is essential to pay them close attention.[32] A commentary could stop there. If it did, it would treat the Song as a closed book and would move outside the Song's text, if it did, only to explain or speculate about the Song's immediate environment, whether textual or otherwise. But this is a Christian theological commentary, and so it cannot stop there. Outside the text of the Song itself, the next context for its interpretation is the canon of scripture as a whole; and so this commentary will identify and discuss verbal, thematic, and tropological verbal consonances and dissonances between what is written in the Song and what is written elsewhere in the corpus of scripture. The principal purpose is to explain the Song as scripture.

Third, discussion of the text as theology, for which the most fundamental question is: What does this tell us about the Lord? Some theology will inevitably have been done in the course of the analysis described in the preceding paragraph, but in this third part, the theology is explicit. I draw for these discussions upon the commentarial tradition, both premodern and modern, as well as upon what I know of the resonances of the text with developed Christian doctrine and with its liturgical and dogmatic use by the church. The Song is, word for word, probably the most-commented-upon book of scripture in the West; this means that it is impossible to read more than a small portion of the commentaries upon it, and equally impossible to provide a systematic treatment of the deployment of the Song in liturgy or doctrine. I certainly attempt neither. What I provide in the way of quotation from or discussion of commentaries, liturgical texts, or doctrinal texts is illustrative only; and it is in the service of developing a theological construal of the Song as a whole and in its parts, not of a history of interpretation or churchly use. The relation between the Song and church doctrine, especially Marian and (therefore) ecclesiological doctrine, is rich and complex: I have learned how to read the Song more fully by learning something of what the church teaches and performs by means of it. It is not merely that the Song reprises and foreshadows what the church teaches (though this is true); neither is it that the church teaches more fully what the Song figures (though this also is true). It is, rather, that what the Song has to teach the church was not fully known to those who composed,

32. "We must begin with the *pleasures* of the Song before progressing to the *truth* of the Song"; Duane Garrett, *Song of Songs*, Word Biblical Commentary 23B (Nashville: Nelson, 2004), 97.

edited, redacted, and canonized it; and that what the Song has to teach the church is not yet fully known to the church. That is why the Song must continue to be read by the church, and not only as an illustration of what it already teaches.

Fourth, and last (and often briefly), I write to you directly, in the second person, identifying what I tentatively take to be the import of the part of the Song under discussion for the ordering of your loves—loves, that is, of yourself, of the Lord, of other people, and of the world and what is in it. Every scriptural text, just because it is a scriptural text, has something of profound importance to say to each of those who read it. You and I are therefore present in it as implicit interlocutors in a way that is not true of any other text.[33] The text confronts us, you and me, demands something from us, and will reconfigure our thought and speech and appetite to the extent that our own particular sins and their concomitant damage do not prevent it from doing so. The beloved's passion in the Song, her desire and her anguish at separation from her lover, will, if you let it, become yours, and in becoming yours reform your loves—not by replicating hers, but by conforming yours to hers (the difference is very important): the text wants that of you, solicits it from you, precisely because it is a scriptural text. A theological reading of the Song ought to take account of this essential presence of the reader in the text, and to the extent that I am capable of doing so, my theological reading does. This text wants to seduce you: it is, in part, my task to return its kiss in such a way as to make it easier for it to have you and for you to be had by it. If the seduction is successful, then you will make your own what the beloved claims: you will know that you are for the lover and the lover for you (2:16; 6:3), and you will languish with love (2:5; 5:8). You are therefore present in my text as well, though of course very differently than you are in the text of scripture; I want to make that presence explicit by calling you out. The commentary's second person, then, is you, whoever you are, reading these words just now; but it is also me, the one who writes them. Every address to you, therefore, includes and implies one to myself.

Approaching the Song in the way just described is not the only way to approach it, and I have no interest in claiming it as the best way. What I offer is one reading among an infinity of possible readings, and one that, like all readings, deploys some controversial assumptions. Among these are the following (there are no doubt more).

I assume that figural reading of scripture is possible, interesting, and, for theologians, unavoidable. There are many reasons for this, among the more important of which are these: that scripture itself self-referentially performs and depicts such reading; that the practice and teaching of the church requires it; and that it is axiomatic for Christian theological interpretation that scripture as a whole and in

---

33. It is trivially true that every text, when read, has its relation to the reader as part of its meaning. But I mean more than this, as should be apparent from this paragraph.

each of its parts is first and last about more than what the surface of its text says. That more is always and necessarily the triune Lord and, necessarily, that Lord's incarnation as Jesus Christ.

But what, in more detail, is figural reading? One event or utterance figures another when, while remaining unalterably what it is, it announces or communicates something other than itself. Eve's assent to the tempter and her consequent taking of the forbidden fruit from the tree figures, in this sense, Mary's *fiat mihi* in response to the annunciation and the consequent incarnation of the Lord in her womb. The second event—the figured—encompasses and includes the first, without removing its reality. The first—the figuring—has its reality, however, by way of participation in the second.[34] This is in the order of being.

Ontological figuration may, however, be replicated at the level of the text, and in scripture it inevitably is. Here, a depiction of a person or utterance or event—say, the lover's praises of the beloved or the details of the construction and ornamentation of Solomon's bed—may figure a textual depiction of some other person, utterance, or event. Christian theological commentators on the Song, as on any other scriptural text, must, in seeking their text's scriptural reverberations, be attentive not only to the sheerly verbal, but also to the figural. Allegory—which may or may not be present in scripture, unlike figure, which necessarily is—differs from figure in that it dissolves the allegorical text into what it allegorizes. Following allegorical method strictly means that an allegorical text's literal sense must be ignored except in so far as it permits understanding of what it allegorizes.[35] The figural text's literal sense—like its ontological reality—does not dissolve in this way: Eve remains Eve, the lovers of the Song remain the lovers of the Song (as will be apparent, I do not read them as if they were figures in a parable), and the text of the Song remains what it is: a constant demand for interpretation whose results are not determined and which may, for Christians, often be uncomfortable.[36]

34. This formulation floats upon deep waters. A sounding into them may be had from Jan Aertsen, *Nature and Creature: Thomas Aquinas's Way of Thought* (Leiden: Brill, 1998); Joseph de Finance, *Être et agir dans la philosophie de Saint Thomas*, 2nd ed. (Rome: Librairie Éditrice de l'Université Grégorienne, 1960); Cornelio Fabro, *La nozione metafisica di partecipazione secondo San Tommaso*, 2nd ed. (Turin: Società editrice internazionale, 1950); Brian Leftow, "Divine Simplicity," *Faith and Philosophy* 23 (2006): 365–80; Christian Moevs, *The Metaphysics of Dante's Comedy* (New York: Oxford University Press, 2005); Fran O'Rourke, *Pseudo-Dionysius and the Metaphysics of Aquinas* (Notre Dame, IN: University of Notre Dame Press, 2005); D. C. Schindler, "What's the Difference? On the Metaphysics of Participation in Plato, Plotinus, and Aquinas," *Nova et Vetera* 5 (2007): 583–618; and Rudi A. te Velde, *Participation and Substantiality in Thomas Aquinas* (Leiden: Brill, 1985).

35. For a very clear statement of the necessity of avoiding ("abolishing") the literal sense in the case of reading the Song, see Joseph B. Soloveitchik, *And from There You Shall Seek*, trans. Naomi Goldblum (Jersey City, NJ: Ktav, 2008), 151–53. Soloveitchik writes as a Jew, expounding the Mishnah and Maimonides on the question of how the Song should be read.

36. In this excessively brief characterization of the figural I follow quite closely Erich Auerbach, "Figura," in his *Scenes from the Drama of European Literature* (Minneapolis: University of Minnesota Press, 1984), 11–76. This essay, though not by a Christian, should be read by all Christian theological interpreters of scripture. For a more detailed interpretation of the practice of Christian

So much, with excessive brevity, for figural reading. Second, and perhaps more controversial, is the assumption that any part of scripture may illuminate any other part. It is this assumption that makes sense of looking for verbal, thematic, and tropological consonances and dissonances between parts of the Song and other parts of the canon of scripture. Such reading has been the usual practice of Christian and Jewish exegetes of scripture. One interesting implication of that practice, rarely observed and discussed, is that it is best practiced by working with one among the versions (see introduction: "Confecting the Song"). This is because verbal reverberations are best sought within the bounds of a single natural language, and this means that I look for them within the bounds of the Latin text of scripture as given in the New Vulgate, since that is the locus of the Song I treat. Looking for consonances and dissonances in this particular Latin version therefore carries with it no prejudice against the many other versions of the corpus, whether in Latin or any other language; neither does it require any particular judgments about the authority of the text I use. The resonances and dissonances I find and comment on sometimes will and sometimes will not be reproducible by those seeking consonance and dissonance between other versions of the Song and other versions of the corpus of scripture.

When I read, for example, in Song 1:3, *oleum effusum nomen tuum* ("your name is oil poured out") and look elsewhere in the corpus of scripture as found in the New Vulgate for connections between *nomen* and *oleum* and for the theological and semantic significance of both terms, what I find may or may not be found by those working in Syriac, Hebrew, Greek, English, Spanish, or what-have-you. That is why the tapestry of theological scriptural interpretation needs work on all the versions: only in that way is what the Lord says to his people by way of scripture asymptotically approachable. Further, in seeking these verbal/theological consonances and dissonances I am guided not only by the corpus of scripture itself, but also by those reverberations already found and given importance by the Western (largely Latin) tradition of commenting upon the Song.

---

figural reading, with special reference to Origen, see John David Dawson, *Christian Figural Reading and the Fashioning of Identity* (Berkeley: University of California Press, 2002). Specifically on the Song as treated by Origen, see J. Christopher King, *Origen on the Song of Songs as the Spirit of Scripture: The Bridegroom's Perfect Marriage Song* (Oxford: Oxford University Press, 2005). Commentators on the Song with historicist or literary interests often dismiss figural reading along with allegorical reading on the dual ground that both (if any distinction is made between them) obscure the particulars of the Song because they treat it as piecemeal support for a general theory arrived at independently and because they advocate reading the text for itself, free from assumptions imported from elsewhere. Jill M. Munro, *Spikenard and Saffron: The Imagery of the Song of Songs* (Sheffield: Sheffield Academic Press, 1995), 10–16, is representative (if a little extreme) in making these criticisms. But neither is defensible: figural reading, as defined, requires rather than calls into question attention to textual and literary particularity; and it is not possible to read a text for itself. See also Kingsmill 2009: 42–44.

SONG OF SONGS

Solomon's Song of Songs (1:1)

Solomon's Song of Songs

The Song opens with a title, "Solomon's Song of Songs," which is suggestive rather than lucid. Solomon's exact relation to the Song is not specified. And the phrase "song of songs" is given no explicit gloss elsewhere in the work. Who sings? Does the title suggest a superlative (the best of all possible songs) or an anthology (a single extended song comprising several or many subsongs)? In what sense is the work a song at all? It contains, certainly, nothing but direct speech, and that often at a high level of impressionistic compression: every word of it, with the exception of the title, is spoken by one or another of its characters, either in soliloquy or to another of its characters. There is no narrative voice, omniscient or otherwise, and no narrative line other than what can be discerned from what the characters say; perhaps that is the sense of "song." There is no mention of songs or singing outside the work's title.[1]

Reading *ad litteram*—paying attention, that is, only to the letter of the Song, to what is written upon its surface and to what a first naïve reading yields by attending to that surface—and assuming that calling the Song a "song" has something to do with its genre, the first explanation that suggests itself is that "song" means lyric. "Lyric" derives from the Greek *lyrikos* ("lyre"), and while the word has no entirely standard meaning as a genre term in poetics, in one of its ranges of meaning it denotes a short (perhaps sung) piece, often in the first person, whose purpose is to express the poet's (singer's) feeling. While there may be narrative content in

---

1. The comments on the Song's title that follow benefit from the extensive and hermeneutically sensitive analysis in Jean Emmanuel de Ena, *Sens et interprétations du Cantique des Cantiques* (Paris: Cerf, 2004), 235–311.

a lyric, it is not the point: the point is empathy and perhaps catharsis, which is to say the engagement of the hearer's feelings by means of the expression of the singer's. The singer and her or his situation need only enough definition and identification to make such effects possible. To ask for more is to make a genre mistake. When a song begins with the words "I want to hold your hand"[2] or "O while I love you pretty baby / you're the only love I've ever known"[3] or "let me be kissed with your mouth's kiss" (1:2), it is a mistake to ask whose hand, whose love, whose kiss, or whose wants are in question. What counts is that there is a desire for someone or something, and that this desire is depicted with sufficient intensity that response—empathetic, cathartic—is possible. The Song, both as a whole and in its parts, fits this definition well: it is a series of short lyrics loosely connected into a longer lyric. So much can be said *ad litteram*.

Attending to the Song as a scriptural book, and asking how songs and singing are represented elsewhere in the canon, permits much more to be said. A scriptural song—which is to say a form of words called that in scripture—is a poetic ejaculation to the Lord in the face of some unusual or dramatic event, whether experienced for the first time or recapitulated as the song is sung subsequently by those who wish to remember the event.[4] Gratitude is typically a song's dominant note: this is true, for instance of Hannah's *canticum*, an outpouring of gratitude for her conception of Samuel (1 Sam. 2), or of Deborah's and Barak's hymn of thanks (*canticum*) for the Lord's great deeds (Judg. 5). It is also true of one of the songs of Moses, in which the Lord's deliverance of the people from slavery is celebrated in a single, extended praise-shout (*carmen*; Exod. 15). But a song's gratitude may also be tempered with lament, as in Moses's other song (Deut. 32), in which, as well as celebrating the Lord's great deeds, he laments the people's inability to respond properly to what the Lord has done for them. And sometimes lament is the dominant or even the only note, as when David laments the deaths of Saul and Jonathan in the Song of the Bow (called a *canticum arcus* or *planctum*, "breast-beating lamentation"; 2 Sam. 1) or when Isaiah, speaking in the voice of the Lord, sings to Israel of the vineyard he has planted in a tone of

---

2. The title of a Lennon/McCartney composition, recorded and released by the Beatles in 1963.

3. The opening lines of Bob Dylan's "Beyond Here Lies Nothin'" from the album *Together through Life*, released in 2009.

4. Origen, *Homeliae in canticum canticorum* (Homilies on the Song of Songs), prologue §4 (Lawson 1956: 47–51), discusses at some length the various texts that might be called "songs" in the Old Testament. Gregory the Great, *Expositio in Canticis Canticorum* (Exposition of the Song) 7 (French and Latin in *Grégoire le Grand: Commentaire sur le Cantique des Cantiques*, ed. and trans. Rodrigue Bélanger, Sources Chrétiennes 314 [Paris: Cerf, 1984], 78–80), writes of five kinds of song in the Old Testament: songs of victory, of exhortation or contestation, of exultation, in celebration of help received, and of joining or union (*coniunctio*). The Song is of the last kind: *per haec dominus familiari amore conplectitur* ("by means of this [Song] one is joined with the Lord in an intimate love"). Compare Rupert of Deutz, *Commentaria in Canticum Canticorum* (Commentary on the Song), prologue (Deutz and Deutz 2005: 8), who writes that scriptural songs are sung to the Lord in gratitude for some *beneficium*, some benefit or favor granted by the Lord.

lament and judgment (*canticum de vinea*; Isa. 5:1–7). But generally speaking, when a scriptural song, a *canticum*, is sung, it acknowledges the Lord's surprising and wonderfully awe-inspiring presence in some event, and does so in the only way that could approach adequacy as a response to the Lord as giver of this gift. Often too a scriptural song is marked in scripture as a reminder to others that the Lord has done whatever it is that the song responds to, and as a gift to them of words with which to engrave this response of gratitude on the tablets of the memory. All this is true of the sequence of New Testament songs that begins with the exchange between Elizabeth and Mary at the visitation and ends with Simeon's acknowledgment that Jesus is the Messiah promised (Luke 1–2).[5] These express surprised gratitude in a poetic language of compressed intensity; and they do so in a way that fits them for what they have become, which is essential parts of the church's liturgy. Many of the songs of the Old Testament have this liturgical function too, for Jews as well as for Christians.

A scriptural song, then, is an act of confession whose principal notes are praise and gratitude, but that may also contain a counterpoint of lament. Its language, like all confessional language, expresses a particular relation of the singer to the Lord and, in expressing it, brings performatively into existence—or performatively deepens and intensifies—that very relation. When Jews and Christians resing Moses's praise-shout, "I will sing to the Lord for he is gloriously magnified: the horse and his rider he has cast into the sea" (Exod. 15:1), or David's lament-song, "How the mighty are fallen" (2 Sam. 1:19); and when Christians resing Mary's "My soul magnifies the Lord" (Luke 1:46), they establish themselves, ever more firmly with each singing, in a new intimacy with the Lord. Quotidian language, whether everyday human chat, the scholar's jargon, or the instrumentalist language of instruction, will not do for this. Language must be heightened, intensified, made prismatic, crystallized, and condensed into poetry. And, in the songs of scripture, it is.

The Song's title prepares the scripturally attuned hearer for all this. To consider the Song as depicting and performing a particular, rather complex, relation of the singer—and of you and me as resingers—to the Lord simply on the basis of its title is not, then, to import into it anything extraneous. It is only to think about what it is called in the light of a broadly scriptural understanding of what it means to sing to the Lord. And that, in turn, is to read the Song as scripture. But the Song does not call itself only a, or the, Song. It calls itself "Song of Songs." What does that mean?

Two meanings at once suggest themselves. The first is the superlative: this work is the song of all songs, the best possible song, the song toward which all other songs tend.[6] The second is the anthological: this work is a collection into

5. Though not explicitly called songs in scripture, these songs have since come to be called *cantica* by the church.
6. German indicates this meaning explicitly in the standard (since Luther) rendering of the title in that language: *Das Hohelied* ("the high[est] song").

one song of a number of subsidiary songs. There is something to be said for both interpretations.

As to the first: the most obvious resonance within the corpus of scripture is with the phrase "holy of holies" (*sanctum sanctorum*), which is grammatically identical to the Song's title (*canticum canticorum*); but this is not the only consonance: consider also "god of gods" (*deus deorum*; Dan. 2:47), "king of kings" (*rex regum*; Ezra 7:12, where Artaxerxes is represented as using this title of himself), and, of course, "vanity of vanities" (*vanitas vanitatum*; Eccl. 1:2; 12:8). The holy of holies is the most holy of all holy places: in the Old Testament the phrase may refer to the innermost part of the tabernacle that accompanied the people of Israel during their wilderness wanderings, in which the ark of the covenant is placed (Exod. 26:33); to the altar for holocausts (Exod. 29:37; 30:10); or to the innermost chamber of the temple of Jerusalem (Ezek. 41:4; 43:12; 45:3). In each of these applications of the phrase, the point is to indicate a place in which the Lord's presence—his scarifying holiness—is most fully evident. Similarly, according to this reading, the Song is the most songlike of all songs, the song in which what it is to be a song is most fully evident and beautifully present.[7]

As to the second, or anthological, meaning: there is no obvious verbal reso-nance elsewhere in scripture for this understanding of the term.[8] What evidence there is to support it is internal to the Song, and it is certainly the case that the text as we have it can be divided into component songs, some in which the lover praises the beloved, some in which the beloved praises the lover, some in which the daughters of Jerusalem question the beloved and receive a response, and so on. But commentators, premodern and modern, Jewish and Christian, have reached no agreement about just where to draw the lines between the component parts of the Song. This is in part because the text as we have it does not provide unambigu-ous signals about voice—which is to say about who is speaking and to whom. It is possible, then, that "Song of Songs" carries with it an anthological meaning as well as a superlative one; but if it does, the superlative one is primary: this is the understanding of the title most consonant with scripture as a whole, though there is nothing further in the Song itself that explicitly speaks to this understanding of the title, and indeed nothing else explicit about a song or songs.

In reading the Song, then, we read the superlative song, the best of all pos-sible songs, the song in which the very idea of singing is apotheosized and most fully represented. This means that all other songs, to the extent that they are

7. On this superlative aspect of the meaning of the Song's title as derivable from its grammatical form, see Origen, *Homeliae in canticum canticorum* (Homilies on the Song of Songs), prologue §4 (Lawson 1956: 46–47).

8. The phrase occurs only in the title of the Song. It was usual, however, for Latin commenta-tors to mention this anthological meaning and sometimes to say that the constituent songs of the Song are marked by the repetition of the *adiuro* formula at 2:7; 3:5; 5:8; 8:4. See Rupert of Deutz, *Commentaria in Canticum Canticorum* (Commentary on the Song), prologue (Deutz and Deutz 2005: 10).

undamaged, participate in this one, which is to say that all other songs figure this one—for figuration is the literary and semantic correlate of the ontological doctrine of participation. A fuller characterization of what this means will have to await commentary upon the Song's content, but it should already be clear that, scripturally speaking, singing is a complex speech-act of confession that may include praise, gratitude, and lament and that establishes a relation of peculiar and profound intimacy between singer and hearer, reconfiguring the being and understanding and aspiration of the singer by conforming her more closely to the Lord to whom she sings. When you sing your praise, lament, and gratitude, you are not only—nor even principally—expressing your feelings or aspirations or beliefs. No, you are reconfiguring yourself as one who praises, one who laments, and one who is grateful, and at the same time making more intimate (more full of kisses and embraces and caresses and delight) your relation to the Lord to whom you sing. Even a theological commentary on the Song must resing it, even if against the will of its commentator; all the more for a true resinging on the part of a devoted reader.

For a Christian reader, this talk of superlatives, of the Song as the best of all possible songs, raises questions. Should we not take the songs of the New Testament—of Mary, of Simeon, of Anna, of Elizabeth, and so on—as songs that in one way or another go beyond this Song? Are they not explicit witnesses to Christ while the Song is only an implicit one? In some sense this must be so: they are explicitly about Christ while the Song is only implicitly so. But the Song has a feature absent in all other scriptural songs: the Lord speaks directly in it as lover, as one who urgently desires the beloved, who hymns her beauty and the pleasure it gives him, and whose desire for intimacy with her is figured as the lover's desire for sexual union with the beloved. All other scriptural songs, including even Mary's, are in human voice only, even if human voice responding to the Lord's acts as lover; in this one, and only in this one, the Lord speaks as lover.

But the Song is not only the "Song of Songs"; it is also "Solomon's." The Song does not say that Solomon composed the Song; neither does it say that he did not. It says only that he is in some respect intimate with it, and it with him. Why?

Solomon is a figure elsewhere in the Song. The beloved's black skin is likened to the color of the skins from which his tents are made (1:5); in 3:7–11 there is a description of Solomon's bed on his wedding day; and in 8:11–12 there is discussion of the yield of his vineyard. There are also other mentions of a king (1:4, 12; 7:6), which suggest—though do not require—the conclusion that he, whether named as Solomon or left unnamed, is the Song's lover. It is possible, then, to read the Song as though it were Solomon's love song to his beloved, and this explains the long tradition of seeing at least that in it; it explains too why some of the more flatfooted among pagan exegetes, for whom it is often the case that there is only one correct reading of the Song, can see only a royal wedding song in the Song. This view is certainly inadequate, but not to be rejected out of hand: the surface of the Song's text, and therefore at least one layer of its meaning, includes the idea that thinking about Solomon may be helpful in thinking through the lover's nature and significance. The text teases here, as so often: Solomon's exact function in it and the nature of his relation to it are important but occluded. But that Solomon has importance for the Song is not unambiguous, even if the kind of importance he has is; and so the reader's attention—and this commentator's attention—must be directed toward the Solomon of the corpus of scripture in order to see what can be learned about the Song from that.

Solomon is, scripturally speaking, the second child of David and Bathsheba whose sexual intimacy began adulterously and was further stained by his father's murder of his mother's first husband in order that their adultery and the child conceived by it might remain hidden. That child, conceived before the murder and the marriage, is cursed by the Lord as punishment for David, and dies; Solomon, their second child, is loved by the Lord, and flourishes (2 Sam. 11–12). He asks for and receives the gift of wisdom from the Lord; builds the first temple in Jerusalem (Jer. 52:20; 2 Macc. 2:9; Acts 7:47); extends and enriches the kingdom (Sir. 47:15–28 [= 47:13–18 RSV]); receives tribute from the principal potentates of the world (Matt. 6:29; 12:42; Luke 11:31; 12:27); marries many foreign women, against the Lord's explicit command; begins to worship foreign gods, prompted by his foreign wives (Neh. 13:25–26); and is punished by the Lord for this by Jeroboam's rebellion and the secession of the northern kingdom (1 Kgs. 1–11; cf. 2 Chr. 1–9). Outside the narratives explicitly devoted to his life, Solomon's name is most often mentioned in scripture as an exemplar of wisdom, of the public glory of the potentate, of the righteous king who honors the Lord (especially by building him a temple), and of apostasy.[9] Solomon is, too, an archetype of the man who loves beautiful and powerful women (Pharaoh's daughter, the Queen of Sheba) and is in turn loved by them. This is no doubt the principal reason why the Song is associated with his name: it is about sexual desire and sexual love, and he is the archetypal lover. But apart from that connection, Solomon has little part to play in the Song. He is at most a hidden presence, not to be taken as either the Song's author or its lover.

Kisses and Loves (1:2–3a)

> Let me be kissed with your mouth's kiss
> for your loves are better than wine
> fragrant with your best ointments.

9. In addition to the Song, another scriptural book is associated with Solomon's name: Proverbs, whose title reads, "The Parables of Solomon, son of David, King of Israel" (1:1). Since Jerome, it has become usual to identify three "books of Solomon" as Proverbs, the Song, and Wisdom of Solomon. But the New Vulgate does not include Solomon's name in the title of the third of these.

Here, in the opening words of the Song proper, there are only pronouns, none gendered, none linked to a proper noun. There is a "me" who wants to be kissed by "your mouth," and "your" skill and desirability as a lover is extolled ("your loves are better than wine"). There is an implied "you," the hearer: you listen, startled, *in medias res*, overhearing the voice of desire. But otherwise, nothing is clear. I assume that the Song's (female) beloved speaks here: her voice runs, probably, through the end of 1:7. The first clear indication of an addressee is in 1:7 ("O man in whom my soul delights"), and on the assumption that when he is addressed or apostrophized it is she who does it, it is she who speaks there. And since there is no clear indication of speaker or addressee until that point—such indications are the usual means, in the Song, of indicating a joint, a place at which there is a shift—I assume that she speaks from the beginning until the end of 1:8, when she becomes the addressee, and he, presumably, the speaker.

While the Song does not exactly open with a kiss (Claudel 1948: 32), it does begin with a triple opening of the lips (Chrétien 2005: 105): of its speaker, of one of the characters in it, and of its hearer, you, whose mouth may open in surprise at what is said, and in imitative sympathy with the lips of the kiss-seeker (→4:2). The intensity and directness of the language ("kiss," "mouth," "loves"—this last rendering *amores*, which can, and here almost certainly does, have an explicitly sexual meaning) reproduces in its hearers the memory and desire it figures; and the absence of narration and scene-setting brings tension with it, an urgent need to know more about who these people are and why, exactly, she wants to be made love to by him. Every cue and clue needs attention: puzzlement opens the ears, and the absence of scene-setting and narration heightens the tension. These are all characteristics of the lyric: we are in the ever-present no-time and no-place of a lover (or a beloved) wanting to be kissed.

Kisses and kissing are mentioned in the Song twice: here at 1:2 and in 8:1. In both cases, she seeks or imagines his kisses. Kisses go with lips (*labia*): these, in the Song, are depicted in such a way as to make it clear that they are principally for kissing. Hers, he says, are "like a scarlet thread" (4:3); they "drip honeycomb" (4:11). His, she says, are "lilies / dripping prime myrrh" (5:13); and when he is praising her throat as "like the best wine," she breaks in, agreeing, and saying that it is "worthy to be sipped by my delightful man / ruminated by his lips and teeth" (7:10). The erotic imagery is very clear and very direct: the redness of her lips makes them desirable; she wants him to use his lips and tongue to nibble, lick, and suck her throat; and each depicts the lips of the other as drippingly and redolently sweet, in the one case with honey and in the other with myrrh (→1:13).

This is unique in scripture. While there is a fair amount of scriptural attention to the kiss, which of course implies the lips, nowhere else is there erotic attention specifically to the lips as a desirable part of the body, capable of giving and receiving pleasure. Elsewhere in scripture the lips are typically mentioned in connection with speech (Ps. 12:3–5 [= 12:2–4 RSV]; Prov. 20:15; Isa. 6:5), and sometimes in connection with eating; they are portals for food going in, and for words coming out, serving as gateways between the inner and the outer. Only once, so far as I can tell, are kissing and speaking lips explicitly connected in scripture: "Those who speak rightly kiss the lips" (*labia deosculatur, qui recta verba respondet*; Prov. 24:26).

In the Song, however, the lips are for the kiss, which, scripturally, is a mark of intimacy. It may be given, scripturally speaking, by the Lord to us and by us to the Lord, as well as by us to one another. The kiss exchanged by humans, whether familial or sexual (and the two are not far apart), is everywhere in scripture. Paul likes to end his letters to particular congregations *in osculo sancto* ("with a holy kiss"; Rom. 16:16; 2 Cor. 13:12); Joseph kisses his long-lost brothers in greeting (Gen. 45:15); Orpah kisses Naomi goodbye (Ruth 1:14); and Judas betrays Jesus with a kiss—even this last marks intimacy of an inverted kind (Luke 22:47 and parallels). Kisses given by us to the Lord and by the Lord to us are also present in scripture. The woman who anoints Jesus's feet and weeps over them is an instance of the former, of a woman kissing the Lord incarnate (Luke 7:36–50 and parallels). Like this, though with valence reversed, is Hosea's typically excitable mention of those who kiss calves as a way of marking their idolatrous intimacy with those false gods (Hos. 13:2). The Lord kisses us, at least parabolically, when the prodigal's father, who certainly figures the Lord, kisses the prodigal upon his return—in fact, not only does the divine father kiss the prodigal, he falls upon his neck, embracing him with passionate joy (Luke 15:20).

When the Song speaks in the first person, as it does here, you, the hearer, can easily and naturally identify with that first-person speaker. This is especially so if you hear the Song as a scriptural book, because part of what it means for a book to be scriptural is that it addresses its hearers. The "me" who wants to be kissed is, therefore, you; and even at this early stage of hearing the Song, you can place yourself in the position of the Song's speaker, the one who wants to be kissed; and if you are attuned scripturally to the meaning of the kiss, you will know it as a gesture of intimacy not only among people, but also from the Lord to his lovers.

The Lord, therefore, your scriptural imagination can tell you, wants to kiss your lips with a passion, to redden them with the redness of his passion for you. The "scarlet thread" of the beloved's lips, stained by the blood of the Lord's passion and inflamed by the heat of his kisses, belongs to the Lord's church and, by extension, to each of its members. The Lord's death on the cross is the deepest kiss of humanity's unclean lips (reflecting Isa. 6:5), extending to all the embrace given to Abraham. Christians reciprocate this kiss most fully here below in drinking the blood-red wine of the Eucharist. The stain of that wine on our lips is the mark of the Lord's blood on our bodies; it is also the mark of his lips on ours, cleaning them with the purifying flame of his passion.

In these kisses, our mundane kisses participate; our desires for our beloveds' lips are what they are because of the Lord's desire for our lips. The intensity of our desires for those human lips, and that the kisses we give to and get from our lovers do not satisfy while being necessary and delightful, is a sign of this participation.

Attending to the beloved's response to and imagination of her lover's lips and kisses can refigure your own kisses and make them more delightful and less idolatrous (the temptation to idolize our lovers and their kisses is almost irresistible). This is one among the Song's many gifts.[10]

The Song's beloved is the one eager for her lover's kisses; and she figures Israel-church just as he, the Song's male lover, figures the Lord. You, whether you are male or female, are, then, identifying with the Song's beloved when you resonate with the Song's first-person voice. But the questions of sex and gender—yours as hearer and that of the Song's voices, male and female—are not of central importance here. You, whatever your sex and whatever the habituated shape of your sexual desires, will find as you hear the Song, whether for the first time or the fiftieth, that you resonate and identify differently at different times; and the text of the Song forces those shifts upon you. If you are female and habituated to love of and desire for males, this does not mean that you can resonate only with the Song's beloved's expressions of desire for her male lover and delight in his male body. Neither, *mutatis mutandis*, if you are a male habituated to desiring the female. The Song's layers of figuration require, if you attend to them closely, transpositions here: as you come to see the beloved as a figure for the Lord's Israel-church and yourself as a member of that body, then her desires come to figure yours, whatever your sex and gender and habits. And the Song's own habit of having the lover and the beloved say identical things to or about one another serves to show the structural similarity of the man's and the woman's desires for one another and the easy possibility, therefore, of resonating with what she says about him and with what he says about her, no matter your own sex.[11] When it comes to yearning, to the remembering and imagination of the pleasures of the other's body, and to the elevation of those pleasures above all others given to the senses, the two are not easily distinguishable; this is a point signaled to the hearer by the occasional interchangeability of their words. This is not to say that their words are always exchangeable: reciprocity does not dissolve into identity, but it does go deep.[12]

Origen, writing in the mid-third century, says that the "kiss" and the "mouth" of this opening verse of the Song signify the Word's power "by which he enlightens the mind and, as by some word of love addressed to her [that is, to his beloved church] ... makes plain whatever is unknown and dark to her. ... It is of this happening that the kiss, which we give to one another in church at the holy mysteries,

10. This paragraph elaborates upon Gilbert of Hoyland's comments on the Song's kisses, conveyed by Chrétien 2005: 112–13. See also Michael Fishbane, *The Kiss of God: Spiritual and Mystical Death in Judaism* (Seattle: University of Washington Press, 1994), chap. 1.

11. This exchange of epithets is seen in 1:2 and 4:10, where first the beloved and then the lover say identical things about one another's "loves." In 2:17 and 4:6, "until the day breathes / and the shadows flee" is in the first case spoken by her to—or at least about—him, and in the second by him to her.

12. For a more extended analysis of the kiss, reciprocity, and exchange, see Jean-Luc Marion, *Le phénomène érotique: Six méditations* (Paris: Grasset, 2003), chap. 24.

is a figure."[13] This is an important connection with the church's liturgical practice, namely the exchange of the kiss of peace at Mass. The way in which Origen puts this suggests a bidirectional double figuration: our exchange of kisses figures the enlightening kiss that Christ gives to his church, her lips open and eager; and the demand for a kiss from the lover with which the Song opens figures that same Christ-kiss, but, as it were, from the opposite direction. Christ's kiss of the church is that which both the Song's scriptural kiss and our liturgical kisses figure.

The opening words of the Song speak not only of kisses but also of "loves," in the sense of the caresses that lovers exchange. These are mentioned often in the Song. Twice (2:5; 5:8) she says that she is "langui[d] with love"; once she promises to give him her "loves" (7:13); and once he says of her loves exactly what is said here, which is that they are "better than wine" (4:10)—which is at least to say that they are deliciously intoxicating.

The acts of love recalled and yearned for by the beloved are praised in gustatory, tactile, and olfactory terms: they are, in the opening words, "better than wine" and "fragrant with your best ointments." Wine has bouquet and taste as well as being intoxicating: it is mentioned six times in the Song: twice in the verses under discussion; in the already mentioned parallel (4:10); at the very center of the Song, where the lovers' consummation of their mutual desire is most explicitly depicted (5:1); where her voice and his almost merge in the likening of her throat to "the best wine" (7:10), which her lover will drink; and where she promises to give him wine in her mother's house (8:2). Wine serves in the Song as an explicit simile and an implicit metaphor for lovemaking, and always as a suggestion of the intoxicating pleasures of that activity (→1:6b).

Similar suggestions of intoxicating pleasure are present in the simile of ointment's fragrance (1:3), though there with emphasis upon the olfactory and tactile, and this trope also occurs several times in the Song (4:10, 14; 5:13), applied to both lover and beloved. Here, the lover's loves are likened to the "best ointments." "Ointment" (*unguentum*) is a regrettably medicinal word in contemporary English: you might use it to salve a wound or to ease a hurt. But in the Song it is not at all medicinal, but rather an instrument and symbol of erotic delight: you might rub it on your lover's body, and in saying, as the speaker does here, that your lover's lovemaking has the fragrance of the best ointments, you remind yourself of olfactory and tactile intimacy and you anticipate the repetition of those delights. But this is not all: "ointment" takes us at once into the sphere of talking and thinking about intimacy with the Lord. The Lord is not explicitly mentioned at all in the Song, but if the Song is read as a scriptural rather than a closed book, then he is everywhere in it. The tropes and figures used in these first words of the Song impel a scripturally versed listener to see, palimpsestlike and in chiaroscuro, desire for

13. Origen, *Homeliae in canticum canticorum* (Homilies on the Song of Songs), prologue §4 (following Lawson 1956: 62, with small amendments). Compare Origen, *Homeliae in canticum canticorum* 1 (Lawson 1956: 269).

and love of the Lord figured by desire for and love of the lover. It is not that desire for the human lover and memory of his lovemaking simply stand, allegorically, for desire for the Lord's love and kisses, to be left aside once we have understood what they represent. Neither is it that the human authors, compilers, and editors of the Song had the Lord's lovemaking in mind when they wrote the words we now read—we know nothing about what they had in mind; what we have is their words, and instead of seeking the chimera of authorial intention we should pay close attention to these words. It is, rather, that the Song's words resonate within the verbal manifold of scripture's corpus, and when you pay attention to those resonances you see, beyond reasonable dispute, that the depiction of human memory, desire, and sexual love in the Song figures both the Lord's love for you and yours for him, and does so in a way that helps us to see that our human loves for one another are what they are because of their participation in his for us and ours, reciprocally, for him.

Anointing is what is done with "ointment," and although the verb "anoint" (*ung[u]ere*) does not occur in the Song, the noun (*unguentum*) occurs four times (1:3; 4:10, 14; 5:13), and it resonates closely with the broad and deep presence of anointing in scripture. That resonance is the principal reason for preserving the word "ointment" as a translation of *unguentum* in spite of the word's medicinal flavor. There are other possibilities ("balm," "salve"), but they lose the resonance with anointing, the preservation of which is essential if the Song is to be understood as a scriptural book. Anointing, first and last, is what is done to signal and seal a special intimacy with the Lord. It is something we humans do to and for one another; but sometimes we do it as the Lord's instruments, and when we do it is the Lord who anoints us.

Consider: "Samuel took a small flask of oil and poured it out on his [Saul's] head and kissed him and said: 'See, the Lord has anointed you ruler over his people Israel'" (1 Sam. 10:1; cf. the account of Moses's consecration of Aaron with the *unctionis oleum* at Lev. 8:1–13). Here Samuel anoints Saul, and in the description of his doing so, a kiss and the act of anointing are brought together—the same concatenation as is present in the Song's opening words (oil is about to be mentioned, in 1:3). Saul's anointing marks and seals him for a special intimacy with the Lord, and in performing the anointing, as well as in marking it with a kiss, Samuel serves as the Lord's agent, as the hands and lips of the Lord.

Consider also: "He [Bezalel] compounded the oil for the sanctifying ointment and incense made of the purest spices according to the arts of the perfumer" (Exod. 37:29). Here, Bezalel, one of the artisans chosen to construct the tent of meeting, the ark of the covenant, and all their appurtenances, mixes the oil (*oleum*) that is ingredient to the ointment (*unguentum*) to be used to anoint the tent and the ark (Exod. 25–37, especially 30:22–35). These material items are sanctified—made holy, given a special intimacy with the Lord—by their anointing. And, as is standard in the descriptions given in the book of Exodus of the materials with which anointing may be done, there is a close link between ointment and oil (Song 1:3).

In the verse quoted, the ointment is a particular kind of oil—oil to which spices and herbs have been added according to a particular recipe. Bezalel's function in preparing the sanctifying ointment is different from Samuel's in anointing and kissing Saul, however: if Samuel's hands and lips were the Lord's at only one remove, as it were (Samuel as secondary cause), then Bezalel's are at two removes at least (tertiary cause, perhaps), because even though he has been chosen and inspired by the Lord (Exod. 35:30–35), he has been given his instructions by Moses, and he does not himself anoint the tabernacle (Exod. 40:9–33). But still, in this case as in Samuel's, the Lord anoints with ointment in order to establish intimacy with himself.

Consider as well:

> There was a sinful woman of the city who learned that he [Jesus] was dining in the Pharisee's house. She brought in an alabaster flask of ointment, and standing behind him weeping she began to wash his feet with her tears. Then she wiped them with her hair and kissed them and anointed them with ointment. . . . Then he [Jesus] turned to the woman and said to Simon: "Do you see this woman? I came into your house and you did not give me water for my feet but she washed them with her tears and dried them with her hair. You did not kiss me, but she, ever since I came in, has not stopped kissing my feet. You did not anoint my head with oil, but she anointed my feet with ointment. Because of this I tell you that her many sins are forgiven because she has taken much delight [in me]. Those who are forgiven little take little delight." (Luke 7:37–38, 44–47)[14]

Here, in the sinful woman's anointing of Jesus, his forgiving of her sins, and his rebuke of Simon, a still more extensive set of connections is made among the terms that form the kiss-ointment-anointing concatenation of the Song's opening words. These verses (and so also the Song) begin with the desire for a kiss and go on from there to praise the lover's lovemakings in terms of ointment. The progression is almost identical in Luke 7, where Jesus's words are strong and direct: the kiss given to the Lord and the ointment poured out on the Lord are good things, worthy not only of praise but also of forgiveness of sin. Such actions of love are the one thing that matters.

With these scriptural themes in mind, the depth of the beloved's words to and about her lover begins to become apparent. If the "best ointments" are those given by the Lord to us—if, as Leviticus puts it, the "anointing oil of the Lord" (*oleum unctionis Domini*; 10:6–11; 21:10–12) is what sets apart the priests of the Lord from others and makes certain actions improper or impossible for them—then the Song's recall of his loves as "fragrant with your best ointments" shows those

---

14. For patristic comments on this Lukan passage in the context of the Song, see Origen, *Homeliae in canticum canticorum* (Homilies on the Song of Songs) 1 (Lawson 1956: 273–74); Gregory the Great, *Expositio in Canticis Canticorum* (Exposition of the Song) 18 (French and Latin in *Grégoire le Grand: Commentaire sur le Cantique des Cantiques*, ed. and trans. Rodrigue Bélanger, Sources Chrétiennes 314 [Paris: Cerf, 1984], 96–98).

who read the Song as a scriptural book that his love for her figures the Lord's for us. She wants to be anointed—set apart, consecrated—by his kisses and caresses, and in wanting that, in recalling that it has already happened, the Song's beloved figures the ideal human beloved, the one who receives the Lord's kisses as they are given and as they ought to be received.

The Name (1:3b)

> Your name is oil poured out
> and so the young girls have delighted in you.

The beloved here continues to speak about her lover, praising his "name" as "oil poured out" and mentioning the "young girls," for the first time (also 6:8) as taking "delight" in the lover because of all the good things about him already mentioned. The "young girls" are not yet identified: you, the Song's hearer, register them as new characters, the first to be labeled with anything other than a pronoun. Shortly (in 1:5) there will be mention of the "daughters of Jerusalem"; and hearers of the Song have mostly, and reasonably, identified the two groups. The Latin word rendered "young girl" is *adulescentula*; in its ordinary usage it means a woman of childbearing, and thus marriageable, age—perhaps fourteen years old. The connotation is of readiness for lovemaking and consequent procreation.

And then there is the name of the lover, a name mentioned only in 1:3 and never given in the Song. The beloved recalls her lover's "name" as "oil poured out," and in doing so echoes, proleptically, the words of Jesus at Bethany not long before the arrest and crucifixion. There, as in the passage from Luke already discussed, a woman anoints Jesus with ointment taken from an alabaster jar; and in Matthew's version of this story, the verb used, *effundere* ("pour out"), is the same as the verb here in the Song (Matt. 26:6–13; John 12:1–8; Mark 14:3–9).[15] Here too we have explicitly sacrificial imagery and, moreover, imagery of preparation for death. Jesus's body is being prepared for death by anointing; and after he has died, the women prepare to anoint it again (Luke 23:56). Anointing with oil is, both scripturally and in the practice of the church, an aspect of preparation for death (Asa in 2 Chr. 16:14; Judith in Jdt. 10:3; 16:7). In seeking the lover's caress as an act of anointing, the beloved seeks to die. Death is a fundamental and universal metaphor for orgasm; it is also proper to the church's thinking about baptism, to which anointing also belongs; and there is ordinary physical death, as part of the approach to which the church gives, as the archaic English has it, "extreme unction."

15. For an interesting analysis of anointing in general, Mary Magdalene in particular, and the Song passage under discussion here, see Bruce Chilton, *Mary Magdalene: A Biography* (New York: Doubleday, 2005), chap. 6.

All these meanings belong to the penumbra of the beloved's words to her lover in these opening verses of the Song. Accepting the Lord's anointing kisses is not a light matter: they bring ecstatic pleasure, certainly, and once your lips have been burned with them they are impossible to forget (Isa. 6:3–7). But seeking them and accepting them will certainly kill you, and in killing you give you life in abundance.

If the language of the Song shows that the beloved's human lover with his loves figures the Lord with his loves for us, then the single mention of the "name" at Song 1:3 is suggestive. It recalls at once the Lord's giving of his name to Moses in Exod. 3:13–18 as *ego sum qui sum* ("I am who I am"), a name that, for Christians, is further specified as the name of Jesus. It is this name above all other names that produces "delight" in those who utter and hear it knowingly. The verb connected with the name, "delight" (*diligere*), together with its derived adjectival and nominal forms (*dilectio, dilecta, dilectus*) lies at the semantic heart of the Song: there are between thirty and forty occurrences, more than any other single word group. This is the same word complex used in scripture to commend a particular attitude toward neighbor, of enemy, and the Lord himself.[16] Translating the verb in question as "delight" communicates a particular flavor to the attitude commended here. "Delight" is what the beloved takes in her lover: her most common epithet for him is *dilectus* ("delightful man"); he, more rarely, calls her the same: *dilecta*. And, close to the end of the Song, *dilectio* is said to be "as strong as death," glossed with *aemulatio* ("zealous desire") and further explained as something ridiculous to the worldly: "If someone should give all the substance of his house for delight / they would despise him as if he were nothing" (8:6–7). I choose the "delight" complex to render the *diligere* complex from Latin to English (and I do so consistently: whenever you read a "delight" word in English, there is a *diligere* word in Latin) rather than, say, the "love" complex (which I reserve for the *amare* complex) for two principal reasons. The first is that I need to distinguish *dilectio* from *amor*, and both from *caritas* (which I render with "loving-kindness"; it occurs only at 2:4 and 8:7): "love" will not do for all these. And the second is that the *diligere* complex in the Song belongs to the erotic register. It is the principal complex of words used to describe the couple's affective response to one another, and for this "love" is, in English, altogether too bloodless. The two do not, first and last, love one another; rather, they delight in one another, and their delight is an element of their desire for one another. This is evident in the words under discussion here: after recalling and anticipating her lover's kisses and lovemaking, and linking his name with the name of the Lord, the beloved tells us that this is why (*ideo*) the "young girls" also "delight" in him. They too hope for (and recall?) his caresses.

16. In John, Jesus tells the disciples that they should have *dilectio* for one another (13:35) and that he has *dilectio* for them just as his Father has for him (15:9). The renderings of the love command in all three Synoptic Gospels use this verb (Matt. 19:19; 22:37–39; Mark 12:30–33; Luke 6:35), as also does Deut. 6:5, which they all echo. In John 21:7 the "beloved disciple" is the disciple *quem diligebat*, the one whom Jesus "loved"—or, if the translation given here were to be followed, it would be the disciple in whom Jesus "delighted."

The Lord prompts delight in those who love him: in you too if you will permit. And the delight is passionate, a movement of desire. This is what those who love the Lord feel for him, and in knowing this, the delight you take in your human lover can be intensified by seeing its participation in a delight much stronger and greater than itself. The Lord's Israel-church, in worship of him, exhibits this delight, and does so with deep sensuality, engaging every sense: hearing with chant, smell with incense, taste with bread and wine, touch with the kiss of peace and (again) with bread and wine on the tongue, and sight with the iconic panoply surrounding the worshipers.

The King's Cellars (1:4)

> Drag me after you—let us run!
> May the king lead me into his cellars
> so that we might exult and rejoice in you.
> Mindful of your loves above wine
> they have rightly delighted in you.

Here, the beloved pleads with, or even orders (the verb "drag" is in the imperative), her lover, as "king," to lead her "into his cellars." This is first to demand of her human lover that he might take her to the place where he keeps his good things (wine, ointment, kisses, caresses); and since the context is one of eagerness for lovemaking, this most naturally and immediately means that she wants to be taken to his private chamber and to bed, there to enjoy the good thing of being made love to by him. It is interesting that it is just here that there is a shift from singular to plural ("me . . . us . . . we . . . they"). She, the beloved, begins to speak not only for herself but for others, for "the young girls" of 1:3, so that they might all together enjoy his lovemaking. This is not an image easily accommodated by those with a strong taste for monogamy, but there it is: the Song, along with the Old Testament in general, does not imagine human loves to be necessarily or ideally one-to-one, especially not when the male lover is a "king," and even more especially not when the figure of Solomon, the ideal-typical lover of many women, is present in the text. You, the hearer, are nudged toward the view that the king—the lover—is not an object of desire exclusive to the beloved, but rather one desired by all beloveds.

There is another lexical sign of the lover as figure of the Lord: he is addressed as "king." The Lord is the king preeminent, the one in whose kingship that of all other kings participate. He is sovereign over the world because he is its creator from nothing; and Jesus too is "king," as he was called by Pilate and the Roman soldiers who crucified him and as he was described on the inscription placed above his cross.[17]

17. For Jesus as king, see the tolling repetition of that word, with mockery and a double irony, in John 19.

The thesis that the beloved is asking for the Lord's kisses finds a final support in Proverbs. While the "cellars" (*cellaria*) into which she begs to be taken (compare the "wine cellar" of Song 2:4) are not prominent in scripture, one text resonates significantly with this one: "Wisdom shall build a house / and prudence shall strengthen it / its cellars are filled with teaching / with all precious and most beautiful things" (Prov. 24:3–4). In asking to be taken into Wisdom's storerooms, the beloved is asking to be instructed by the Lord in what is beautiful: she is submitting herself, body and mind, to divine instruction.[18]

These first verses of the Song, when considered in terms of what their figural weight tells us about the beloved, foreshadow themes more prominent later in the Song, most especially that of desire's urgency, accompanied by the sense that what the beloved wants has not yet been fully attained. She hopes, subjunctively ("let me be kissed . . . may the king lead me"); she demands, imperatively ("drag me after you"); and she anticipates the pleasure that will follow ("so that we might exult").

It is not difficult to see how these themes apply to the Christian and to the church: for both, the triune Lord's intimate caresses are, in the order of being, unbroken. The Lord does nothing other than offer his embraces to the church, as is intimated by some of the descriptions given to her: she is Christ's bride and the Lord's beloved. She is also Christ's body, his presence here below, and no more intimate connection than that with the Lord is imaginable. The same intimacy of embrace is given without cease by the Lord to the individual Christian. I, like all Christians, have been baptized and anointed in confirmation, the water and oils of those rites caressing my body and running blindingly into my eyes; I eat and drink Christ's body and blood, participating thereby in his sacrifice and being conformed thereby to him; and at every moment the Lord bids me welcome, battering my heart and calling me to "get up, O my beloved, / my dove, my lovely one, and come" (2:10) and encouraging me to open myself to him (5:2) so that I might be fully loved by him.[19] These are constants. But in the orders of knowing and seeming, the Lord's caresses are often absent: the church can seem to wander without guidance and to be damaged by sin within and persecution without; I can seem to myself to be abandoned, lost in a dark wood (see the opening of Dante's *Inferno*). The world is broken and bloody, and in such a world both the church and its members can cease to feel the pressure of the Lord's lips, whether through their own fault or as a result of the damage abroad in the world. It is this

18. It is worth noting that the temple of Solomon, the Lord's dwelling place, has *cellaria* (1 Chr. 28:11).

19. I take the Lord's bidding from George Herbert's "Love III": "Love bade me welcome: yet my soul drew back, / guiltie of dust and sinne"; in *The English Poems of George Herbert*, ed. Helen Wilcox (Cambridge: Cambridge University Press, 2007), 661. And the Lord's battering of my heart from the fourteenth of John Donne's "Holy Sonnets," in *John Donne: The Complete English Poems*, ed. C. A. Patrides, Everyman's Library 5 (New York: Knopf, 1991), 443. Both poets, but Herbert especially, made frequent use of tropes from the Song.

seeming absence of the Lord's love that explains the urgent desire on the part of the Christian and the church for its return, a desire tensively figured by the urgent imaginings of the beloved in these opening verses of the Song. Christ's body, collectively and figuratively, never loses the sense that the Lord's loving has been partly withdrawn from it and therefore never loses the desire for its full return and for a consummation not yet experienced.

The back-and-forth between singular and plural in 1:2–4 enriches a reading of the Song's beloved as figure for both the church and the Christian. She is the principal figure, and her anticipation of further kisses is in the foreground of these verses, and of the work as a whole. But the "young girls," later identified as the "daughters of Jerusalem," are with her. In speaking of herself the church cannot avoid also speaking of her members. When the beloved says "they have rightly delighted in you," she, as figure of the church, speaks figuratively of us, her members.

Black But Lovely (1:5–6a)

> I am black but lovely
> O daughters of Jerusalem
> like Kedar's tents
> like Solomon's skins—
> do not think me swarthy
> for the sun has darkened me.

She, the beloved, continues to speak, but now addressing the "daughters of Jerusalem," who receive their first mention here and who are, you are likely to assume, the same as the "young girls" of 1:3; the daughters will be named seven times in the course of the Song (1:5; 2:7; 3:5, 10; 5:8, 16; 8:4). She is, she says to them, "black but lovely," a formulation that suggests that being black is not ordinarily lovely: she is lovely in spite of her blackness. The parallelism of "Kedar's tents" and "Solomon's skins" is on its face unclear. It might recapitulate that of "black but lovely," in which case "Kedar's tents" would be black, and hence superficially ugly, while "Solomon's skins" would be lovely, and perhaps therefore white. There is a clear change of tone here, as well as of addressee. The Song to this point has been ardent, redolent of the memory and anticipation of physical intimacy and pleasure. But now, doubt and regret and apology enter. The beloved acknowledges that things are not as they should be and that she needs to explain her blackness and its surprising coexistence with her beauty.

The term "black" (*nigra*, here in the feminine) occurs elsewhere in the Song only as an ingredient in her praise of his hair, which she calls "raven-black" (5:11). At that place, blackness is unambiguously positive, as it also is in Jacob's praise of the color of Judah's eyes as "darker than wine" (Gen. 49:12). Blackness can also serve, scripturally, as a sign of threat and danger, as in the threatening blackness of the Day of the Lord (Ezek. 30:18; 32:7; Rev. 6:12; cf. Lam. 4:8, for a black-white contrast produced by the sufferings of the Day of the Lord) or the black horse of the apocalypse (Zech. 6; Rev. 6:5). The only other scriptural mention of black skin is in Job, and there it serves as a very clear sign of distress: Job laments that his skin has "blackened" (*denigrata*) upon his body (Job 30:30), and this is perhaps the most illuminating parallel to the Song's use of the trope. Job's blackened skin epitomizes his distress and suffering; so also the beloved's blackness epitomizes hers. In both cases too blackness is extrinsic, brought upon the one suffering it by external causes, as is made clear by Song 1:6. All this supports the reading suggested by the text's surface, which is that the "but" in 1:5 is adversative: being "lovely" does not, in the Song, naturally suggest being "black." Rather the opposite.

Explaining this feature of the text—that the beloved is "lovely" even though she is "black"—Origen writes: "The question is, in what way is she black and how, if she lacks whiteness, is she fair. She has repented of her sins, beauty is the gift conversion has bestowed; that is the reason she is hymned as beautiful. She is called black, however, because she has not yet been purged of every stain of sin, she has not yet been washed unto salvation; nevertheless, she does not stay dark-hued, she is becoming white."[20] This establishes the grammar of virtually all Christian theological interpretation of the Song. The beloved, however she is identified, is not yet what she will be; her blackness labels what about her will be transfigured.

The beloved's likening of herself to "Kedar's tents" and "Solomon's skins" is also illuminated by examination of the broader scriptural uses of these terms. Kedar (the Hebrew form of the name; the Latin is Cedar) is Ishmael's second-born son (Gen. 25:13; 1 Chr. 1:29), which means that he descends from Abraham by Hagar rather than by Sarah (the main story of Hagar and Ishmael is scattered through Gen. 16–22); Ishmael is circumcised along with Abraham's household and in that way recognized as a legitimate descendant and therefore as a Jew; furthermore, the Lord promises both Hagar and Abraham that Ishmael will father a great nation; but Ishmael is not the recipient of the covenant promise given to Isaac, Abraham's son by Sarah, and is eventually sent away. His descendants are thereafter associated with Edom, Egypt, and Arabia. His "tents" become, therefore, a symbol of exile and absence: they are in a place far from the promised land, and to live in them or near them is to live far from the Lord's presence, whether in the ark and the tent of meeting, or later in the Solomonic temple (Ps. 83:7 [= 83:6 RSV]; 120:5). It is also to live in a place often mentioned among those whose inhabitants will, when the Day of the Lord comes, come to Jerusalem to recognize and worship him (Isa. 42:11; 60:7; cf. 21:16; Jer. 49:28; Ezek. 27:21).

20. Origen, *Homeliae in canticum canticorum* (Homilies on the Song of Songs) 1 (Lawson 1956: 276).

"Solomon's skins" are rather more puzzling. The Latin word rendered "Solomon" here is *Salma*, which is not the usual form of his name, but rather (probably) an abbreviation of it; but the word occurs nowhere else in scripture. If "Kedar's tents" represent exile and wandering, then, perhaps, "Solomon's skins" represent the stability of place—and that certainly fits the scriptural vision of Solomon as the builder of the first temple in Jerusalem (following Claudel 1948: 35–36). Discussion of this verse by the commentators of late antiquity tends to connect it with Jesus's mention of the lilies of the field as being clothed more gloriously than Solomon (Matt. 6:28–29).[21] On this reading, "Solomon's skins" are gloriously beautiful and also (assuming the white lily) likened to something white by contrast to the blackness of "Kedar's tents."

The beloved draws a distinction between being "black" (*nigra*) and being "swarthy" (*fusca*). The latter term occurs only here in scripture, and its connection with the explanatory claim that "the sun has darkened me" suggests that it means something different from "black." To be "swarthy" is, in this context, to be intrinsically dark skinned, independently of external circumstance, and this the beloved denies of herself; while to be "black" is simply to be dark skinned, whether intrinsically or otherwise. Her mention of the "sun" as the cause of her swarthiness shows this: she was not, the implication is, always "black," and she may again cease to be when she ceases to be exposed to the sun. Whatever it is that separates her from the lover, whatever it is that makes her seem to herself to be unworthy of him and to have to explain that unworthiness to the "daughters," is temporary and expungeable.

The interpretive possibilities here are rich. You, as hearer of the Song, can identify yourself as the hesitantly apologetic lover of the Lord, "black" in your ignorance and foolishness and disordered loves, and very conscious of that fact; but you also know yourself to be "beautiful," confident that you are indeed, nonetheless, the Lord's beloved. The Lord's visible Israel-church, too, knows itself as a *corpus permixtum*, a body whose members are both sinners and saints and whose appearance is therefore simultaneously beautiful and ugly, but nonetheless the Lord's beloved.[22] And Mary, while not herself sinful,[23] doubts, at first, whether what is promised to her at the annunciation can really happen and does not (so the description in Luke 1 may be read) judge herself worthy that it should happen to her. This Marian oscillation—doubt, uncertainty, acceptance, delight—is

21. See Theodoret of Cyrus, *Explanatio in canticum canticorum* on Song 1:4 (Hill 2001: 45; *Patrologia Graecae* 81.70).

22. Augustine emphasizes this meaning of "black but beautiful" in *De doctrina christiana* 3.32.45 (*Sant'Agostino: La Dottrina Christiana*, ed. and trans. Vincenzo Tarulli, Opere di Sant'Agostino 8 [Rome: Città Nuova, 1992], 182–84).

23. In saying this I assume the truth of the dogma of the immaculate conception, defined by Pius IX in 1854 in *Ineffabilis Deus*. The idea of Mary's immaculate conception is much older: the liturgical feast of that name was established as a universal feast by Sixtus IV in 1476, and for at least a millennium before that the idea of Mary's freedom from sin's stains, from *maculae* (→4:7), was canvassed by theologians.

constitutive of our love affairs too; the Song's beloved's awareness of her blackness and beauty at the same time participates in Mary's, as also does the church's and your own.

Guarding the Vineyards (1:6b)

> My mother's sons were angry with me
> they placed me as guard of the vineyards
> but my vineyard I did not guard.

The beloved continues to speak to the daughters of Jerusalem. She makes enigmatic reference to her "mother's sons"—presumably to her brothers—immediately after her acknowledgment of and apology for her blackness, and perhaps in explanation of it: she has been made by her brothers "guard of the vineyards," and she has failed to guard her own vineyard. This, perhaps, is why her brothers were "angry" with her; but it is equally possible to read the text as though their anger was their motivation for making her the vineyards' protector. The tone continues to be one of apology and regret, almost of lament: something has gone wrong in the past (all the verbs are in the past tense), and she, for reasons not given, describes it. The events are described in such compressed terms that the hearer's puzzlement about what is going on is unavoidably deepened: we have already, in the space of a few dozen words, moved from expressions of panting desire for kisses and lovemaking through memories of delight and urgent anticipation of its repetition to painful regret.

Elsewhere in the Song the beloved mentions her "brother," but in that place only in imaginative key, as someone she would like her lover to be so that she could freely kiss him in public; and she frequently mentions her "mother" and her "mother's house" and "bedroom," with a complex set of meanings (→3:4; 6:9; 8:1–2). The new term of central importance is "vineyard" (*vinea*), which occurs twice in 1:6; one of the phrases there, "my vineyard" (*vinea mea*), occurs verbatim also at 8:12—almost as close to the end of the Song as this occurrence of the phrase is to the beginning. The speaker of the phrase in 8:12—"my vineyard is before me"—is on the face of things unclear, but it is possibly the beloved; and attributing the same words here, in 1:6, to her supports that reading. The meaning is that she claims a vineyard for herself at the Song's beginning and at its end, regretting her failure to protect that vineyard at the beginning and (perhaps) celebrating its presence and fertility at the end (→8:11–12). It is certainly the case that the trope-patterns in the first few verses of the Song—vineyards, guards, brothers, sisters—occur also in its last few verses, which is some small evidence in support of the view that the Song has an approximately chiastic structure, with 5:1 at the center. But what, more broadly, is the significance of vineyard talk, in the Song and in scripture?

"Vineyards" are frequently mentioned in the Song. Sometimes, they are elements in its pastoral imagery. When she imagines or recalls his voice calling her to him in the spring, the "flowering vineyards" (2:13; cf. 6:11; 7:13) are among the signs of spring's fertility; and on two occasions (1:14; 7:9) the vineyard is used as a trope in the couple's praise of and delight in one another's bodies. In those cases too the vineyard serves to suggest beauty and fertility. But this is not the meaning of "vineyard" here or in the obscurities of 8:11–12. In both places, there are images of ownership and protection, supplemented in Song 8 with images of financial exchange—payment is made for the fruit of the vineyard. At this point it is enough to say that in both texts the vineyard is itself good and is productive of more goods, that it needs stewardship and protection in order to flourish, and that stewardship may fail.

In scripture outside the Song, vineyards are often included in the list of good things that belong to the promised land (Deut. 6:11; Josh. 24:13) and described as gifts given by the Lord, freely and without consideration of the merits of those receiving them. The point of this motif is to emphasize the importance of showing gratitude for such gifts (Jesus depicts himself as the true vine in John 15:1–6). More relevant for understanding the vineyards of Song 1:6, however, is the motif of the vineyard as Israel: the Lord has brought a vineyard out of Egypt and planted it in a new place (Ezek. 17; cf. Ps. 80:9 [= 80:8 RSV]; Isa. 1:8; 5:1–7). This theme is often connected with lament for the corruption and apostasy of Israel, and that in turn is often depicted by means of images of uprooted vines, vineyards with walls broken down, and vines with branches hacked off or burned to the ground (Jer. 2:21; 12:10–11; Ezek. 19:10–14; Matt. 21:33–44 and parallels [parable of the tenants]). The following passage is typical (the Lord is speaking): "I planted you as a vineyard set apart / with nothing but good seed / why then have you turned away / and become branches of an alien vine?" (Jer. 2:21).[24]

If, scripturally speaking, the vineyard is sometimes a type of the people of Israel or of the promised land (and these two are sometimes so closely connected that it is not useful to attempt to separate them), then it is something capable of flourishing or of corruption and decay. It is, therefore, something that needs close watch, which may be described in terms of the protection the beloved was supposed to give the vineyard or in terms of the watch- or guard-tower and walls built to protect it (Isa. 5:2; Matt. 21:33 and parallels). It is to this sphere of scriptural discourse that Song 1:6 belongs: the beloved is implicated somehow, whether by her own fault or as a result of the actions of others, in failure properly to protect the vineyard-Israel, and this fits well with the tone of apologetic regret in these verses.

The scriptural resonance of most note here is from Ezek. 19, where, in the extended figure of the vine given as part of lamentation over Israel's king, a vineyard

24. On the church as vineyard, see *Lumen Gentium* 6 (Latin and English in Tanner 1990: 851–52).

and a mother are brought together. The vine, representing the people of Israel, is there likened to the mother of the king ("your mother was like a vine / planted by the water"); her strongest and tallest branch is the king. "But she was uprooted in wrath . . . / her strong branch was ripped off and withered up / fire consumed it" (Ezek. 19:10–12).

She—the mother, the vine—is now alone in the desert, without a king. In Ezekiel this is an oracle about the destruction of the monarchy. The beloved's lament that she has not protected her vineyard (Israel?), even though it was given into her charge, belongs to this pattern of thought, even if enigmatically; and it may be too that the still more enigmatic mention of her mother and brothers should awaken scriptural echoes of the laments of Israel for her lost sons and daughters. The context of Song 1:5–6 is in any case thoroughly communal: the beloved speaks to the daughters of Israel, regretting the past's damage, and implicitly apologizing for it, even if the particulars of that past and its damage are left unclear.

The beloved's figuring of Mary is only enigmatically visible in 1:1–6. Mary is, in the New Testament, not a figure of passionate desire so much as one of serene acceptance. When the gift of pregnancy is offered to her, she accepts it, but the texts in which that acceptance is described say nothing of her desire preceding the act of acceptance, nor of her delight in what follows it. She seeks, certainly, to understand what has happened, and to that extent seeks greater intimacy with the gift she has been given (she holds these things in her heart and ponders them; Luke 2:19). And the scripturally rooted churchly tradition of depicting and meditating on Mary's grief as she stands at the foot of the cross places emphasis on her grief at separation from Jesus; it is figured dimly by the beloved's eagerness for reunion in these verses of the Song (*stabant autem iuxta crucem Iesu mater eius*; John 19:25).

Suppose, in accord with the line of interpretation already established, we see the beloved as church-Mary—the Marian church and the ecclesial Mary—and her lover as the triune Lord. Much more can be seen in these verses when they are read through that lens. The church, stained as she is by the failings of her members and by her implication in and contribution to the world's damage, confesses herself to be "black," but not intrinsically "swarthy": she has been darkened by what is extrinsic to her while being intrinsically *formosa* ("lovely"). Mary too confesses her *humilitas* before the Lord (Luke 1:48) and, thereby, her unworthiness to receive the Lord into her womb. It is exactly that confession that makes her worthy to receive the gift: these are the caressing words of love given back to the lover. In the Song the confession of unworthiness is made not directly to the lover, to the Lord, but rather to the "daughters of Jerusalem"; and in Luke's Gospel too, Mary confesses her unworthiness to her relative, Elizabeth. The Marian church is a communal body, returning the Lord's love with words of love not in the solitary flight of the alone to the alone but rather in the communion of saints, bound together by the gift of the Lord's love. When the Song's beloved confesses to the daughters, then, she figures both Mary's song sung in Elizabeth's company and the constant song of the church.[25]

Recall, however, that the Song's beloved does not allegorize the Marian church: she figures it, and often, as here, does so enigmatically (drawing upon *videmus enim nunc per speculum in aenigmate*; 1 Cor. 13:12). This means that while the beloved can be understood more deeply by considering her as a figure, not everything said of her finds its ready equivalent in what is said of Mary or the church. It is not so easy, for example, to see in what sense Mary has failed to protect her vineyard, even though the instances in which the church has so failed are numerous and not difficult to see. The motif of the vineyard and of the beloved's mother may therefore not be obviously or easily deepened by placing them in a Marian frame.

There may, however, be one more Marian connection worth mentioning: the early-medieval European practice of making black Madonnas, that is, icons or statues of Mary with black skin. Whether or not this practice had Song 1:5 among its roots, the verse and the practice were certainly taken from at least the twelfth century onward to be mutually illuminating and supportive.[26] This is another and significant sign that the Song's beloved figures Mary. It is at least true that Mary has been adored in a guise suggested by this description of the Song's beloved.

If the lover figures the triune Lord and the beloved figures Mary-church, while yet remaining who they are by avoiding the allegorical dissolution into what they figure, then human love and more specifically human sexual desire remain the Song's first topic. And about that the first half dozen verses of the Song are suggestive. They point the hearer first to what everybody knows about those matters,

25. Another interpretation of the beloved's blackness is prominent in the Christian commentarial tradition. It identifies the daughters of Jerusalem, to whom the beloved, understood as the church, protests her loveliness in spite of her blackness, as the synagogue, or the Jews; and it contrasts her real beauty, obscured to the people of Israel by her being a gentile (her blackness), with their apparent beauty (they are not black) but real ugliness. Origen, *Homeliae in canticum canticorum* (Homilies on the Song of Songs) 2.1 (Lawson 1956: 91–104), provides an elaborate example of this line of thought. This is not an interpretive position I wish to defend: it is too intimate with a kind of supersessionism that the church now clearly teaches is not the proper position to take with respect to the relations between the church and the people of Israel.

26. There is no clear scholarly consensus on why there came to be Madonna images with black skin in the Mediterranean world (especially France, Italy, and Spain) by the high medieval period. The subject attracts idiosyncratic and speculative thought. For some information on the location and history of such images, as well as speculation about their origin and meaning, not all of it reliable, see Ean Begg, *The Cult of the Black Virgin* (London: Arkana, 1985); Lucia Chiavola Birnbaum, *Black Madonnas: Feminism, Religion, and Politics in Italy* (Boston: Northeastern University Press, 1993); Sara Jane Boss, ed., *Mary: The Complete Resource* (London: Continuum, 2007), 458–75; Sophie Cassagnes-Broquet, *Vierges noires* (Paris: Rouergue, 2000); Marie Durand-Lefèbvre, *Étude sur l'origine des vierges noires* (Paris: Durassie, 1937); Malgorzata Oleskiewicz-Pieralba, *The Black Madonna in Latin America and Europe* (Albuquerque: University of New Mexico Press, 2007); Miri Rubin, *Mother of God: A History of the Virgin Mary* (New Haven: Yale University Press, 2009), 181–85; Monique Scheer, "From Majesty to Mystery: Change in the Meaning of Black Madonnas from the Sixteenth to Nineteenth Centuries," *American Historical Review* 107 (2002): 1412–40.

which is that the memory of lovemaking and the imagination of its repetition are at least as important for us as its performance. We are constituted as beings in time and as beings who are capable of being aware of ourselves as such. This is what makes memory and anticipation important for us, and it is remarkable that in the Song lovemaking is depicted almost entirely through their lens and not in terms of how the kiss and the caress seem as they are being given and taken. Hearing the Song as a depiction of human desire can intensify an awareness of this interesting fact about ourselves as lovers and beloveds. It reminds us that what we want when we want to be loved and to give love is not fully available to us in the performance of those acts. The intensity and complexity of human romantic and sexual need cannot find its fulfillment in the circumincession of two (or more: recall that she wants to share her love of him with the young girls, and not only her love of him but his making of love with her) human bodies and minds. If that circumincession were limited to its performance it would not be human lovemaking. In order to be that it needs to be placed in the order of time as an object of memory and anticipation and in the order of narrative as an event about which the right story can be told.[27] Even when attention is restricted to the Song's surface, therefore, the horizon it points to is open. The human desire to love and be loved, to caress and be caressed, exceeds its own fulfillment and indicates its own insufficiency. It begs for a story and for the memories and hopes that enframe stories. Every act of human physical love is therefore already and inevitably figural. The only question is: what does it figure?

The theme of regret for damage suffered and effected, evident in 1:5–6, is also a common element in human loves. To be the recipient of someone's love—to become a beloved—is typically to be surprised, in large part because the beloved does not seem to herself or himself to be worthy of this gift. There is nothing about him in his own eyes to make it reasonable to expect that she will love him, offer herself to him, show him by what she says and does that he is, to her, a beloved. A response to the offer, the offer in which the lover says, "Here I am: I love you," usually, almost inevitably involves something like what the Song's beloved says in 1:5–6, which is a complex admixture of regret and lament for unworthiness ("I am black . . . my vineyard I did not guard") and delight in lovability ("but lovely"). The presence of the one without the other makes it impossible to receive the offer of love and therefore impossible to be a beloved. Were you to respond to the gift of love with an unruffled sense of your own beauty and worthiness to be given that gift, you would not be a beloved—one who can return love—but rather a demigod receiving homage. And were you to respond to the lover's gift to you of your new condition as a beloved with nothing but a sense of your own unworthiness and ugliness and filthiness, then too, you could not be a beloved but

27. Flaubert's Emma Bovary shows this very well: she tells the wrong stories about loving and lovemaking, but she is completely and fully human in seeing the need to make a narrative of her lovemakings, to dramatize them and herself as agent in them, and to locate their emotional and physical force principally in remembering and anticipating them.

only a mirrored wall of self-hatred from which all offered love would be reflected directly back to its offerer.

The Song's beloved's eagerness for the renewal of her lover's embraces, together with her knowledge of herself as simultaneously damaged and delightful, ugly and beautiful, can, if we let it, reconfigure our own mode of being as lovers and beloveds.

> The Bride then beholds the Bridegroom; and He, as soon as she has seen Him, goes away. He does this frequently throughout the Song; and that is something nobody can understand who has not suffered it himself. God is my witness that I have often perceived the Bridegroom drawing near me and being most intensely present with me; then suddenly He has withdrawn and I could not find Him, though I sought to do so. I long, therefore, for Him to come again, and sometimes He does so. Then, when He has appeared and I lay hold of Him, He slips away once more; and when He has so slipped away, my search for Him begins anew.[28]

Seeking Him (1:7–8)

> O man in whom my soul delights
> show me where you graze
> and where you rest at noon
> so that I might not begin to wander
> after the flocks of your companions.
>
> If you do not know
> O most beautiful of women
> then go out and depart
> after the flocks' traces
> and graze your young goats
> close by the shepherds' tents.

In 1:7, though the voice remains hers, the addressee shifts again from the daughters of Jerusalem to the "man in whom my soul delights." Her question to him marks the beginning of an extended dialogue between them, in which the transfer of voice from one to the other is not ordinarily marked by explicit identification of the speaker, but rather of the addressee. In 1:8, he, the lover, answers her directly, identifying her with the superlative epithet "most beautiful of women." This is the first time his voice is heard. She does not know where her lover is, or at least where he is about to go ("show me where you graze / and where you rest at noon"), and she needs to know so that she might not get lost, "wander[ing] / after the

---

28. Origen, *Homeliae in canticum canticorum* (Homilies on the Song of Songs) 1.7, in J. Christopher King, *Origen on the Song of Songs as the Spirit of Scripture: The Bridegroom's Perfect Marriage Song* (Oxford: Oxford University Press, 2005), 16.

flocks of your companions"—which is to say, presumably, not after his flocks, not where he will be. That she wants to avoid: her desire is to be where he is. His answer is made directly to her, but is on its face enigmatic: she must follow "the flocks' traces"—those of his flocks?—and then pasture her goats "close by [his?] shepherds' tents" if she wants the answers to what she asks, and thus to find him. The imagery is throughout pastoral (flocks, grazing, goats, shepherds), and the tone is one of eagerness to replace separation with presence.

She calls him here the "man in whom my soul delights," a phrase that occurs verbatim five times in the Song (1:7; 3:1, 2, 3, 4), which accounts for five of the six occurrence of *anima* ("soul") in the Song, The sixth is in 5:6 ("my soul melted"). In all six of the occurrences, she is speaking directly to him, showing herself as responsive to his love, as aroused by him and full of desire for him. It is her favored term for herself as responsively beloved and eager to love. In this usage, the Song's beloved uses the term "soul" very much as it is used elsewhere in scripture, where it occurs very frequently.[29] In its barest and most reduced sense it can serve as a reflexive pronoun ("me" or "myself") or as meaning simply "a person" or "someone" (2 Pet. 2:14); and sometimes it indicates what it is that makes a human being (*homo*) alive rather than dead (Acts 20:10, 24). But it usually carries a heavier affective load, depicting its user as personally responsive to an offer made by another person. That person is often the Lord, and when a person's soul responds to the Lord, whether with joy or anguish, she (or he) acknowledges and represents herself (or himself) as a creature. The paradigmatic instance of this usage, for Christians, is Mary's response to Elizabeth's hymn of praise ("blessed are you among women") at the visitation: "My soul [*anima*] proclaims the Lord's greatness, / and my spirit [*spiritus*] exults in God my savior" (Luke 1:46–47). Mary has earlier been addressed by the angel, and she now responds to Elizabeth and to John's leaping in Elizabeth's womb by praising the Lord exactly as a beloved does. The Song's beloved's repeated use of the term "soul" for herself as one who returns her lover's love verbally figures Mary's use of the same word to represent herself as one who has joyfully accepted the Lord's love, and by accepting it has returned it. The beloved's very language here participates in Mary's; and because of the intimacy between Mary and the church, it is easy for the church to see itself in the Song's beloved's words as it has in Mary's.

He, the lover, "graze[s]"; he takes his "rest at noon"; and his companions have "flocks." Grazing is an important activity here, and the verb that denotes it (*pascere*) occurs six times in the Song. She asks him here to show her where he grazes, and he replies by telling her that if she doesn't already know she should graze her "young goats / close by the shepherds' tents." Both he and she are shepherds, grazing their flocks. But not only that: there is even a suggestion that grazing may not be only, or even principally, something that shepherds make possible for their flocks. Her

---

29. *Anima* occurs more than one hundred times in the New Vulgate's Psalms, and more than eight times in its Sirach.

first question to him about grazing suggests that it is something he does for himself; and this impression is strengthened by examination of the verb's other occurrences in the Song. She addresses him as one who "grazes among lilies" (2:16), and she describes him, probably to the daughters of Jerusalem, as her "delightful man" who has gone "to graze in the gardens / to gather lilies" (6:2–3). And he praises her breasts as "doe-born twins / grazing among lilies" (4:5).

Grazing is much talked of elsewhere in scripture. Usually, it is something shepherds do for their flocks, and it can often serve as shorthand for the entire range of pastoral activities: leading the flock to a safe place, protecting it from predators, finding good grass for it, watering it, and so on. To "graze" (*pascere*) is something that "pastors" (*pastores*) do. The Lord, scripturally speaking, is the pastor of pastors: all other pastoral activity stems from and participates in his; and so he is often the subject of the verb, as also are his appointed leaders of the people. Joseph, for instance, speaks of the Lord who has "grazed" (*pascit*) him from childhood on (Gen. 48:15); the Lord commands the ravens to "graze" (*pascant*)—feed, nourish—Elijah (1 Kgs. 17:4); the psalmist hymns the Lord who "grazes" him (*dominus pascit me*; Ps. 23:1); the Lord can threaten to stop "grazing" (*non pascam vos*) his people (Zech. 11:3–9); Jesus tells Peter to *pasce agnos meos*—"graze my sheep" (John 21:15); and Jesus takes the image of pastor, one who grazes, to himself (John 10:11). In scripture, therefore, to graze is most fundamentally a pastoral activity performed by the Lord for his people. Reading the Song as scripture means that this fundamental meaning of the verb must be taken seriously: when the beloved asks her lover to "show me where you graze," we must read the question as one addressed to the Lord as pastor.

In his instruction to her, he tells her not merely to follow the "flocks" but to follow their "traces" (*vestigia*). This word occurs only here in the Song, though fairly often elsewhere in scripture, where it most often means "footstep" or "track," whether belonging to a human person or to the Lord (Josh. 22:29; Job 11:7; cf. 1 Pet. 2:21 [an exhortation to follow Christ's *vestigia*]); but sometimes also, in an extended metaphorical sense (Sir. 21:7; 42:19), the trace of something no longer present or otherwise hidden. The word carries with it a sense of the lover's—and the Lord's—half-hiddenness: he is not where she wants him to be, in front of her, kissing her; but his whereabouts is not entirely hidden, either: there are always traces to follow. The word can serve as a potent trope for the nature of the Lord's absent presence to us.

In the Song, uniquely in scripture, grazing is connected with lilies: four of the six uses of the verb in the Song make that connection explicit, and lilies are mentioned four more times in the Song. The Song's talk of lilies accounts for more than one third of all scriptural mentions of those flowers.[30] In the Song,

---

30. Most mentions of lilies in scripture are either in passing, as when some artifact is likened to a lily in shape or beauty (1 Kgs. 7:26; 2 Chr. 4:5) or in the enigmatic Psalm titles, where the term may refer to a metrical or musical form (Ps. 69; 80).

lilies are connected with grazing, whether his or hers, as already mentioned; and the word is used as a trope of praise for the beauty of the lovers or of parts of their bodies. She speaks of herself as "a valley-lily" (2:1), and he immediately picks up the word and returns it to her, describing her as "a lily among thorns" (2:2). She, in praising his appearance to the daughters of Jerusalem, says that "his lips are lilies / dripping prime myrrh" (5:13). And he says of her belly that it is "like a heap of wheat / fortified by lilies" (7:3). In all these cases, the lily is something beautiful, standing out from what surrounds it because of its beauty. The lily's beauty is natural: it has grown without human artifice and is therefore an instance of the Lord's unmerited gift of beauty. It shows too that some things in the created order are more beautiful than others, and that this is explicable by the Lord's choice to make it so. The prophets sometimes use the word in this sense: Hosea speaks of Israel blooming like the lily in response to the Lord's election (Hos. 14:6 [= 14:5 RSV]); and Isaiah of the desert blooming with lilies (Isa. 35:1; cf. Sir. 39:19 [= 39:14 RSV]; 50:8). And the same range of meanings is evident in the sole instance of Jesus's mention of lilies: they do no work, but they are glorious in contrast to other, less beautiful flowers (Matt. 6:28; Luke 12:27). This is true too of the beauty of the beloved and her lover in the Song: they are radiantly, unmeritedly, and supremely beautiful like the lily—and indeed like the Song itself, the Song of Songs.

What, then, is to be made of the connection between grazing and lilies, and especially of the image of grazing among lilies? This, in the Song, is something the lover is said by his beloved to do. Might the Lord do this? Perhaps. If the lily is his beautiful creation, then for him to graze *inter lilia* ("among lilies"; 2:16; 6:3) and *lilia colligat* ("to gather lilies"; 6:2) is to delight himself in his creation, to provide nourishment for himself in contemplating its beauty, a beauty that exists only by participation in him. And more is suggested. If she, the beloved, is "a valley-lily" and "a lily among thorns" (2:1, 2), then in saying that he grazes among lilies she says that he grazes upon her, in the dual sense of nourishing her and delighting in her. Who, or what, in the created order, is the Lord likely to graze upon in this dual sense? The scriptural sense of grazing provides the first answer: the people of Israel. Jesus's command to Peter, *pasce agnos meos*, and his taking to himself the title "pastor" provide the second answer: the Lord's sheep, the lilies in which he delights and among whom he grazes, are the disciples of Christ, which is to say the church.[31] And that the Song's beloved also figures Mary provides the third answer: she, as lily, is his special delight; she, as lily of unsurpassed beauty, exceeds all beloveds in beauty; and he grazes upon her body—as the Song will go on extensively to show—with the delight of one who has chosen her to bear his child.[32]

31. On the church as sheepfold, see *Lumen Gentium* 6 (Latin and English in Tanner 1990: 851–52).
32. Since the fifteenth century, and with foreshadowings much earlier, it has been usual to depict Gabriel offering Mary lilies in paintings of the annunciation.

A Mare among Pharaoh's Chariots (1:9)

> To a mare among Pharaoh's chariots
> I have likened you, O my beloved.

The lover has just told the beloved how to find him. Now he begins to praise her. These are his first words in praise of her in the Song, and the first among many uses of his preferred epithet for her: "beloved" (*amica*). He likens her to "a mare among Pharaoh's chariots," a phrase that finds its first scriptural resonance in Exod. 15:1–18, which is another scriptural song, that of Moses.[33] The verbal resonances are direct and explicit: there, as here, Pharaoh's chariots (*currus*) are mentioned with their horses (*equi*); Moses and, immediately afterward, Miriam sing there of the Lord's destruction of those chariots and horses by submersion in the Red Sea. Here in the Song, the horse is female, *equa* rather than *equus*, and in likening the beloved to "a mare among Pharaoh's chariots" the Song is profoundly suggestive: Pharaoh's stallions, representing an idolatrous slave empire out for the blood of its escaped slaves, were drowned. This mare, the Lord's beloved, is greater than they, overcoming their instruments of violence ("chariots") by her beauty and by her having received and acceded to the Lord's loving promise (→6:12). She, like Israel in Exodus, can be ridden by the Lord onward into the land of promise. She, the mare, is a symbol of beauty and power, as also, perhaps, of fertility. By means of his love for her, the Lord gets what he wants, which is finally the redemption of the world, a redemption wrought first by his irrevocable love for the people of Israel and then by his equally irrevocable love for Mary, out of whom comes his son, and thereby the church.

The perfect tense of the verb *assimilavi* is worth noting. The lover has "likened" her: that is, he has already done so in the past, in a single complete action. The Song often shows, by the tenses of its verbs, that the present love and desire of the couple is rooted in a deep past. You have already been told that the "young girls have delighted" (1:3) in the lover and that she, the beloved, "did not guard" her own vineyards (1:6); and there are many such indications yet to come. The past in question, as the reference to "Pharaoh's chariots" shows, is that of the Lord with Israel: that is the historical prism through which their present love is refracted. Your loves too, your desire for an intimacy with your "beloved," has that history as its true past: the Song here begins, if you will permit it, its work of reconstruing your understanding of your own loves in a properly ecclesial direction, as participant in the Lord's love for Israel-church and for you as a member of that body.

Earrings and Necklaces (1:10–11)

> Your cheeks are beautiful with earrings
> your neck with necklaces—

33. Moses's song is not called a *canticum*, but rather a *carmen*.

> we shall make earrings for you
> silver-chased.

He continues to praise her in direct address, rhapsodizing now about particular parts of her body, her "cheeks" and her "neck." A good portion of the Song is about the body. She praises his body, in its parts and as a whole, at length (5:10–16); and he praises hers in the same way, at considerably greater length and with more repetition (4:1–6; 6:4–7; 7:2–7). In addition to these extended treatments, there are numerous occasional references to this or that part of the body. This is, at one level, easy to understand. Lovers are interested in one another's bodies, indeed absorbed by them. They gaze into one another's eyes, they kiss one another's lips, they lick and suck and graze upon every inch of one another's skin, driven by a desire to inhabit and be inhabited by the other's physical being, an urge to become one flesh; and they may imagine the body of the absent other with sufficient intensity that its particulars are as vivid to them in absence as in presence. Their own bodies become transformed by this attention in two ways: by responsive attunement to the body of the other, and by movement from the capacity to be a beloved lover to the actuality of being one, a movement that can be received only as gift from a lover. Lovers' bodies are remade, coming into their own exactly as lovers' bodies by being for another a source of excessive delight. All this requires detailed and (from the perspective of those not in love) sometimes excessive and unseemly attention to bodily particularity—her breasts, his thighs, their lips, and so on. The Song depicts this, as it must. It is, after all, an erotic lyric. And, as always in such cases, the tropes and images used by her for his body and by him for hers can seem to hearers as often comic as stirring.

The lovers, body-obsessed, remain what they are in the Song. But what they are is a window open to the Lord's love gift and our (possible) loving response. This is in part because the Song is a scriptural book, and as a result must be read in that way, as a gift of the Lord to his people. But that is not the only reason for reading the Song's hymns to the body as hymns also to the soul's intoxicated desire for the Lord and to the Lord's passion for us. There is, in addition, the sheer excess of human sexual love, its radical disproportion to its biological and social functions, its deranged openness to configuration in almost any direction (there are necrophiles, fetishists, practitioners of bestiality, those sexually obsessed with the bodies of children, and so on)—meaning that it forces upon anyone who wants to give it serious thought the question of why our bodily passions, our sexual desires, are like that. What, for example, does a lover writing poetry to and about his beloved's breasts mean? How can we account for the radically excessive nature of Dante's response to Beatrice, or of Kierkegaard's to Regine? The Song is not in the least unusual in portraying sexual desire as it does, and in hymning the body as it does. It is, in this at least, a representative instance of a particular, culturally specific grammar of depicting human sexual love.[34] All these instances—and our own early twenty-first-century versions of them—show the Lord's presence by their very excess. In addition, then, to the demand placed upon you, its hearer, by its status as scripture, the Song's depiction of bodily desire calls for attention to the meaning of its excess—a meaning only finally accountable by seeing its participation in the excess of the Lord's desire for us—just because it is such a depiction. Whatever human beings attend to repeatedly and with concentrated and excessive passion has written upon it with special clarity the Lord's presence.

So far, these are general claims about the depiction of the body in the Song. They would be true of any hymn of bodily desire for the body. The depiction of the body in the Song offers, however, considerably more than this: it offers a particular construal of the meanings, functions, and possibilities of the body and its parts according to which those parts incarnate (make bodily) the very fabric of our existence before the Lord and before one another. The Song's depiction of the desiring and desired body provides a schema whereby the meaning of what we are and what we want is simultaneously laid bare and ornamented.[35] Attention to the particulars of that schema was, for more than a millennium, one of the main ways in which Western thinkers thought about the body and its desires. It is not that the Song provides a crackable code, according to which each body part has a single meaning, and the body as a whole is depicted as an internally complex allegory of what we are. On that model, the neck might be the thing that can be stiff or flexible, showing our capacity for resistance to or acceptance of the Lord and one another; or the breasts might be what provide or fail to provide nurture if sucked, thus showing our capacity to feed one another as the Lord feeds us. Rendering the Song's treatment of the body comprehensible would, according to that way of thinking, mean nothing more than providing the relevant equivalences and making the appropriate substitutions. But this is not how the Song treats the body, and certainly not how the commentarial tradition glosses the Song's depictions of the body. It is, rather, that the Song gives a flexible, trope-constituted picture of bodiliness, according to which one and the same body part is shown to be capable of figuring our relations to the Lord and to one another in very different ways; and in which different body parts may have the same figurative capacity (paraphrasing Chrétien 2005: 68, who is quoting and paraphrasing Haymon d'Auxerre).

Christian hearers of the Song's lovers' praise of one another's bodies and their parts can scarcely avoid finding this material suggestive and figurative of the broadly

34. For a splendid treatment (with pictures) of the ancient Near Eastern grammar of the desired and desirous body, of which the Song is an instance, see Othmar Keel, *Das Hohelied*, Zürcher Bibelkommentare AT 18 (Zurich: Theologischer Verlag, 1986).

35. I draw here heavily and gratefully upon Chrétien 2005: 8, 36, and passim, for these formulations. Also in the background here are John Paul II's catecheses on the Song; for the question of the language of the body, see *Man and Woman He Created Them: A Theology of the Body*, trans. Michael Waldstein (Boston: Pauline Books, 2006), 552–60.

Pauline christological understanding of the body and its members. When Paul writes of the church as Christ's body, and of its many members linked one to another as parts of the same whole, given to one another as members exactly because of their participation in that whole, what he has to say about the ecclesial body affects how our particular living bodies are understood, and also how we read other scriptural treatments of the body and its parts. The complex and fluid relations of one body part to another—of hand to arm, of lips to tongue, of skin to blood—together constitute an integral organism that is what it is because it participates in the body of Christ. The parts complement and ornament one another without competing, and they cannot be properly defined (or praised) without reference to their relation to other parts. They are what they are only because of the relations they bear to the other parts, and in this way they image, very imperfectly, the individuation-by-relation that constitutes the Lord as the most holy Trinity (1 Cor. 12:12–31; cf. Col. 3:15; Rom. 6:13, 19; 12:5; 1 Cor. 6:15; Eph. 4:25; 5:30; detailed analysis in Chrétien 2005: chap. 2).

This complex view about the body's nature and the individuation of its parts yields theological understanding of the Song's treatment of the parts of the body. It shows why that treatment does not lend itself to interpretation as a monovalent allegorical code: if any member of the body may have multiple beauties and uses and may share those with other members, and if the beauties exhibited by any member can be accounted for only by appeal to the relations they bear to the beauties of other members, then there can be no such code. That is how it is with the members of Christ's ecclesial body, as well as with the members of his fleshly body. To kiss any single member of the beloved's body is to kiss all of her because she is fully present in each, each being constituted by its relation to all. The eucharistic version of this view is the Catholic Church's teaching that receiving Christ under either species (bread or wine) is receiving him completely.[36] The christological-ecclesial understanding of the body and its parts also illuminates the Song's shifting and overlapping and repetitious praises of particular body parts: what is said of one may be said of another, and what is said of his may also be said of hers. Such a lack of clear boundaries and precise differentiation is to be expected if the implicit understanding of the body and its parts in the Song is ecclesial-christological. This is also why you, as hearer of the Song, can have your understanding of and response to your lover's body reconfigured no matter what your own sex and gender are.

So much in general about the body in the Song. Specifically mentioned in 1:10, the first body part to be hymned are the beloved's "cheeks," which are "beautiful with earrings." Elsewhere in the Song the lover says twice that the beloved's cheeks are "like a fragment of pomegranate / through your veil" (4:3, repeated verbatim at 6:7). And she, in praising his body to the daughters of Jerusalem, says that

36. Many Christians not in full communion with the Bishop of Rome do not accept this teaching and have eucharistic practices at variance with it.

"his cheeks are like seedbeds of spices / ointment piled up" (5:13). Those tropes will be taken up in more detail at the appropriate place. They have in common at least an appeal to the eyes: the cheeks are good to look at, a visual feast (those "pomegranates") that promises much sweetness when the other senses engage them more closely—when, that is, the cheeks are touched or tasted. The "cheeks" are mentioned very rarely elsewhere in scripture: there is no developed scriptural symbolism of the cheeks,[37] and they are given more attention in the Song than anywhere else in scripture.

The beloved's "neck" is also mentioned here, also beautiful and also adorned, this time with "necklaces." Her "neck" is praised three times in the Song, while the lover's is not mentioned at all. In addition to being necklace adorned (1:10), it is twice likened to a "tower." In the first case, the imagery is of fortification and invulnerable strength: "Your neck like David's tower / built with battlements / hung with a thousand shields / with all the armor of the strong" (4:4). In the second, her neck is "like an ivory tower" (7:5).[38] The imagery of fortification and impregnability is found as well in 8:9–10, where the images of "rampart" and "battlement" are used to describe the beloved and her breasts are said to be "like a tower." Her neck is, then, beautiful and strong, straight and worthy of ornamentation, incapable of conquest and therefore incapable of bending to a conqueror.

Elsewhere in scripture this grammar of the neck is underscored and deepened.[39] Your neck (*collum* usually, but also, and effectively equivalently, *cervix*) is the place where your status, your relation to others, can be indicated. It can be yoked by an oppressor, indicating subservience and even slavery (Sir. 51:34 [= 51:26 RSV]; Jer. 27:11; 28:10; cf. Matt. 11:29 on Jesus's yoke); and it can be adorned to indicate that you occupy a place of honor (Gen. 41:42; Prov. 3:22; Dan. 5:29). When the lover likens the beloved's neck to a well-fortified tower (→4:4), then, he is best construed as saying not that she is hard to approach or that her neck is inaccessible (in 7:10 he says that he wants to nibble her throat, and she enthusiastically agrees that he should), but that it, and thereby she, as figured by it, will yield herself to none but himself. She (her neck) cannot be mounted, her battlements scaled, by

37. Following: "Mais il est clair qu'il n'y a pas vraiment de symbolisme des joues dans la Bible en dehors du *Cantique*" (Chrétien 2005: 165). There is, of course, Isa. 50:6, in which the prophet claims of the servant that he freely gives his "cheeks" (*genae*) to those who pluck at his beard. The word *maxilla* (literally "jawbone") occurs more frequently than *gena*, but even for that there is not much figural resonance.

38. Is this the origin of the "ivory tower" cliché in English? And if so, how did it migrate from praise of the Song's beloved's neck to the familiar modern sense of seclusion or separation from the world? Among early English versions of scripture, the King James (Authorized) Version renders the phrase thus: "Thy neck is as a tower of ivory." The Douay-Rheims gives: "Thy neck as a tower of ivory." The Coverdale Bible: "Thy neck is as it were a tower of yuery." The Wycliffe: "Thi necke is as a tour of yuer." The *Oxford English Dictionary* records no uses of the phrase earlier than the seventeenth century and no use in the modern sense prior to the nineteenth; but this seems unlikely.

39. In this paragraph I draw from and elaborate upon Chrétien 2005: 125–41.

anyone but him: his yoke, and only his, goes around her neck, just as his lips and teeth, and only his, leave their marks on her throat.

Both "cheeks" and "neck" are praised by mention of their adornments in 1:10. "Earrings" (*inaures*) ornament her cheeks, and her throat is necklaced. The earrings are mentioned only here in the Song, while the "necklaces" (*monilia*) are mentioned twice more, once as something to which the curves of the beloved's thighs are likened (7:2) and once as constituents of her torque (*torques*), a more elaborate throat ornament composed of many necklaces (4:9).[40] In all these cases—and throughout the Song—the beloved's adornments are unambiguously positive, and not least because her lover makes them for her, or at least promises to (1:11). He wants her decorated, made more beautiful by what he gives her and in that way more pleasing to him and more capable of exciting his desire for her.

Consider this text from Ezekiel, where the prophet speaks in the first person as the Lord, addressing the people of Israel as his beloved:

> And I passed you by and saw you, and it was clear that your time had come for love. I spread my cloak over you and covered your nakedness.[41] . . . I swore you an oath and entered into a covenant with you, and you became mine. Then I washed you with water and cleansed you from your blood and anointed you with oil. I dressed you in multicolored cloth, shod you with sandals of fine leather, girded you with a linen sash, and clothed you with silk. I adorned you with ornaments, put bracelets on your wrists, a torque around your neck, a golden ring upon your forehead,[42] pendants in your ears, and a splendid crown upon your head. And so you were adorned with gold and silver, dressed in linen and silk and multicolored cloth. You ate finely milled flour and honey and oil, and you were splendid and supremely fit to be a queen. And your name became known among the peoples because of your beauty: you were made perfect in my splendor, which I had placed upon you. (Ezek. 16:8–14)

The Lord's beloved here is Israel, as the context in Ezekiel makes clear: she is likened to a girl menstruating for the first time, and the Lord to a man who prepares her for lovemaking. She becomes his by covenantal pact, and then he washes and anoints her body, dresses her gorgeously, and ornaments her. She is then not

---

40. In Song 4:9 a *torques* can have several *monilia*, and since the usual meaning of *monile* is "necklace," it seems reasonable to offer "torque" as a calque of *torques*, given that "torque's" range of meanings includes neck ornaments made of several bands of metal twisted together. One of these bands might then be a *monile*. Precise differentiation among these various terms for jewelry is difficult for us, as it already was for those who rendered the old Hebrew text into Greek and for Jerome's Latin rendering.

41. The Latin of Ezek. 16:8 is *ignominiam*, which is more literally "shame" or "dishonor" or (by calque) "ignominy." But the meaning here is pretty clearly that she is naked, and thereby shamed.

42. Translating *inaurem super os tuum*. *Inaures* is also the word in Song 1:10–11, there translated "earring," which is its ordinary meaning. Given its connection with *os* ("mouth/face," here rendered "forehead") in Ezek. 16:12, it must mean simply "golden ring."

only "comely" (*speciosa*), a word applied to the beloved in the Song as well (2:13; 5:15), but also renowned as such. Her "splendor" (*decor*—cf. 1:16; 2:14; 6:4; 7:7) is reflective of and participatory in his: it is his gift to her, and ornamentation is among its important constituents.

This elegantly illuminates the Song's references to the beloved's ornamentation by her lover. What is said of his desire to ornament her ("we shall make earrings for you / silver-chased") is said also of the Lord and Israel; his delight in her and his choice of her requires that she be made ready for an intimacy with him given to no one else, and this must be his gift, not something she can do for herself. This, in significant part, is what election means: the beloved is set apart from other women exactly by being given gifts not given to others. For Christian readers, the extension to the church, and then to Mary, is natural and almost inevitable. Both can properly be understood as "perfect in my [the Lord's] splendor, which I had placed upon you."

Ornamenting the female body is not, however, usually depicted in scripture as a good thing, being most often connected with whoring after gods other than the Lord (Gen. 35:4; Exod. 32:2; Hos. 2:15 [= 2:13 RSV]; Jer. 4:30).[43] When body ornamentation is depicted negatively in this way, it is always described as something the woman does for herself, and not as something her lover does for her.[44] There are no doubt echoes here of a patriarchal social order. But speaking theologically, the point is much more fundamental: it is that ornamentation is a gift, to be received as such if it is not to be idolized. We (men and women) are beautiful, to the extent that we are, because the Lord has given it to us to be so. Choosing to adorn our bodies with gold and silver for our own purposes would be to expropriate that gift; but delightedly accepting the ornaments the Lord provides is nothing but good because it is to acknowledge the Lord as our lover and to return his love. Hence the beloved's necklaces and earrings: the lily is not gilded by his gift of them to her, but rather its beauty perfected—Ezekiel's words, *perfecta eras in decore meo* ("you were made perfect in my splendor"), apply preeminently to Israel-church-Mary, but also, by participation, to each of us to the extent that we choose to allow ourselves to be adorned by the Lord and prepared for his love.

When you offer ornaments to your beloved, or receive them from your lover; when you decorate your body in anticipation of your lover's pleasure in it; when you give thought and attention to the adornments appropriate for the increase of delight that each of you takes in the other—when you do these things, you are acting as the Lord acted for Israel and as Christ did for the church.

43. Many of the same body ornaments depicted positively in the Song are in these texts depicted negatively.

44. The account of Judith's self-ornamentation in preparation for her bedazzlement of Holofernes (Jdt. 10) is an interesting mixed case. She ornaments herself for deception, but does so knowing what she does and that the final purpose of the deception is good. This is, I think, the only half-positive depiction of self-ornamentation in scripture.

On the King's Couch (1:12–14)

> While the king was on his couch
> my spikenard gave off its scent.
> A sachet of myrrh is my delightful man for me
> he lingers between my breasts;
> a henna cluster is my delightful man for me
> in the vineyards of Engaddi.

She responds to his words of praise to her in 1:9–11, though initially not in the voice of direct address but rather with third-person memories or anticipations of bed—she recalls that they have been "on his couch" together—and lovemaking, as in the first few verses of the Song. Naming him again as her "king," she recalls or hopes for his lingering between her breasts, saturating her images of physical intimacy with those of sweet-scented herbs and ointments ("spikenard," "myrrh," "henna"). He is her "delightful man"—the one who gives her delight: again, the explicitly sexual vocabulary—but she distances him by not yet matching his vocatives and second-person verbs with her own.

She smells, she says of "spikenard" (*nardus*), which is, botanically speaking, a fragrant unguent derived from plants of the valerian family—usually *Nardostachys grandiflora* or *Nardostachys grandimans*. The word occurs in the Song only here and at 4:13–14, and always with reference to her pleasing and erotically exciting perfume. *Nardus* is rare in scripture as well, the only other occurrences being in the stories of Jesus's anointing with it (→1:3a), at Bethany by Mary, perhaps Martha's sister (as John 12:1–8 has it), or by an unnamed woman (as in Mark 14:1–9). In both versions of the gospel story, emphasis is placed on the expense and purity of the spikenard used, and on the connection of the anointing with Jesus's death and burial. Spikenard is therefore used as a preparation for both sex and death; and that Jesus is anointed with it by a woman preserves and deepens its connection with the former. To anoint Jesus's body with spikenard is to prepare it for that act of love that is his death, a preparation best done by a woman.

Gregory of Nyssa, writing at the end of the fourth century, is lyrical and suggestive on the connection between the "spikenard" of the Song and that of the Gospels:

> This [the spikenard of the Gospels] is perhaps the same as the bride's spikenard [of Song 1:12], which gave off the bridegroom's scent. In the Gospel, it is poured out upon the Lord and fills the house with its scent. Here [in the Song] it seems to me that the woman's spikenard foreshadows by a kind of prophetic inspiration the mystery of his [the Lord's] death. The Lord bears witness to what she has done when he says, "She has come beforehand to bury me" [Mark 14:8]. . . .
> In the Song, the spikenard gives to the bride the sweet scent of the bridegroom; in the Gospel, however, the perfume that fills the whole house becomes the

fragrant chrism of the whole body of the church in the entire inhabited world and in the entire cosmos.[45]

This line of interpretation—a commonplace in later patristic commentary—emphasizes not only the sweetness and diffusion of the spikenard's scent and its connection with love and death, but also its ecclesial meaning: when the Lord's Israel-church loves him by returning his caresses "on his couch," then the effusion of sweetness that results can fill the world. This sweetness is the presence of Israel-church, and Gregory depicts it with words whose very form imitates that of Christ. The "chrism" he mentions, *chrisma* in Greek, is related morphologically and etymologically to *Christos* ("the anointed one"): what has anointed the body of Christ as preparation for his death is figured by the Song's beloved's "spikenard"; both are recapitulated by and participated in by the church's presence in the world; and the circle of resonance is closed when the church further recapitulates what the beloved does on the couch and what Mary did at Bethany by using chrism in the liturgies of baptism and confirmation. In your baptism you were (probably) smeared with chrism; and in so being you were behaving as the Song's beloved did when she returned her lover's embraces on his couch.

The Song's beloved goes on to describe her lover in herbal terms, first as a "sachet of myrrh" lingering between her "breasts." Myrrh (*myrrha*) is an aromatic gum from the tree *Commiphora schimperi*; it was widely used in the premodern Mediterranean world as an ingredient in perfumes and oils of various kinds, as well as a component of incense. This word occurs frequently in the Song (3:6; 4:6, 14; 5:1, 5, 13, in addition to this occurrence), on her lips for him (as here), and on his for her (as especially, in 5:1, where their intercourse is depicted). Her fingers are said to drip with it as she opens herself to him (5:5), and she describes his lips as dripping with it (5:13) when she describes his delights to the daughters of Jerusalem. Myrrh carries with it the most explicitly sexual connotations of the three herbal unguents mentioned in these verses: its first level of meaning is as symbolic representation of the bodily fluids involved in sexual intercourse (→5:1; →5:3–7).[46]

45. Author's translation from the third of Gregory of Nyssa's late-fourth-century *Homiliae in canticum canticorum*; Greek in *Gregorii Nysseni Opera*, vol. 6: *In Canticum Canticorum*, ed. Herman Langerbeck (Leiden: Brill, 1960), 92–93. Compare Rupert of Deutz, *Commentaria in Canticum Canticorum* (Commentary on the Song) on Song 1:12, where a contrast is made between the stink of Eve's pride in ignoring the Lord's command and the sweet smell of humility represented by spikenard. By the former we were turned away from the Lord; by the latter we turn back to him (Deutz and Deutz 2005: 176–86).

46. The explicitly sexual uses of myrrh are evident elsewhere in scripture, as well. In Esth. 2:12 myrrh is mentioned as among the unguents used to prepare the bodies of those who will have sex with King Ahasuerus; there it represents both purification and erotic beautification. But there are also more everyday mentions of myrrh as effectively a household perfume (Prov. 7:17; Ps. 45:9 [= 45:8 RSV]).

This deeply sexual meaning exhausts the implications of myrrh neither in the Song nor in the corpus of scripture. In 4:6, the lover ends a hymn of praise to his beloved's body by saying, "I shall go to the mountain of myrrh / and to the hill of frankincense," and while the meaning is not quite clear, the place to which the lover intends to go is a cool refuge, a place of retreat and quiet and recovery.[47] There is also a connection between myrrh and incense. In 3:6, the daughters speak, asking, "What is this ascending through the desert / like a wisp of smoke / spicy with frankincense and myrrh?" The image is one of burning incense ascending to the Lord, and myrrh is mentioned as one among the herbs that scent the incense, without, however, being given any special qualities or significance. A connection between myrrh as concomitant of sexual union—and especially as trope for the bodily secretions connected with that union—and myrrh as ingredient to incense ascending to the Lord is at least possible and perhaps likely: in both cases, myrrh accompanies intimacy and serves as synecdoche for it.

Myrrh bears yet another set of scriptural connotations: it is connected with the anointing of the ark of the covenant (Exod. 30:22–25) and, by resonant extension, with the unguents used to embalm Jesus's body after it had been taken down from the cross.[48] To anoint the ark is to mark the Lord's presence there, a presence that is also, and necessarily, a kind of absence, because the Lord does not live in temples made with hands. His presence cannot be constrained or limited to any particular place, which means that the anointing of a particular place as where the Lord (preeminently? exhaustively?) must be is a complex gesture. It is required: the Lord does inhabit the ark; but its failure is inevitable: the Lord is not subject to the necessities of location. The embalming of Jesus's body with a mixture that includes myrrh intensifies this complex structure. The flesh taken down from the cross is dead; myrrh plays its part in marking that fact, in sanctifying an absence, and in doing so with the special poignancy produced by the dead Jesus being a man, gone (they think) from those, like Nicodemus, who loved him as such.

The third herb mentioned by the beloved as she recalls being in bed with her lover is "henna." Her *dilectus*, the man in whom she takes delight, is "a henna cluster" for her. This word (*cyprus*) has much less extensive scriptural resonance: in the entire corpus of scripture it occurs only in 1:14 and 4:13, on both occasions in close proximity to "spikenard." Botanically speaking, henna is a shrub belonging to the loosestrife family; it was used in the premodern Mediterranean world, as now, to make dyes and cosmetics. At 1:14, the beloved's likening of her man to a "henna cluster" suggests that he beautifies her, painting her with his colors.

47. In Mark 15:23, myrrh-mixed wine is offered as an anesthetic to Jesus hanging on the cross. He refuses it. Here too, perhaps, as in Song 4:6, there is a weak connection between myrrh and the cool quietness of pain's removal—a link that approaches that of myrrh with death.

48. The embalming mixture used by Nicodemus (including myrrh) is mentioned in John 19:39. Myrrh is among the gifts brought to the baby Jesus by the Magi (Matt. 2:11), marking both the identity of his body as the Lord's tabernacle and his future violent death.

Her lover, she says, lingers between her "breasts." The lovers are in bed together, and this is part of what they do together. He wants to be between her breasts: he "linger[s]" there; and she wants him to do so: it is her voice that delightedly speaks of his presence there. The first and obvious sense is that her breasts give him sexual pleasure and that his pleasure in them pleases her. This is a meaning all lovers can understand, and the Song here, as throughout, blesses the sexual and sensual delight the two take in each other's bodies. Her breasts are mentioned often in the Song: the beloved says that he, her king and her lover, "linger[s]" between them like "a sachet of myrrh" (1:13); they are "like two fawns / doe-born twins" (4:5; 7:4); they are like "clusters" of ripe fruit on the palm tree or on the vine (7:8–9); and they are "like a tower" upon the "rampart" of her body (8:10). These tropes emphasize her breasts' beauty and fertility, as well as their attractiveness to her lover: he wants to climb the palm tree "and seize its fruit" (7:9). The likening of her breasts to "two fawns" in 4:5 and 7:4 emphasizes their graceful mobility (→2:7).

Mention of the breasts as synecdoche for female beauty, sexual attractiveness (Ezek. 16, 23; Hos. 2), and capacity to feed and nurture children (Job 3:12; Ps. 22:9; Isa. 28:9; Joel 2:16) is almost universal and is certainly present elsewhere in scripture. Figural extension of these meanings, and especially of the breasts as givers of nourishment, is also present elsewhere in scripture, most notably in Isaiah's rendering of the Lord's injunction to Israel to suck at Jerusalem's breasts and be filled with the consolation that comes from them (Isa. 66:7–14). Here, as often, the beloved and Jerusalem—itself a synecdoche for Israel—merge, each figuring the other.

The nutritive trope, the breasts as giving suck, is present also in the New Testament, where Mary's nourishing breasts are blessed by an unnamed woman in Luke's Gospel.[49] Jerusalem, Israel, church, and Mary, then, all have breasts and all are sources of nourishment for their lovers. What nourishment do they provide? What comes into the mouths of those who suck at them? The first and most obvious answer is that the nourishment derived therefrom is the words spoken by the Lord to his lovers. To suck at the church's breasts is to ingest the words the Lord has given to her and that she in turn transmits to her lovers. Recall here the Song's repeated emphasis on the twoness of the beloved's breasts: they are "doe-born twins" (4:5; 7:4). What does the church have two of that nourishes and consoles her members? There are two testaments, two collections of the Lord's word to Christians, which together form the canon of scripture; from those two testaments nourishment is drawn. Their words can be sucked and licked and chewed, as babies do to their mothers' breasts and as lovers do to their beloveds'; this repeated and delighted attention to what the Lord has said is among the most important activities undertaken by the people of the Lord, Jews and Christians both. The church appoints individuals among its members to make this repeated

49. Jesus rebukes the woman for saying *"Beatus venter, qui te portavit, et ubera, quae suxisti"* (Luke 11:27), or at least transfers the blessing she offered to him and his mother to all those who hear and act upon what the Lord says.

sucking at scripture's nipples both nourishing and delightful: they are preachers and teachers.[50] This commentary, in a small way, is intended to exemplify what the Song here recommends: a repeated sucking at scripture's breasts.[51]

If we take seriously the figuration of Mary's breasts by those of the beloved in the Song—and the scriptural resonance (of the Song with, inter alia, Isa. 66 and Luke 11) permits this, opens it before us as a possible mode of thinking—then we can turn the significance of the beloved's breasts in a different direction. Mary's breasts nourished Jesus, who is, according to Christian doctrine, the Word, the one in whom all words, scriptural and otherwise, participate. His desire for the nourishment of his mother's milk, and for the growth and strength and increase in wisdom given him thereby (Luke 2:40),[52] shows not our desire for the Lord and his words and Word, but the Lord's desire for the nourishment we can provide him. The Lord's desire for us is a fundamental theme of the Song, and it is one of its distinctive features that it paints this desire in unrestrainedly physical terms. The Song's lover wants to suck and enjoy and get nourishment from the beloved's breasts, and this serves as figure for what the Lord wants from us—from you and from me. An extended theology of the Lord's desire for us cannot be developed here, but the Song is one of the central scriptural sources for it. What the Song does show, beyond reasonable theological dispute, is that if the Lord does desire us, then this desire can be neither depicted nor understood as unrelated to our physical being. If we are, as the Christian tradition almost unanimously asserts, not souls adventitiously embodied, but rather bodies formed by the soul, constitutively and essentially physical beings, then if the Lord desires us at all, he does so as what we are, which is to say as bodies ensouled. Jesus's sucking at Mary's breasts, like the Song's lover's lying between his beloved's breasts, can serve to remind us of that fact.

This double reading of the breasts—as figuring Israel-church's provision of nourishment to the Lord's lovers, and as figuring Mary's provision of nourishment to the Lord—serves to support the view that the grammar of the Song's depiction of the body is not allegorical. It is not that one of these two figural readings is right, not that the breasts in the Song really figure nourishment and delight that goes from the Lord to us, nor that they really figure nourishment and delight that goes from us to the Lord. No, it is that both readings (and no doubt more) are to be affirmed, because both respond to the resonances of the Song's text with the text of scripture, and both are consonant with the grammar of the faith.

50. For detailed and rich discussion of the breasts in the Song, see Bernard of Clairvaux's twelfth-century *Sermones super cantica canticorum* (Sermons on the Song of Songs) 9–10 (English in *Bernard of Clairvaux on the Song of Songs*, trans. Kilian Walsh and Irene Edmonds [Kalamazoo, MI: Cistercian, 1971], 1.53–68; Latin in *Patrologia Latina* 183.815A–824A).

51. I drew in this and the immediately preceding paragraphs on Chrétien 2005: 201–23 and Kingsmill 2009: 75–78.

52. For an interesting study of patristic and medieval commentary on this verse and on the complexities of the idea that the incarnate Lord could increase in wisdom, see Kevin Madigan, *The Passions of Christ in High-Medieval Thought: An Essay on Christological Development*, Oxford Studies in Historical Theology (Oxford: Oxford University Press, 2007).

Even this is not all that can be said about the breasts in the Song. Recall that reading the Song will, if you let it, reconfigure your loves. If you are a woman, it may do that with respect to your own breasts: they are proper objects of delight, attraction, and nourishment for you and your children and your lovers. They participate in Mary's breasts, from which Jesus sucked; the church's scriptural breasts, from which we all suck; and the breasts of the Song's beloved, which in turn refigure all breasts. When your breasts are desired and delighted in, whether for nourishment or sexual pleasure or a more diffuse sensual delight, then you participate as female beloved in Mary and the church in ways not possible for a male human being. If you are male, without breasts, then your desire for your mother's and lovers' breasts is here affirmed and intensified: in such desires you figure human desire for the nourishment that comes from Mary and the church; and you figure also the Lord's desire for us. Sex with its desires is in these ways deepened and given resonance. And for both men and women, if you come to see, as the Song encourages you to do, that the delight of lovers in one another's bodies (here specifically of the man in lying between the woman's breasts and of the woman in having him do so) figures the delight of Christians in scripture, then your own love of scripture and what it has to offer might be reconfigured. Our desires for one another's bodies are among the most intense we know, and they are not exhausted, but rather intensified, by being acted upon. To see that these desires are only figures of the intensity and delight that belongs to sucking at scripture might be a first step toward coming to make that source of nourishment more seductively attractive to you than it now is.

A final point about the breasts. It may seem that thinking about them in the ways evident in the immediately preceding paragraphs serves to underline a rigid essentialism of gender with respect to sensual and sexual desire, and therefore also with respect to the modes in which the sexual desires of men and women differently figure and participate in the Lord's desires. After all, breasts are a secondary sexual characteristic of women and not of men; they are one of the distinguishing features, therefore, of the human female. But matters are, scripturally (and otherwise), more complicated. It is true that the version of the Latin Song under discussion in this book speaks of breasts only as belonging to her, the beloved (and possibly her sister, in 8:8), and therefore does not play with the thought that the lover, the man, might also have breasts or think of himself as doing so. But other versions of the Song, notably the Latin version produced by Jerome at the end of the fourth century, do just that, reading "breasts" for "loves" in 1:2, and thus putting into the beloved's mouth praise of her (male) lover's breasts.[53] This presence of a reference to male breasts in the Vulgate meant that large portions of the Latin commentarial tradition on the Song had perforce to say something about

---

53. Jerome's rendering is found also in the Septuagint and in other Greek versions of the Song. The Latin of the New Vulgate appears to have been emended to accord more closely with the Masoretic Text.

what it might mean that the beloved ponders and desires her male lover's breasts; and this in turn prompted much theological consideration of the exchangeability of male and female desire, a theme also present elsewhere in the Song, where the couple often echo one another's sentiments and praises verbatim. This is a theme that will come up at various points in the commentary to follow.

These verses, 1:12–14, contain the second mention of a place in the Song (the first was "Kedar" in 1:5), namely "the vineyards of Engaddi."[54] "Engaddi" was an oasis town on the western shore of the Dead Sea, about forty miles southeast of Jerusalem. In the Song it is mentioned only here, and its connection with the beloved's praise of her lover while she is in bed with him—it is where he is "a henna cluster" for her; where, therefore, he makes her beautiful with his lovemaking—means that it must stand in the Song for a beautiful and fertile place. This connotation is, on the whole, supported by its other mentions in scripture. In Wisdom's hymn of praise to herself in Sirach, for instance, she likens herself to a tall and flourishing palm tree in Engaddi (Sir. 24:18 [= 24:14 RSV]; see Kingsmill 2009: 50–53), and this connection with palms is found also in an alternative name in 2 Chr. 20:2 ("Asasonthamar," which is latinized Hebrew meaning "the pruning, or cutting, of the palm tree") given to it. A similar connection is present in the mention of Engaddi in Ezekiel's vision of the waters flowing out from Zion: fishermen at Engaddi will, when the waters of the sea have been purified and made fertile, be able to spread their nets and haul in an abundance of fish (Ezek. 47:10). The oasis character of Engaddi is underscored by its location *in deserto*: when the towns allotted to the tribe of Judah after the conquest are listed, Engaddi among them, this is how it is characterized (Josh. 15:62); and the same is true for its mention as the place where David, in a cave, has Saul at his mercy (1 Sam. 24:1-2 [= 23:29–24:1 RSV]). When, therefore, the beloved locates her lover's lovemakings as occurring in Engaddi, she emphasizes not only their fertility and beauty, but also their contrast with what surrounds them. That is desert, where there is only thirst and destitution; in the lover's bed, caressed by his hands and encircled by his arms, she finds the oasis.

Her Dove-Eyes #1 (1:15)

> O my beloved—
> see how beautiful you are
> see how beautiful you are
> your dove-eyes.

54. Seventeen places are mentioned in the Song: Amana (4:8), Baalhamon (8:11), Bathrabbim (7:5), Bether (2:17), Carmel (7:6), Damascus (7:5), Engaddi (1:14), Gilead (4:1; 6:5), Hermon (4:8), Heshbon (7:5), Israel (3:7), Jerusalem (1:5; 2:7; 3:5, 10; 5:8, 16; 6:4; 8:4), Kedar (1:5), Lebanon (3:9; 4:8, 11, 15; 5:15; 7:5), Sanir (4:8), Tirzah (6:4), Zion (3:11). Generally speaking, places are important in the Song for their symbolic associations, not for the geographical imagination.

He responds to her with a half-incoherent love mutter. The repetition of "see how beautiful you are" caresses her with words as an echo of the caresses of the body she has been recalling and hoping for. He is dazzled by her beauty, appreciative and desirous of it, calling attention to it ("see") as though he hopes to persuade her of how beautiful she seems to him and, therefore, that she is beautiful. It is a commonplace of human love that your own beauty becomes apparent only when you see how beautiful you seem to your lover. It is a gift of love to permit the beloved to see herself as beautiful: beauty, in the realm of desire, is, like flesh, a gift word. You become flesh when you are caressed as such by a lover; you become beautiful when you are desired as such by a lover; without that caress and that desire, you are neither because you have not received the gift that provides them. All this is true most fundamentally and essentially of the Lord's love for his Israel-church: she is beautiful because he has given her the gift of being desired as such, and the lover's apostrophizing of his beloved in these terms here serves as an aphoristic summary of that love gift.

The lover uses here a refrain, "your dove-eyes," repeated verbatim by him at 4:1. She uses the same trope, though as a simile rather than a metaphor, at 5:12. The eyes are often praised and attended to in the Song: such attention is an important part of the Song's grammar of the body. In addition to the connection of eyes with doves, he also says that her eyes have "wounded [his] heart" (4:9), and he asks her to "turn your eyes away from me / for they disturb me" (6:5). The lover also uses the similitude "fishpools in Heshbon / in the gate of Bathrabbim" (7:5) for his beloved's eyes. And there is in addition a vocabulary of gazing and looking in the Song, most notably when she, the beloved, perhaps speaking in soliloquy, says of him: "He is the very one who stands behind our wall / looking [*respiciens*] through the windows / gazing [*prospiciens*] through the lattices" (2:9).[55]

The beloved's eyes in the Song are both beautiful and dangerously disturbing. Their beauty is shown most clearly in being likened to doves. He calls her *columba* ("dove") no fewer than four times in the Song (2:10, 14; 5:2; 6:9), and on four of these occasions it is not just "dove" but *columba mea* ("my dove")—the endearment signaling both her beauty and her intimacy with him. Likening her eyes to those of doves, as is done in the words under discussion here, underscores their beauty, but also that her eyes are apostrophized as synecdoche for herself. Her eyes may be praised in this way because in them—in their gaze and in the attractiveness of that gaze to his—is evident herself in peculiarly concentrated form. Lovers, when kissing or making love, may gaze intently into one another's eyes, or may close their eyes exactly to avoid doing so, to signal that the weight of such intimacy is unbearable. In either case, the significance of the eye, and especially of its dark pupil in which the lover finds himself reflected and in

55. For the grammar of the eyes and the gaze, I draw in part on Chrétien 2005: 143–64. See also Gregory of Nyssa's fourth homily in *Homiliae in canticum canticorum* (Greek in *Gregorii Nysseni Opera*, vol. 6: *In Canticum Canticorum*, ed. Herman Langerbeck [Leiden: Brill, 1960], 105–7).

which the depths of his beloved open themselves unfathomably before him, is acknowledged and responded to.[56]

But what, more exactly, is the connection between eyes and doves? What does the trope show? The fullest answer within the Song is 5:12, where his eyes are "like doves' / above rivers of water / milk-washed / beside completely full streams." The similes and the syntax here are on their face obscure. The most natural reading is that "milk-washed" (smoothly white?) modifies "doves" and that the compound expression ("milk-washed doves") is then the subject of the predicates "above rivers of water" and "beside completely full streams." The whole—doves so described—is what his eyes are like: they are beautiful and smoothly white, they fly above the waters, and they (perhaps) perch beside those same waters.

Dove talk elsewhere in scripture strengthens and deepens this impression. In Gen. 8:6–12, Noah three times sends out a dove from the ark as the floodwaters begin to recede. The first time it returns without having found any dry land; the second time it brings back an olive branch; and the third time it does not return. And then, in the Gospel accounts of the baptism of Jesus, the Spirit descends over the waters of the Jordan *sicut columbam* ("like a dove") (Matt. 3:16 || Mark 1:10 || Luke 3:22; John 1:32). In both stories—of Noah and of Jesus's baptism—the dove is over the waters; and in both it serves as the bringer of something supremely good, something that stands in contrast to the waters, which in both stories serve as a Janus-faced symbol, suggesting both the purification that necessarily comes before rebirth and the chaos that is overcome and left behind as rebirth happens: the floodwaters recede, permitting Noah to repopulate the earth; and the newly baptized Jesus rises from the Jordan's waters, ready to begin redeeming the world from the chaos of sin. When the Song's lover apostrophizes his beloved's "dove-eyes" (1:15), and when she apostrophizes his as "like doves," the words vibrate with these deep scriptural resonances.

All that is deep background to the Song's mention of the beloved's "dove-eyes." Less distant is the frequent scriptural use of the dove as synecdoche for Israel as the Lord's beautiful beloved (Jer. 48:28; Hos. 7:11; 11:11) and the occasional use of it to represent any beautiful woman—as, most strikingly, when Job gives the name *Columba* to the first of the daughters born to him following the restoration of his fortunes, daughters whose beauty is unrivaled in the world (Job 42:14–15). Scriptural doves, however, do not figure only beauty; they also figure mourning, because, no doubt, of the mournful coo of the dove. And so, likening the beloved's eyes to those of doves adds grief to the beauty of intimacy with the beloved's face. As well as offering the soulful gaze, the eyes cry: and the beloved's grief at separation from the lover is as much a theme of the Song as her delight in his presence. She is beautiful like a dove and she mourns like a dove; the two

56. On the phenomenal significance of the eye and its pupil, see Jean-Luc Marion, *In Excess: Studies of Saturated Phenomena*, trans. Robyn Horner and Vincent Berraud (New York: Fordham University Press, 2002), chap. 5.

are inseparable and are bound by the dove image. In the same way, Noah's dove figures the recovery of the land and its repeopling; but rejoicing at the dove's nonreturn is threaded through with the certainty that sin, too, will reestablish itself—Noah immediately shames himself by being drunk and naked before the gaze of his son. So too with Jesus's dove: he is recognized by the Spirit for who he is, and his salvific work thus begun; but that work involves bloody suffering and death, and the dove's words of approbation have that as their subtext too.

Elsewhere in scripture, eyes, both the Lord's and ours, are mentioned hundreds of times. Most frequently, the meaning is simple and literal: the eyes of the body, the fleshy orbs in the head. But the eyes often also stand for the whole person, whether the Lord or some human being. Moses, for instance, asks for favor in the Lord's eyes (Exod. 33:13), and Esther asks King Artaxerxes whether she is acceptable in his eyes (Esth. 8:5). In both cases the question is not only about whether their visual appearance is pleasing, but also about whether they find acceptance in every way. The eye also often represents human (and divine) desire: what your gaze turns to is what you find interesting, what you want, what concerns you. It is with this meaning that Jesus calls the eye "the light of the body" (Matt. 6:22 || Luke 11:34) and advocates plucking it out if it gives offense (Matt. 5:29; 18:9). When the lover praises his beloved's eyes in the Song, he praises her whole person, and especially her as one who can herself desire, who can reciprocate his desirous gaze with her own.

In Genesis, Adam and Eve have their eyes opened by eating the fruit of the forbidden tree, as the serpent promised would happen (Gen. 3:5–7); but in that case they cannot endure one another's gaze and shield themselves from it by putting on clothes. This shows that the eyes of love can burn as well as caress and that the lover's gaze can be difficult to endure precisely because it strips the beloved naked and exposes her as herself a lover, but one who is, usually, unwilling to give herself over to love, and thus also unwilling to look back at the lover without reservation. In the letter to the Hebrews it is terrifyingly said that all creatures are naked before and fully open to the Lord's eyes (Heb. 4:13); and Isaiah's response to seeing the Lord of Hosts in the temple is one of agony: his eyes cannot endure it (Isa. 6). This illuminates the threatening and dangerous nature of the eyes in the Song. The beloved's eyes have wounded the lover's heart (4:9); and he asks her to turn her gaze away from him because they disturb him (6:5). It is especially interesting that the dangerous eyes belong to the beloved, not to the lover. It is he who has been wounded by her gaze, not she by his. The scriptural tropes of damage and danger run in the other direction: it is we who are damaged by a too-direct exposure to the Lord's gaze, not he by ours. So far as the Song's human lovers are concerned, this is no difficulty: it is a cliché of love poetry to speak of the dangers of bewitchment by a woman's eyes, while enchantment in the other direction is a much less common theme. But if we take seriously the naming of the Song's lover as the Lord, we learn something here, once again, about the intensity with which the Lord desires us and the anguish with which he responds to a deceitful or obstinate or blind beloved's gaze. If you or I or the Lord's Israel-church look at the Lord with the fluttering eyelashes of the coquette or the stony gaze of someone convinced of her ability not to reveal herself fully to her lover, then we wound him, which is further evidence of the depth of his love for us.

The phenomenology of the loving gaze is a complex matter, certainly, and a full account of it requires theology because the human gaze turned to the face of the beloved human other is what it is only because of its participation in the Lord's gaze turned directly and unceasingly toward the face of each of us. The Song, read as a depiction not only of the exchange of gaze between human lovers, but also as a depiction of the Lord's—the lover's—gaze turned toward each of us as his beloved, makes a contribution to such a phenomenology. This phenomenology is deepened still more, and made more beautiful, if the beloved is understood as not only a human woman, which of course she is, but also as Mary and the Lord's beloved Israel-church, which she figures. The Lord's gaze is turned upon Mary in the annunciation, and she responds to it by returning it without reservation, which is to say by looking back at the Lord without withholding anything. In giving her assent to what the angel offers she gets as close as any human being can to returning the Lord's gaze without having to avert her own, without having to do what Isaiah does in the temple. It is with her in mind, and this return of the Lord's gaze, that the church asks the Lord not to look at the sins of the members of Christ's body, but rather to attend to the faith of the church.

There is as yet, here in Song 1, nothing of the tension and terror of the gaze in the Song. Here the lover is with his beloved, praising her eyes and thereby also herself, without reservation. Her response, about to come (1:16), suggests that she is similarly without reservation. But the anguish will come. Later (6:5) he will ask her to turn her eyes away from him because they disturb him. But that is not yet.

The Flowerful Bed (1:16–17)

> O my delightful man—
> see how beautiful you are
> and splendid!
> Our flowerful bed—
> our cedar-beamed house—
> our cypress-paneled ceilings.

She responds to his endearments with equally passionate ones of her own, addressing him directly and returning his compliment to her beauty by calling him "beautiful" and (again) her "delightful man," who is "splendid." She then mentions their "bed" and "house" in lyrical terms, as the places in which they enjoy one another's beauty. The tone is again excited, the phrases disjointed, expressive of images without connection as though she is, whether in reverie or to him, recalling a succession of images of the place they have made love ("our flowerful bed") and the house they have lived in ("our cedar-beamed house— / our cypress-paneled ceilings"). This, again, is lyric, not narrative: the image-laden words flash discretely upon the screen of your consciousness as their hearer, bound by no chronological order (we are again in the tenseless present) but laden with a deep sensual affect.

This is the only place in the Song in which the adjective "splendid" (*decorus*) is applied to him. Elsewhere, in the feminine, it is applied to her face (2:14), to her in likeness to Jerusalem (6:4), and to her in her pleasures (7:7). The word occurs frequently elsewhere in scripture, most often as an adjective applied to particular people (Rachel [Gen. 29:17], Joseph [39:6], David [1 Sam. 16:12], Jonathan, Esther) as an indication of their radiantly attractive physical beauty. The word can also be applied to places (Carmel [Isa. 35:2], Tyre [Ezek. 27:3]) and, on a few occasions, to artifacts (the temple's marble floor [2 Chr. 3:6], ornaments for camels' necks [Judg. 8:21], Aaron's vestments [Exod. 28:2, 40]). But most fundamentally it is a term used for the Lord: he is "splendid" (1 Chr. 16:29; Ps. 30:8 [= 30:7 RSV]; 93:1) and can give his splendor to others, choosing especially to ornament or decorate his people with a splendor that participates in his own. Splendor is the Lord's gift, and human splendor is always participated, which is to say that it belongs to us only by way of our participation in the Lord and his splendor.

The participated nature of the splendor that belongs to creatures can be recognized by us for what it is. When we do recognize it in this way, we return it to the Lord, worshiping him *in decore sancto* ("in holy splendor") (1 Chr. 16:29). It is also possible for us to fail to recognize creaturely splendor as creaturely, and thereby to idolize it, to, as Hosea nicely puts it, give splendor to *simulacra*, to things that imitate, but are not, the Lord (*Israel . . . decoravit simulacra* in Hos. 10:1). When the beloved calls her lover not only beautiful but also splendid, she figures the nonidolatrous worship of the Lord that the people of Israel and the church ideally offer. Again, the beloved's offering of this endearment to her lover is not dissolved or erased by it figuring the people's adoration of the Lord. It remains what it is: a human expression of sexual and emotional passion. Because it so remains, it can, if read well, reconfigure your endearments and embraces as well, for the Song addresses those first and most directly. If you let it, if you read it for what it is, you will begin to find the endearments you give to your lover, male or female, deepened by the recognition that your lover's worthiness to receive them is gift, as is your capacity to offer them. In recognizing that, your lovemakings begin to participate in the church's and Israel's worship of the Lord and are thereby intensified and made more moving.

The "bed" (*lectulus*) is mentioned here for the first time in the Song. There are two subsequent occurrences: she, lying in her bed apart from him, dreams and remembers (3:1); and he mentions and describes "Solomon's bed" (3:7). The bed, in the Song, is not easily distinguished from the "couch" (*accubitum*; 1:12) or the "litter" (*ferculum*; 3:9): all are places for reclining, sleeping, and (perhaps) eating. The "litter," as its mention in 3:9 makes clear, is also for being carried about on—which does not necessarily rule out any of the other activities mentioned. For the Song, all these are also places for sexual love: the beloved has recalled her embraces of the "king" on the "couch," and elsewhere in scripture the same word is used for something on which lovemaking may occur (most dramatically, it is on an *accubitum* that Haman plans to rape Esther in Esth. 7:8); and "Solomon's bed" is mentioned in the context of preparations for his marriage. In mentioning their bed to him—perhaps they are in it, embracing; the text permits but does not require that reading—she reminds him and herself and us that they are lovers.

It is a beautiful bed. To call it "flowerful" is to observe and underscore that beauty, and to connect it to desire and fertility: the bed blooms with the lovers' desire, and the blooms are beautiful to both the eye and the nose, as is the flesh of lovers to one another. But it is not only a beautiful bed, a fertile playground for lovemaking; it is also in a magnificent house, whose beams are of "cedar" and whose ceiling is of "cypress." These decorations are mentioned elsewhere in scripture, where they belong to Solomon's Temple (1 Kgs. 5–6) or to the palaces of the first kings of Israel. Cedarwood and cypress, taken together, suggest magnificence, solidity, beauty, luxury, and sweetness (Behemoth's tail in Job 40:17; David's cedarwood house in 2 Sam. 5:11; purification in Lev. 14). To say that the flower-adorned lovers' bed is in such a house is to say at least that it is in a king's house, and to suggest the house of the Lord himself. Once again, the text pushes beyond its first and surface meaning and draws the attuned reader toward a deeper one, according to which the beloved is in the temple, accepting and rejoicing in the Lord's caresses as do both the church and Israel.[57]

Cedar trees resonate in scripture in another way as well. The *cedri Libani* ("cedars of Lebanon") are mentioned often in the Old Testament, and while the context sometimes suggests admirable magnificence and grandeur and solidity (Judg. 9:15 and passim), the cedars of Lebanon are also sometimes listed among the world's magnificences that can and will be destroyed by the Lord on the day of judgment (Zech. 11:1–2). To observe that the lovers of the Song make love in a house that is "cedar-beamed" suggests that human loves, however magnificent and delightful and luxuriant, are not independent of the Lord. If they are pursued as though they were, they will end in destruction.

In this double cedrine resonance, positive and negative, the Song shows itself as scripture: its first meaning—the beauty and magnificence of human loves—is at the same time underscored and erased by its second—the endless delight of the love of the Lord. Human love participates in the Lord's love, and that is why in recalling the lovers' bed she recalls not only it but also its participation in the Lord and her own embraces as given and received by the Lord; but human love can easily be idolized, separated from the Lord, and the dual valence of its

57. For temple imagery and its significance, see Gary Anderson, "To See Where God Dwells: The Tabernacle, the Temple, and the Origins of the Christian Mystical Tradition," *Communio* 36 (2009): 42–68. See also, with special reference to temple imagery in Song 4, Kingsmill 2009: 252–55.

decorations reminds the Song's reader of that. Your sexual loves are valorized and elevated and deepened by the Song; and at the same time you are warned of the possibility of misconstruing them.

The Lord's invitation to become his beloved in his flowerful bed and to accept his caresses there is made directly to you, the Song's reader.[58] But it can be made to you only because it was first made to the people of Israel and then, with special intensity, to Mary. She, the Lord's preeminent beloved, was and is a woman of that people, and she accepted the Lord's caresses precisely as such, so that she might conceive and give birth to a Jewish son through whom the kisses given to Israel might be extended to the whole world. The flowers on and around the Lord's *lectulus floridus*, upon which Mary reclined as she returned Gabriel's annunciatory kiss with the full passion of her *fiat mihi*, a responsive kiss open-mouthed and open-wombed, have never left Mary. The church crowns and garlands her with them in May, and from a very early period Christians have thought and written much about the flowers whose beauty and meaning figures Mary's: it has, for example, been standard in Western iconography since Trent to depict the annunciation as lily laden.

Field-Flower and Valley-Lily (2:1–3a)

> I am a field-flower
> and a valley-lily—
> like a lily among thorns
> is my beloved among daughters—
> like an apple among forest trees
> is my delightful man among sons.

Her voice continues in 2:1, in the first person, applying in the indicative mood two flowery appellations to herself. She is *flos campi* ("a field-flower") and *lilium convallium* ("a valley-lily"), images of natural beauty located firmly in the world of the pastoral, where flowers grow uncultivated in a realm tamed and ordered by human creative effort. He responds at once (2:2), intensifying her floral image and using it to contrast her favorably with all the other blooms. Not only is she "a valley-lily," but also one whose beauty outshines that of all other flowers, for which the "daughters" serve as synecdoche. They may be blooms too, but they, when compared to her, appear as if they were "thorns." The Song's voice then (2:3a) returns to her, and she returns his compliment, at first still in the present tense and indicative mood. If she is "a lily among thorns," then he is "an apple

---

58. On the bed see, lyrically, Bernard of Clairvaux, *Sermones super cantica canticorum* (Sermons on the Song of Songs) 46 (English in *Bernard of Clairvaux on the Song of Songs*, trans. Kilian Walsh and Irene Edmonds [Kalamazoo, MI: Cistercian, 1971], 2.241–47; Latin in *Patrologia Latina* 183.1004A–1008B).

among forest trees," which is to say the best among the trees of the forest, a tree capable of offering her shade under which she has happily "sat." The compliments include, as well, an exchange of epithets: she calls him her "delightful man," and he calls her his "beloved."

Here, following hard upon the mention of the "flowerful bed" (1:16), is the first concentrated occurrence of flower imagery in the Song. It is a thread that runs through much of the work. The generic "flower" (*flos* and cognates, verbal and adjectival) occurs nine times in the Song, mostly in descriptions of the out-doors, whether wild or cultivated; it is only in 2:1 that the word is used directly of the beloved. The lily's (→1:7) beauty is natural, and this is part of the point of mentioning it as "a field-flower," one that has grown without human artifice and is therefore an instance of the Lord's unmerited gift of beauty; it may therefore serve as a trope for election: Israel is beautiful like a lily because the Lord has chosen to make her so. This is true too of the beauty of the beloved in the Song: she is radiantly, unmeritedly, and supremely beautiful like the lily—and indeed like the Song itself, the Song of Songs. The Marian resonance lurks so close to the surface that it is almost explicit. To say that the beloved is to other women as a "lily" is to "thorns" is to say that her beauty is of a different order than that of all other women: an appropriate gloss would be *benedicta tu inter mulieres* ("blessed are you among women") (Luke 1:42).[59]

The "apple" tree to which she likens him here, comparing him to one "among forest trees," serves the same function in her praise of him as does the lily in his praise of her: the lines are strictly parallel. The apple tree, then, is the best among the trees of the forest; all the rest of them when compared with it are like thorns to lilies. But the apple is a more complex symbol than the lily, both within the Song and in scripture. Apples are mentioned three times in the Song in addition to here. She is just about to ask her lover to "fill" her "with apples" (2:5); he says that the scent of her mouth is like that of apples (7:9) and, puzzlingly, that he "enlivened" her (or possibly "raised [her] up") "under an apple tree" (8:5). In the first three cases (2:3, 5; 7:9), apples are unambiguously good; the last is more complicated—it could be read "under an evil tree," which is only one among its interesting complexities (→8:5b). Elsewhere in scripture, "apple" (*malum*) occurs rarely (only at Prov. 25:11 and Joel 1:12),[60] and without much resonance. One important difference between the lily and the apple is that the former is pleasing to the eyes and the nose (and perhaps also to touch), whereas the apple pleases all those senses and that of taste as well. She, it seems, wants to taste him as well as to look at him and smell him—this aspect of the trope is about to be taken up in the Song—whereas there is no parallel implication for his desires as directed at her.[61]

---

59. The more familiar (to Catholics) formulation in the Ave Maria is *benedicta tu in mulieribus*.

60. There are ripe possibilities for strong reading caused by *malum* also being a noun meaning "evil," and this word occurs frequently in scripture.

61. Theodoret of Cyrus puts this distinction well in his *Explanatio in canticum canticorum* on Song 2:3 (Hill 2001: 56–57; *Patrologia Graecae* 81.88), and I take it from him.

The exchange of endearments here partakes of the ordinary grammar of love's election. In loving, bringing a beloved into being, she (or he) is constituted for the lover as someone unique, "distinguished" (5:10) from all others, as she says of him; or "most beautiful" (*pulcherrima*) (1:8; 5:9; 6:1), as he (and the daughters of Jerusalem) call her; or "set apart" (*electa/us*) as is said of both of them (5:15; 6:9–10). Claims of this sort, which lovers make to one another (usually when alone), do not, for us, mean that we think of those to whom we say them as, according to some external and public checklist of criteria, more beautiful or more important or more interesting than anyone else. We mean, instead, that they are these things for us: we have elected them, chosen them, set them apart, and in that way constituted them as our beloved. This is what the Song's couple does in these words. But it is not all they do, for they figure the Lord and his beloved Israel-church, as well as Mary in whom that church finds its most concentrated and intense mode of being. The Lord does set Israel apart, thinking of her as "most beautiful"; and he does distinguish Mary from all other women. But his action of so doing is not a matter only for him and his beloveds; it is material to all, whether members of Israel or the church or not, because the Lord's beloved is also the world's beloved, whether or not the world knows it.

Under His Shade (2:3b)

> I sat under his shade—that of the man I desired—
> and his fruit was sweet to my throat.

Beginning with these words, there is a series of mood and tense shifts. The couple has been exchanging endearments in the present tense, but now she begins to speak in the past tense of things that have already happened: she has "sat under his shade," pursuing still the image of the apple tree, but now in the past tense; and when she was there, "his fruit was sweet to my throat," which is to say that her aspiration to taste him, foreshadowed immediately before, as well as to touch and smell him, is here recalled as having been achieved (the demand for food, for fulfillment by taste, will come up again shortly). Among the more interesting and disconcerting features of the Song as a literary work is this kind of shift, unexplained and cinematic. Much of what the beloved says can be heard as memory, reverie, soliloquy, or dream, and that is certainly true of these words. Is she speaking them to him or to herself? The feel of the text, its texture, suggests the latter. It is certain that she speaks them directly to you, and in hearing them you can begin to see more clearly what it means to be shaded by your lover's spreading branches, and how you enjoy the taste of his (or her) fruit—the fruit of his body. And doing that is to understand your delight in your lover as participant in your delight in the Lord.

Here again, scriptural resonances point to the figuration of the Lord's love for Israel and church and Mary by the Song's lover's love for his beloved. When she sits "under his shade" she gives herself over to him as lover and protector in an act of self-abandonment that delights her. So does each of us when accepting the Lord's caress. The metaphor of the lover as shade tree under which the beloved sits does not end there. "Shade" (*umbra*), also rendered "shadow" in this translation, occurs in the Song only here and in the twice repeated formula "until the day breathes / and the shadows flee" (→2:17; 4:6). Elsewhere in scripture, "under the shade" (*sub umbra*) is a standard trope with the meaning of protection. You might be under Egyptian (Isa. 30:3) or Babylonian (Bar. 1:12) or Assyrian (Ezek. 31) shade, ignominiously for a Jew; or you might be under the shade of the all-powerful one, which is to say of the Lord (Ps. 17:8; 91:1; Lam. 4:20; Ezek. 17:22–24), a place than which there can be no better and no safer and no more delightful. A similar range of meaning is present in the verb *obumbrare*, which is found in Luke's Gospel among the words Gabriel speaks to Mary: "The Holy Spirit shall come upon you, and power of the Most High shall overshadow [*obumbrabit*] you" (Luke 1:35). Origen is representative of (and perhaps the originator of) a wide and deep stream of patristic commentary that makes much of this connection between the shade of the Song's beloved and the overshadowing announced by Gabriel to Mary:

> And indeed how could "his shade" not yield us life when, at his bodily conception, Mary was addressed in these words: "The Holy Spirit shall come upon you / and the power of the Most High shall overshadow you" [Luke 1:35]? If, therefore, there was overshadowing by the Most High when his body was conceived, then it is proper to say that "his shade" will give life to the Gentiles. And his bride properly wants to sit under the shade of his apple tree; doubtless she wants this so that she might participate in the life that is in "his shade."[62]

The beloved also says in the words under discussion here that her lover's "fruit was sweet to [her] throat." Elsewhere in the Song, the throat (*guttur*) is itself depicted as something to be licked and tasted, most strikingly when he says to her, "Your throat is like the best wine"; and she at once responds, "Worthy to be sipped by my delightful man / ruminated by his lips and teeth" (7:10). She also says that "his throat is supremely smooth / and completely desirable" (5:16): each of them wants to taste the throat of the other as well as to use the throat to taste good things. These tropes connect the throat first with eating and drinking, but only as the occasion for considering the body as itself figurally good to eat and drink. She wants to eat and drink his throat, and to have him do the same to hers, because the throat is, among other things, the organ of eating and drinking (Job 34:3; Prov. 24:13) and of talking (Ps. 115:7; 149:6). This is certainly one of the standard scriptural ways of talking about the throat, and the Song's usage

62. Author's translation of Rufinus's Latin version (the Greek original does not survive) of Origen, *Homeliae in canticum canticorum* (Homilies on the Song of Songs) 3.5.11–12 (Lawson 1956: 182; French and Latin in *Origène: Commentaire sur le Cantique des Cantiques*, ed. and trans. Luc Brésard, Henri Crouzel, Marel Borret, Sources Chrétiennes 376 [Paris: Cerf, 1992], 530).

participates fully in it. These directions of thought merge with one another, and in that way the throat becomes the focus for taste, inner and outer. Israel and the church have a taste for the Lord, as he does for them.

Human lovemaking engages all the senses. The Song constantly emphasizes this, here by picking out the gustatory. We want to taste our lovers as well as see and touch and smell and hear them. The same is true of the liturgical love-making that the church offers to the Lord. There too, every modality of sense is engaged, and it is in receiving the consecrated bread and wine in the mouth that the gustatory comes most obviously into play. Christians exactly lick and suck and ingest the Lord and find his taste good. This is figured here by the Song. What is also figured—and what may be difficult for contemporary tastes fully to accept or understand, gnostic haters of the body that most of us are—is the Lord's reciprocal gustatory delight in us: we taste good to him too: Christ sucked at Mary's breasts.

Loving-kindness (2:4)

> He led me into his wine cellar
> loving-kindness was his banner above me.

Her memory/dream/reverie continues, still in the past tense. She recalls that the lover has led her into "his wine cellar," a place in which all good things can be found, including, presumably, the good of lovemaking, the satisfaction of all the senses (→1:4). There, "loving-kindness" (*caritas*) was raised as his "banner" (*vexillum*) or battle standard over her. This image of the "banner" raised by the lover over his beloved does not recur elsewhere in the Song. It is a military trope—the Latin word might equally well be translated "standard" or "ensign," and almost all its occurrences elsewhere in scripture have this meaning (Num. 2; cf. Jer. 6:1). But there is one important passage, a reading of which in conjunction with this verse of the Song is at least suggestive: the account of Joshua's defeat of the Amalekites in Exod. 17. The battle goes the way of the Israelites so long as Moses, on a hill above the plain of battle, is able to hold up his hands. When, as the day advances, he tires and lets his hands drop, the Amalekites begin to prevail. And so he sits down on a stone, and Aaron and Hur hold up his hands for him until the sun sets and the battle is decisively won by Joshua and his army. The passage ends in this way:

> Then the Lord said to Moses: "Write this down in a book so that it might be remembered, and speak it before Joshua's ears: I will erase the memory of Amalek from under the heavens." Moses also built an altar there and named it *Dominus Nissi* (the Lord is my banner), saying: "Because a hand has been raised against the Lord's seat there will be war from the Lord against Amalek from generation to generation." (Exod. 17:14–16)

The meaning of this is not transparent, and the versions (Hebrew, Greek, Latin, English) differ significantly among themselves. The New Vulgate provides a transliteration (*Nissi*) of a Hebrew word meaning (something like) "banner" or "military standard" and then parenthetically glosses it with *vexillum*. It is the Lord who is a banner, and in saying that he is so, in such a context, the text emphasizes the Lord's capacity to provide protection, in this case against the Amalekites, with whom conflict continues until they are effectively exterminated (Num. 24; Deut. 25; 1 Sam. 15; 27; 30; 1 Chr. 4). The other details—the significance of Moses's raising of his hands during the battle and the echo of that action and stance in what Moses says about the hand and the Lord's seat/throne (whose precise meaning remains obscure)—do not matter much for our purposes here. What does matter is that the Lord is here called, by synecdoche, a banner.

In the Song, the banner is said to be the lover's "loving-kindness," his *caritas*. This word occurs only here in the Song and once in the final chapter, where she (probably; but the identification of the speaker is not certain) says that "many waters have not been able to extinguish loving-kindness" (8:7). We have, then, a closely woven set of connections between the Lord as protective banner—*vexillum* as synecdoche for *Dominus*—and *caritas*. This should make your scripturally attuned nerves sing with excitement: to say that the lover's protective banner is one of loving-kindness is a hairsbreadth from saying explicitly that the lover is the Lord whose loving-kindness binds us to him with the "chains of perfection" (*vinculum perfectionis* in Col. 3:14; cf. Hos. 11:4). The Lord loves us with excessive loving-kindness/*caritas* (Eph. 2:4), and the Song's play with the banner of protectively passionate loving-kindness under the tree of the Lord's shade figures exactly that truth.

Languishing (2:5)

> Sustain me with raisin cakes
> fill me with apples
> for I languish with love.

The beloved's voice shifts now to the imperative. She has been remembering, tranquilly but happily; now she demands: "sustain me . . . fill me." She wants to be fed, to be filled to satiation with delicious things.

"Raisin cakes" (*uvae*) are mentioned in scripture much more frequently than "apples" (→2:3b). Both foods are luxurious and sweet, delicacies that lovers might properly feed to one another and ask to be fed with.[63] The verbs suggest a little more. To ask to be sustained (*fulcire*) is to ask more than simply to be fed: it is to

63. The word translated "raisin cakes" in Song 2:5 is *uvae*, which occurs very frequently in scripture, sometimes meaning dried grapes—raisins *simpliciter*, we might say—sometimes unripe grapes, and sometimes raisins formed into some kind of sweetmeat; hence "raisin cakes." Hos. 3:1

ask to be supported or aided in time of trouble, to be given help that one could not provide for oneself. The Lord is sometimes said in this sense to sustain those who call upon him (Ps. 18:19 [= 18:18 RSV]), in something like the same way that pillars sustain or support a roof (1 Kgs. 7:35–36; 2 Chr. 24:12). And to ask to be filled (*stipare*) is to ask to be crowded, crammed, stuffed, or engorged with whatever-it-is, so that there is no room for anything else.[64] The verb does not, in nonscriptural Latin, so far as I am aware, ordinarily have a sexual sense; but it is easy enough to see how it might be given one.

Given these extended senses of the verbs, the beloved is asking her lover to treat her as only the Lord can, to give her sustaining support of a kind that fills her completely and that no one other than he can give. Here too, the Song's love play has several levels. First, there is the connection between sex and food, a connection familiar to all cultures and all lovers: it is not only that lovemaking is like eating (the body of the beloved as a feast); nor only that some of the actions of eating are replicated in lovemaking (chewing, sucking, nibbling); nor even that the vocabulary of lovemaking and eating overlap so much (as they explicitly do in the Song at this point). It is that lovemaking and eating both figure and find their fulfillment in receiving and returning the Lord's kisses and caresses and in that way being sustained and filled by him. This theological understanding is not merely in accord with what the Song here says: the Song's words, considered as scriptural words, are among the principal causes of this view among Jews and Christians; and the theological understanding is given depth and beauty by the Song being first and explicitly not theological.

This close connection between lovemaking and eating, a connection present throughout the Song, finds its fullest enactment not in our sexual exchanges, but rather in the Eucharist. There, we eat, eating what we are; and both the fact of eating and the fact of what is eaten are sheer gift, outside the realm of exchange. In eating the body of the Lord and drinking his blood, we bring what the Song here figures to its proper end, at least in this fallen life here below. In this eating, and only in this, are we filled.

The beloved demands to be sustained and filled, gastronomically and sexually, because, she says to her lover, "I languish with love" (*amore langueo*), a phrase also present, verbatim, in 5:8, when she instructs the daughters of Jerusalem to tell her lover, if they can find him, that this is her condition. She means that she is sick with love, weakened by it, lying, we might imagine, with tear-filled eyes upon a bed of grief, hoping for a union with her lover that at the moment she lacks. The word, verbally and nominally (*languere, languor*), occurs very frequently in scripture, and mostly to indicate rather straightforwardly a lack of bodily health. *Languores* are what Jesus heals (Matt. 4:23–24; 9:35; Luke 4:40; John 5:3) and

is interesting here: *uvae* seem to be a food connected especially with adultery—a figure, therefore, for sensual indulgence that separates from the Lord.

64. *Stipate* in Song 2:5 appears to be the only occurrence in scripture of an active verbal form from *stipare*.

what the likes of Jehoram (2 Chr. 21) and Joash (2 Chr. 24) suffer from as they come to their unpleasant ends.

But why should she be languid? Doesn't she have a lover whose embraces she has just been recalling? Lovers will not find this very puzzling. Any love affair, whether within marriage or out of it, follows these patterns, and they often come hard upon one another or are intertwined inseparably with one another. As a kind of sadness can follow orgasm and depression childbirth, so human loves are always intimate both with active agony and the quietness of languor. There is a theological reason for this, and it is among the virtues of the Song to depict it with intensity: human loves, no matter how intense and deep, are always unsatisfactory because they always promise what they cannot deliver. They promise eternal, unbroken bliss, the gaze of your beloved that you can return unflinchingly and in full and forever and that, in being so returned, remakes you as the lover you could not have been were you not to have been looked at in that way, as one who can love and be loved.[65] But in fact your lover is always flawed, as you are; her (or his) gaze and yours cannot fully meet; your caresses are mutual gifts, yes, but ones from which something is always withheld. As your lips meet your lover's they open into a void of expectations that cannot be met.

They can be met by the Lord's loves, but those too are not fully and finally available here below. Human loves and desires, most intensely the sexual ones, figure and participate in our desire for the Lord and his for us. Among their virtues is to throw into sharp relief what they cannot provide exactly by providing what they can. And the Song shows us this precisely in its disjointedly breathless literary form. Rupert of Deutz comments: "Languishing with love for the absent delightful one, O people of the world, I can be consoled in no other way than by the one in whom we should believe, and in believing have eternal life."[66]

Even Mary, the beloved who most fully returns the Lord's embrace, languishes with love. Scripture does not use this vocabulary for her, but the church does: she languishes when her son dies; she languishes because she knows that he will; the very acceptance of the Lord's embrace brings languishing with it, and this inevitability means that we all "languish with love" and demand, therefore, to be sustained and filled with the "raisin cakes" and "apples" the Lord has in his gift.

Embracing (2:6)

> His left hand under my head
> his right embraces me.

---

65. I draw here, though at some considerable distance and in ways he would probably not approve, upon the analysis of erotic love given in Jean-Luc Marion, *Le phénomène érotique: Six méditations* (Paris: Grasset, 2003).

66. Author's translation of Rupert of Deutz, *Commentaria in Canticum Canticorum* (Commentary on the Song) on Song 2:5 (Deutz and Deutz 2005: 208).

This sentence, still apparently in her voice, shifts tense again, back to the present from the past; it also shifts mood, from the imperatives of 2:5 to the indicative. There is also a probable shift of addressee: in 2:5 she seems to have been addressing her lover directly, but here, perhaps, she lapses back into reverie or soliloquy. It is also possible to read the whole of 2:3–6 as a dream-soliloquy, in which what counts is not the narrative or dramatic setting of the words—the tense and mood shifts make it effectively impossible to construct any such setting—but rather their lyrical and figurative meaning. And that is, at the literal level, clear enough: she reports that she is being embraced by her lover in an archetypal posture preparatory for or consequent upon sexual intercourse: his left hand supports her head, ready for the kiss; and his right pulls her body close to his, in tight embrace.[67]

This sentence is found again, verbatim, at 8:3; and there, as here, it is immediately followed by one of the Song's refrains, in which someone, presumably the lover, adjures the daughters of Jerusalem not to "enliven or awaken" the beloved (largely verbatim at 2:7; 3:5; 5:8–9; 8:4). I provide a fuller discussion of this refrain immediately below; I mention it here to indicate that the verbatim repetition of 2:6–7 at 8:3–4 provides a structural marker within the text of the Song. It brings a speech by the beloved (2:3–5 || 7:11–8:2) to an end and marks a transition to a new lyric, without apparent connection to what has gone before. The occurrence of the "left hand . . . right hand" formula here, then, signals to the Song's hearers at least that a significant transition is at hand.

The "left hand . . . right hand" formula has a significant echo in what the book of Proverbs has to say about Wisdom (*sapientia*): "Long life is in her right hand / riches and glory in her left" (Prov. 3:16). Wisdom, feminine in gender in Latin, is among the titles of the second person of the Holy Trinity; the gifts of her hands are therefore also the gifts of his, and Prov. 3:16 became, after Origen, a standard point of reference for explaining this line of the Song.[68] On this reading, the lover's posture promises not only caresses, but also particular gifts: "long" or eternal life as the gift of the right hand, and the riches and glory of participation in the Lord as the gift of the left.

First Adjuration (2:7)

> O daughters of Jerusalem—I adjure you
> by the does and hinds of the fields

67. See Othmar Keel, *Das Hohelied*, Zürcher Bibelkommentare AT 18 (Zurich: Theologischer Verlag, 1986), for numerous reproductions of depictions of lovemaking from the ancient Near East earlier than or contemporary with the early stages of the Song's confection. Many of these represent exactly the posture mentioned here.

68. See Origen, *Homeliae in canticum canticorum* (Homilies on the Song of Songs) 1.1 (Lawson 1956: 200–203; French and Latin in *Origène: Commentaire sur le Cantique des Cantiques*, ed. and trans. Luc Brésard, Henri Crouzel, Marel Borret, Sources Chrétiennes 376 [Paris: Cerf, 1992], 584–95).

> not to enliven or awaken this delightful woman
> until she wishes.

A shift of addressee, and also of topic.[69] Someone in the first person, without explicit sign of identity and no mark of gender, addresses the "daughters of Jerusalem" about "this delightful woman," whom you, the Song's hearer, immediately assume to be the beloved whose voice has been speaking immediately before. This assumption leads naturally to another—that the Song's male lover is now speaking. He gives them a charge, which is "not to enliven or awaken this delightful woman," this *dilecta*, "until she wishes." In this way we learn that she is asleep; we are not told why or how this came to be. And he charges or adjures them to this effect "by the does and hinds of the fields." Twice more (3:5; 8:4) the lover speaks to the daughters of Jerusalem about her using this formula, and in the second of these instances the formula is preceded, as it is in 2:7, with a description of the posture of lovemaking: "his left hand under my head / his right embraces me" (2:6). And in one further place (5:8–9), she speaks to the daughters about him, in something close to the same formulaic words.

You are likely to be puzzled by many things here. The adjuration formula brings to an end a brilliantly lit vignette in which the beloved and the lover exchange compliments; she remembers lovemaking's caresses and asks for more; she is heavily languid with love; and the lover conjures the daughters not to excite or awake the apparently sleeping beloved. Her languishing and apparent sleep are not explained, but simply mentioned. There is union, and then there is separation; there is delight, and then there is languor, love's heavy, sick, sleepiness.

The English verb "adjure" is legal in both etymology and use, and this is true as well of the Latin verb (*adiurare*) it calques. To adjure someone is to put them under oath as in a courtroom and thereby to threaten them with penalty should they fail to do whatever it is they are being adjured to do. The verb is a performative: that is, its formulaic utterance ("I adjure you") brings into being a new reality, in much the same way that the formula "I promise" does. The utterance of an adjuration has the effect of placing a legal or quasilegal obligation upon those to whom it is uttered: adjuring someone places them, therefore, in a new relation to the adjurer.[70] When the lover adjures the daughters of Jerusalem he does something

---

69. These verses are read by contemporary translators of the Hebrew text as though the word rendered *dilecta* means "delight" rather than "delightful woman" (so RSV). Commentators, then, generally attribute these words to the beloved rather than the lover (so Roland Murphy, Cheryl Exum, Marvin Pope, Christopher Mitchell, Othmar Keel, and others). The Latin text, however, can be read only as said to the daughters about the (female) beloved and thus (very likely) as spoken by the (male) lover. See 5:8–9 for a closely similar formula, there spoken by the beloved to the daughters.

70. For *adiurare* as quasilegal performative, see Gen. 24:3, 37 (Abraham adjuring his servant not to seek a wife for Isaac from among Canaanite women); Num. 5:19–21 (on the rite for a woman charged with adultery, in which she is adjured with an oath of imprecation, *iuramentum maledictionis*, specifying the dreadful results should she undergo the rite while guilty); 1 Sam. 14:24–30 (Saul adjures his soldiers not to eat before sunset); Matt. 26:63 (the high priest adjures Jesus to say

severe and thereby signals the importance of what he adjures them to do, which is to refrain from enlivening or awakening her. But what do these verbs mean? What, more exactly, is the lover adjuring the daughters not to do?

The two verbs "enliven" (*suscitare*) and "awaken" (*evigilare*) are close in meaning and scriptural use, but by no means identical. The former is most often used to denote the action of bringing into being something that did not previously exist, whether a baby by sexual intercourse (Gen. 38:8; Ruth 4:10; Matt. 22:24; Mark 12:19), a prophet by divine inspiration (Deut. 28:9; 2 Chr. 36:22; Ezek. 34:23), anger by harsh words, or a resurrected person by prophetic or divine action or by conjuration (1 Sam. 28:11–15; Sir. 48:5; 2 Macc. 7:9).[71] It is hard to find an English verb that covers all these cases; "enliven" perhaps comes closest. In the second case, "awaken," the scriptural range of meaning is much less broad, and with very few exceptions denotes the opposite of sleeping and dreaming (Gen. 9:24; 2 Kgs. 4:31; Luke 9:32), though it may also have the connotation of watchfulness and alertness (Ps. 35:23; 44:24 [= 44:23 RSV]).

Given these meanings of the verbs in the lover's adjuration to the daughters of Jerusalem, his charge to them can be read simply as an adjuration not to wake her up. She sleeps, and it is (by implication) his task to wake her, not theirs. But there are further layers of meaning: they are not to encourage her to watchfulness or vigilance; they are not to arouse or awaken her sexually; and they are not to bring her to life from death, to inspire her, that is, with the breath of life. All those actions too are for him rather than for them, and there is a deep claim to exclusivity here: he is for her and she for him, without intermediaries or obstructions (compare the formula in 2:16; 6:3; 7:11). As the deer imagery in the adjuration also suggests, they thirst for one another, and it is their mutual task to slake this thirst, a task in which the daughters have no part. Her further responsiveness to him must wait "until she wishes," until she is again prepared for him.

The people of Israel and the church share this thirst, and the Lord, their lover, makes the same exclusive claim upon his beloved that all lovers make. They sleep, however: they are not always in his arms, returning his kiss open-mouthed, breathing him in, opening themselves to him. They sleep in the sense that, often—usually, almost always—they cannot see him, cannot find him, wander lost without him in regions of desolation. It is interesting and remarkable that this first adjuration comes abruptly after an intense exchange of endearments and caresses, the usual culmination of which for human lovers is sexual intercourse, the unity of the flesh. Instead, she sleeps; he acknowledges her sleep and waits for her to wake, waits for her to want him. Their endearments and caresses rise almost to a peak of passion

whether he is the Christ); Mark 5:7 (the Gerasene demoniac adjures Jesus not to exorcize him); Acts 19:13 (some Jewish exorcists unsuccessfully attempt to exorcize evil spirits by adjuring them in Jesus's name). On adjuration, see Marvin H. Pope, *Song of Songs: A New Translation with Introduction and Commentary*, Anchor Bible 7C (Garden City, NY: Doubleday, 1977), 385.

71. *Suscitare* is used frequently in every stratum of the New Testament as a verb to describe what God—or the Lord or the Father—has done for Jesus.

and then, stammeringly, fall away into quiet separation. This is a constant theme of the Song, and it is often jarring, as it should be.

Mary too, the Song's most perfect beloved, sleeps. Her son is crucified, raised, and ascends; she lives on here below, without him. And at the end of her life, she sleeps—which may or may not be a metaphor for death; the crucial point for the Marian reading of the Song is not to arrive at a conclusion about the exact nature of the events prior to Mary's bodily assumption into heaven, which is a dogma of the church, but only to see how the particulars of the text can be illuminated by understanding them to be about her—and is then awakened into eternal life by her son.[72] Knowing that the Song's beloved figures Mary permits the deepest possible penetration into the text. The lover's charge to the daughters of Jerusalem, who in this interpretive context can be understood as Mary's acolytes, her serving maids (which includes all Christians), makes clear to them—and thus to us—that it is only the Lord who can enliven and awaken us, whether from the sleep of death or the sleep of separation. That "enliven" (*suscitare*) is also the standard verb used in the New Testament for Jesus's resurrection should be recalled here. It shows that the lover's—the Lord's—charge to the daughters of Jerusalem implicitly promises that he will enliven (resurrect, bring to life from death) us, as he already has done for Mary, and for the church, and for the people of Israel. The beloved's sleep of separation will eventually become the wakefulness of life eternal, when we are ready—when we wish for it to happen. The Lord is here shown to be one who offers us this constantly; all we have to do in order to receive the gift of his kisses, which is to say of resurrection, is to wish that it may be so. Ordinarily, of course, we do not so wish, and in this we remain separate from Mary, who did, not only in her acceptance of what was offered at the annunciation, but also in her dormition and assumption.

The placement of the adjuration formula is important. Here in 2:7 it concludes a series of endearment exchanges between the lover and the beloved (1:9–2:6). Those exchanges have a rhythm: they move from memory to yearning to anticipation to something close to fulfillment in 2:5–6; and then, suddenly, they cease. The lover stops speaking to and with the beloved and instead addresses the daughters. A pause is marked, and when the beloved speaks again, as she does in 2:8, the two are no longer together but once again apart, anticipating their meeting and lovemaking. The affair between the two has no smooth trajectory in the Song: it stammers and stutters, moving from intimacy to separation and back to intimacy. The adjuration formula is used here, as elsewhere, to mark these pauses. In this stammering structure (advance, pause, retreat, advance, stop, advance again), the Song is like (and not accidentally) the eucharistic liturgy, which is

72. Mary's assumption into heaven is celebrated by the church on August 15. The Eastern churches also call the feast that of Mary's dormition, thus focusing on her sleep (or death) prior to her assumption. For English versions of the most important patristic homilies on this subject from the seventh and eighth centuries, see Brian E. Daley, trans., *On the Dormition of Mary: Early Patristic Homilies* (Crestwood, NY: St. Vladimir's Seminary Press, 1998).

also a stammering approach to intimacy with the Lord. We prepare ourselves to approach the table to receive the Lord not by simply standing and walking into his arms, but by stutteringly acknowledging our unworthiness, making pleas for forgiveness, praising the Lord and expressing our joy in being sought by him, and then again falling to our knees as we recall who and what we are. Only after the stammering pauses can we open our lips for his kiss. The Song's repetitive use of the adjuration formula participates in and figures this fundamental structure of the liturgical act of love.

The lover's adjuration of the daughters is not only to do, or more exactly to refrain from doing, something particular. It is also performed "by"—in the name of—something: "the does and hinds of the fields."[73] What of them? This is the first reference to deer—"does and hinds"—in the Song. These animals—the *cervidae*—have a prominent place in the Song; four different words are used for them, and together these words are used seventeen times. Almost half of all mentions of the *cervidae* in scripture are found in the Song. The four terms are: "hart" (*cervus*), "hind" (*cerva*), "doe" (*caprea*), and "fawn" (*hinnulus*). It is not clear in any of the Latin versions (the New Vulgate is very close to the Vulgate on this) exactly what genus and species these terms are meant to indicate, but that is not important for coming to some understanding of their use in the Song in any case. It is clear that two of the words ("hart" and "hind") refer to adult animals, and two ("doe" and "fawn") to young ones. It is also clear that two ("hart" and "fawn") are masculine in gender, and two ("hind" and "doe") feminine.

Among these words, the one used most frequently (seven times) is "doe"; the lover likens the beloved or her breasts to a doe or does four times (2:7; 3:5; 4:5; 7:4), and the beloved likens him to a doe three times (2:9, 17; 8:14). The other deer words cluster around this one. "Hind," used twice of her by him (2:7; 3:5), occurs always together with "doe"; "fawn," used three times by her of him, and twice by him of her breasts (2:9, 17; 4:5; 8:14), is found in every case in close proximity to "doe"; and the same is true of "hart," used only three times by her of him (2:9, 17; 8:14). None of the deer words occurs without being clustered in these ways, and this means that no very precise differentiation among them is evident on the surface of the text. In the adjuration formula that concerns us here, "does and hinds" appears pleonastic; and this is true throughout the clusters of deer talk in the Song.

But none of this as yet tells us how to take the doe-hind-hart-fawn tropes—for of course that is what they are. Outside the adjuration formula under consideration here, the terms are endearments and words of praise. She twice likens him to "a doe or fawn among harts" (2:9, 17), and in both cases in contexts where she is praising his beauty and agility. The same is true when she says to him at the very end of the Song "be like the does / and like the fawns among the harts / upon

---

73. In what follows I draw gratefully upon Jean Emmanuel de Ena, *Sens et interprétations du Cantique des Cantiques* (Paris: Cerf, 2004), 380–407.

the spice mountains" (8:14). When he compares her breasts to "two fawns / doe-born twins" (4:5; 7:4), the implications are similar: her breasts are beautiful and they move with grace. These meanings for deer are present also in the rest of scripture—where too there is no clear distinction among these four *cervidae* terms (1 Chr. 12:9 [= 12:8 RSV]; Sir. 11:32 [= 11:30 RSV]; 27:22 [= 27:20 RSV]; Gen. 49:21; 2 Sam. 22:34; Ps. 18:34 [= 18:33 RSV]; 104:18; Isa. 35:6). The *cervidae* are often mentioned in scripture as clean, edible animals (Deut. 12:15, 22; 14:5; 15:22), and this adds to their positive overtones.

Two scriptural texts deepen and extend the meaning of deer talk beyond beauty and agility. The first is: "O God, my soul desires you / as the hart desires spring water. / My soul thirsts for God, the living God— / when shall I arrive at and appear before God's face?" (Ps. 42:2–3 [= 42:1–2 RSV]). The (masculine) hart's thirst for water serves as synecdoche for the (feminine) soul's thirsty desire for the Lord. When the lovers liken one another to deer in the Song, this theme lurks in the background: their beauty and agility and passion participates in the soul's passion for the Lord, and in seeing this the Song's hearers find its words opening before them into a figuration of the soul's search for the Lord. Each of them, in the grace and beauty and energy with which they seek the other, shows the hearer something of what it is like to seek the Lord and be sought by him. Lovers want more than anything else to be face-to-face with one another; just so with our properly ordered desire for the Lord and (it is extremely important to recall) his for us.

The second scriptural text contains the only occurrence of *hinnulus* ("fawn") in scripture outside the Song. In Prov. 5 a father warns his son against consorting with prostitutes because they will alienate him from the woman (or wife: the text can be read in either way) of his youth and cause him to become "a laborer in alien houses" (*et labores tui sint in domo aliena* in 5:10). In those ways he will consume and waste his very flesh. Better than that would be to drink from his own wells—to "rejoice with the woman of your youth, / your dearest hind [*cerva carissima*] / and most graceful fawn [*gratissimus hinnulus*]. / Let her blandishments intoxicate you always, / and take intimate delight in her love" (Prov. 5:18–19; Kingsmill 2009: 54–56). These tropes of inebriation and delight in love occur in the Song as well (5:1); but the point of interest here is the characterization of the beloved as hind and fawn. So to characterize her—as the pair characterize one another in the Song—is to indicate that she is a proper beloved for her lover, the one he should love rather than dissipating his affections and himself among the prostitutes. She is for him and he for her, as the Song elsewhere says (2:16; 6:3; 7:11), and calling her *cerva* and *hinnulus* supports this pattern of scriptural resonance.

If she is soul and Israel and church and Mary, then the application to her of these epithets of grace and beauty and agility show that she is his unique beloved, chosen from all others. And, correspondingly, to say of him, as she does, that he is doe and hart and fawn is to say that he is her proper beloved, the one toward whom her loves are properly turned and for whom she does and should thirst—as, recall, the deer thirsts for pure water.

This reading of the deer tropes in the Song suggests that the lover of Israel-church thirsts for his beloved as much as she for him, for he is a deer every bit as much as she. This conclusion should be embraced. The Lord desires us as much as we him: the Song sings of reciprocal loves, of the Lord's for you, as hearer of the Song, as much as of yours for the Lord, being formed as you are by hearing the Song into being a better lover and a better beloved.

But, to return to our text, the adjuration formula of 2:7: the mention of "does and hinds" is not applied straightforwardly there to the beloved. The deer are, rather, those beasts in whose name the lover adjures the daughters. Given the range of meanings of deer talk in scripture, one interpretive possibility immediately suggests itself. It is that the lover-Lord adjures his beloveds (the daughters) in the name of the "does and hinds" because that trope connects his particular beloveds (the daughters, you, me) with his supreme beloved (Israel-church-Mary). She, the supreme beloved, the *gratissimus hinnulus*, is the one in whom the particular beloveds (the rest of us) participate; he loves her because of her peculiar and unsurpassable grace and beauty, and he loves them according to the extent that they participate in and belong to her. Adjuration—conjuration—by the "does and hinds," then, is adjuration by what all the Lord's beloveds share. He calls them by their grace and beauty and loveliness to acknowledge his special relation to the supremely graceful and beautiful and lovely one by refusing to "enliven or awaken" her "until she wishes." You too are adjured in this way: reminded, that is, of what you share with Mary's Israel-church and placed, performatively, into a particular relation to that beloved—one of service and participatory delight.

Sleeping and waking is an important and at first blush puzzling theme in the Song. The daughters are adjured not to "awaken or enliven" the beloved three times (2:7; 3:5; 8:4); she speaks of herself as seeking her man "in my bed—night by night" (3:1), and perhaps "bed" here means or goes with sleep. And then in 5:2 she says of herself that she "sleep[s] with wakeful heart" immediately after the pivotal description of the couple's lovemaking described in 5:1. Many of the disconcerting shifts of tone and mood and voice and addressee carry with them the flavor of the dream vision, in which causal connections are absent or idiosyncratic. In a high proportion of the Song's words spoken in the beloved's voice, you can easily and defensibly hear the voice of a sleeper recounting her dreams, and this is especially true if you listen to, or read, the Song complete, without veils (like this book) to shelter you from its strangeness. Hearing the beloved as asleep, or as recounting her dreams, is only one possibility among many for reading it; but it is an important one.[74]

74. It is a position quite often advocated by premodern commentators, as for example by Honorius Augustodunensis, who, in his *Sigillum Beatae Mariae*, offers a consistently Marian reading of the Song according to which she is depicted there as sleeping and dreaming of the Lord (3:1–5:1), and thereafter awakening in heaven, following the assumption, being addressed face-to-face by Christ. See *The Seal of Blessed Mary*, trans. Amelia Carr (Toronto: Peregrine, 1991); and Rachel Fulton, *From Judgment to Passion: Devotion to Christ and the Virgin Mary, 800–1200* (New York: Columbia University Press, 2002), 268–80.

Sleep is closely associated with memory: in dream you remember, often in disconnected and unfathomable ways; and the frequent past tense of the beloved's voice is illuminated by the dream reading. She moves often from anticipation ("let me be kissed"; 1:2), to memory ("I sat under his shade"; 2:3), to direct, present-tense address ("show me where you graze"; 1:7). But there is a predominance of past-tense formulations on her lips in the Song as a whole (strikingly, in the gradual shift from present to past in the sequence in 5:2–5), and so, perhaps, also a predominance of dream discourse.

Attention to the sleep-dream-memory threads in the Song also deepens and nuances the Marian reading of the text. Mary, according to the tradition of the church, sleeps before her bodily assumption into heaven, a condition known as the dormition; from that sleep (which may also be death) she is awakened to assume her proper place in heaven as its queen. During her dormition she may be thought to dream. And the Song's dreams may figure hers. When the beloved adjures the daughters not to wake her, on this reading, he—Christ, her son—adjures them to let her continue to dream of her son and of what he has done for the world.

His Voice and Gaze (2:8–9)

> The voice of my delightful man—
> look—he comes
> leaping among the mountains
> skipping over the hills
> like a doe or fawn among harts.
> He is the very one who stands behind our wall
> looking through the windows
> gazing through the lattices.

Following the formulaic pause of 2:6–7, the voice of the beloved resumes. It is not marked as such, but its topic is "the voice of my delightful man," which suffices to identify it as such. There is no direct indication of her audience, though in the first-person plural of the phrase "our wall" (*parietem nostrum*) there is a suggestion that she is not alone, and that the "wall" and "windows" and "lattices" about which she speaks may belong to the couple (as in "our flowerful bed" in 1:16), or that she is speaking to—or among—the daughters of Jerusalem. Perhaps it is to them that she says "look—he comes"; it is certainly to us, the Song's hearers, that she says this. Her words are full of eager expectation. Her lover is coming to her, quickly, "leaping" and "skipping"; and then he is there, "looking through the windows / gazing through the lattices."

She imagines him coming to her "leaping" and "skipping." The verb "leap" (*salire*) occurs only here in the Song, as does "skip" (*transilire*), its close cognate. These verbs occur rather rarely in scripture too, and not much help is to be had from the few instances there are.[75] The connotations are of urgency and agility and perhaps also of youth, as is suggested by the connection of these verbs with the lover's likeness to "a doe or fawn among harts" (a phrase she repeats in 2:17), which is to say to a young animal among older ones (→2:7).

The lover is present but invisible to the beloved: she is inside and he outside, he looking at her "through the windows . . . through the lattices," but she unable to see him. Windows and lattices are mentioned together in scripture several times (Judg. 5:28 [Sisera's mother looks through them, waiting for his return]; 1 Kgs. 6:4 [Solomon's Temple built with both]; Prov. 7:6 [the author sees through them a young man keeping an appointment with a prostitute]), sufficiently frequently that the connection is unremarkable: a window opening (unglassed) might be protected with wooden latticework, whether shutterlike or not; peering through lattices then yields a partial and checkered view, shaded and shadowed.

If the lover is the Lord and his beloved his Israel-church, then there are rich possibilities for thinking about additional meanings for these phrases. The Lord's partial or full invisibility to us is one: he is there and can see us, but we cannot see him. The Lord may seem to choose to conceal himself from us: he "stands behind our wall" (a word that occurs only here in the Song). But this is a barrier we have erected, and its presence here may suggest that it is our actions rather than the Lord's that separate us from him. We have enclosed ourselves by sin in a place in which the Lord's voice can be heard, yes, but where he cannot be seen. There are, however, openings even in this wall, openings that let in the Lord's light. Through those openings he approaches more closely to us, and through them he speaks to us. On this reading, scripture itself, and especially the words of the Song under discussion, serve as just such openings: in reading or hearing the Song we are looked at by the Lord as our lover through the windows and latticework of scripture. A conceit, it may seem, but a nice one. The Song here performs what it figures: an opening to the "voice"—and proleptically the vision and the touch—of the Lord.

She begins to express her delight at her lover's approach by saying, "The voice of my delightful man." In the Song, mention of the voice is always positive. It is what the two use to exchange endearments, and so it is for them a mode of intimacy. His approach is signaled by mention of the voice, and his departure by its fading into absence. She hears him before she can see him, and so his voice is, for her, a provocation of desire that she hopes soon to find realized in more intimate ways. Voice and speech stand, therefore, as prelude to sight, touch, and taste. In this, the Song's use of *vox* and its verbal cognates is like that of scripture in general, in which they occur hundreds of times. The Lord, of course, speaks to the people

---

75. In 1 Kgs. 18:26 the prophets of Baal "leap" around their altar, which is a negative use. Similar is Prov. 14:16, in which it is the *stultus*, the stupid one, who "skips," showing excessive confidence in his strength and understanding. In Isa. 35:6 it is the lame who "leap" in that day, the day of salvation—as, approximately, also in Mal. 3:20 [= 4:2 RSV]. In 2 Sam. 22:30 || Ps. 18:30 [= 18:29 RSV] David gives thanks to the Lord that he has been given strength enough to "skip" over walls.

of Israel and to the church as lawgiver and as lover, or perhaps better as the lover who gives law; and the Lord calls and names (usually *vocare*) his chosen, whether as individuals or as a people, with a voice (Moses in Exod. 3:4; Isaiah in Isa. 6:8; Jesus in Matt. 3:17 ‖ Mark 1:11 ‖ Luke 3:22; 9:35). In calling and naming and addressing his people, the Lord remains (usually) invisible: his voice is, in a sense, overheard, as we, without seeing them, can hear people on the street or in the next room or on the telephone. But the Lord's voice presses always toward visibility, something that happens in the incarnation, when the Word (the *verbum* of God) takes flesh and becomes visible. Even before that, the Lord's *vox* hovers on the edge of visibility, and sometimes this dialectical tension between the invisibly spoken word and what can be seen is evident in scripture, as when the people of Israel see the Lord's *voces* (literally "his voices," his words): these become visible after he has given them the law at Sinai.[76]

This dialectic between the invisible voice and its approach toward visibility illuminates the Song's use of *vox*. In 2:8–3:5 the beloved never sees her lover. He is close, and she can hear his words; but he is not within sight and cannot be touched. Earlier in the Song, when their intimacy is largely depicted as face-to-face and flesh-to-flesh (1:12–2:7), there is no mention of the voice. They speak, of course; but their words are spoken face-to-face and do not need to be labeled "voice," in the way they are here. When the Song speaks of voice, separation hovers always in the wings, and the anticipation and memory of that separation are not detachable from hearing what is said. Just so—or at least approximately so—with the Lord's address to the people. As the Song's lover speaks and is gone, so the Lord speaks from a cloud and then speaks no more. And as the Song's beloved yearns not only for her lover's voice but for his touch, so we also yearn for the Lord's caresses. In heaven, Augustine speculates, there may be no need of language or of speech, which is the same as to say that *vox* will have come to an end.[77] This suggestively supports the view that talk of the Lord's voice is also and at the same time talk of his partial absence.

He Urges Her (2:10)

> And my delightful man speaks to me—
> "Get up, O my beloved,
> my dove, my lovely one, and come—

---

76. *Cunctus autem populus videbat voces et lampades et sonitum bucinae montemque fumantem; et perterriti* (Exod. 20:18): "And all the people saw the voices and the flashes and the trumpet blasts and the mountain smoking, and they were terrified." English versions made from the Hebrew, reading (I assume) a different text, generally have "thunder" where the New Vulgate has *voces*. See the discussion in Jean-Louis Chrétien, *The Call and the Response*, trans. Anne A. Davenport (New York: Fordham University Press, 2004), 39–43.

77. On Augustine's speculations about speech in heaven, see Paul J. Griffiths, *Lying: An Augustinian Theology of Duplicity* (Grand Rapids: Brazos, 2004), chap. 4.

The beloved's voice continues, addressing (perhaps) the daughters of Jerusalem if we remain within the Song, but also you, the Song's hearer. She tells you that her "delightful man" speaks to her, and his words, reported by her, are in the vocative, the case of direct address to his "beloved," whom he also calls here his "dove," his *columba*. "Get up," he urges her—the voice is imperative—and "come." The refrain is repeated in 2:13, and the lover's words to his beloved, reported by her, extend, probably, to the end of 2:15. Talk of the beloved as a "dove" is common in the Song; the term has already been applied to her eyes (1:15), and he calls her "dove" four times in the Song (2:10, 14, 5:2; 6:9), a figure that suggests, scripturally, intimacy, delight, special favor, and also mourning (→1:15).

Talk of "getting up" (*surgere*) is also frequent in the Song: she is twice commanded by her lover to do this (2:10, 13), and twice (3:2; 5:5) she describes herself as about to do so or as having done so, once from her bed of separation from her lover, and once so that she might open the door of her room to him, permitting him to come in and make love to her. The verb is always one that implies separation in the Song, as well as an urgent desire to end that separation: to be told to "get up" is to be told to stop being alone and to come to your lover. It is also a verb that implies sadness and the possibility of failure: the separated one might choose not to get up; and even if she does get up, she might not find her lover. When in 3:2 she gets up from her solitary bed to seek her lover, there is at first a period of wandering through the streets of the city before she finds him; and when in 5:5 she gets up to open her door to him, it is to find that he has "turned aside and gone away" (5:6). When the lover commands his beloved to "get up" in 2:10, all this is in play: they are apart; he wants her to be with him; but the attempt to come together may fail.

You, like the Lord's Israel-church, are called by him to "get up" and to "come" to him. He wants you as his beloved because you are already his "dove," his beautifully winged one whom he can send out to discover where there is dry land to be found among the chaos waters of the flood (drawing on Gen. 8:6–12), and because you are already his "lovely one" (→1:5). But there are things for you to do and places for you to go: the lover-Lord is about to entice you into the garden (Claudel 1948: 68–69).

Spring Comes (2:11–13a)

> for already winter has gone away
> the rain has departed and withdrawn
> flowers have appeared in the land
> the time of pruning has arrived
> the turtledove's voice is heard in our land
> the fig tree has put out its figs
> and the flowering vineyards have given off their scent.

She began to report his words in 2:10; they continue here, as they will until at least 2:14, and possibly as far as 2:15. His (reported) words to her began with direct address ("get up"; 2:10) and continue here in seductive pastoral mode. It is spring, "flowers have appeared in the land . . . the flowering vineyards have given off their scent," and he wants his beloved to be with him, as fertile and beautiful as the land in which he wants them to walk and make love.

The "turtledove" and the "fig" are mentioned in the Song only here, but rather frequently elsewhere in scripture. The former turns up almost always in the context of prescriptions about sacrifice, as a beautiful thing to be offered;[78] and the latter as representative of fertility and beauty and security.[79] They both belong to the standard repertoire of scriptural images for the order and harmony of the created order, and of its gifts of food and beauty to the human part of that order. When things are as they should be, ripe figs drop from the trees ready to dissolve as sweet delights on the tongue while turtledoves coo and field-flowers fill the air with their scent and the eye with their color. The lover urges his beloved out into this vernal paradise, so that she will there offer her beauty to him as the figs and flowers and turtledoves do.

The paradise he wants her to enter is a highly cultivated one, prepared and worked and shaped by human effort: it contains vineyards and cultivated fig trees, and the lover notes that "the time of pruning has arrived," thereby confirming that the lovers' garden is one of artifice and that, by implication, their love is a work of cultivation. When the Lord seeks and finds Israel and the church, he does so on ground carefully prepared and intensively worked; and the exchange of embraces between lover and beloved is in the same way a matter of cultivation. There is nothing spontaneous or wild or impulsive about the courtship or the lovemaking. He has chosen her and prepared her and adorned her (recall 1:10), and her response to him is equally a matter of cultivation. The Song's consistently positive use of the pastoral correlates with its abjuration of the wild and uncultivated, and with it of the romantic idea of the attraction of soul mates that has only to be acknowledged and acted upon. That desire is cultivated intensifies the delight that lovers take in one another rather than reducing it—the savor of the wine made from "flowering vineyards" and the sweetness of the figs produced from carefully pruned fig trees is much more intense than anything given by the uncultivated wild. The theological point here is that Israel is cultivated as the Lord's beloved rather than being recognized as the one whom the Lord loves. This does not mean that he loves her any the less.

78. In Gen. 15:9 the *turtur* is among the creatures Abram is instructed to sacrifice to mark the establishment of the covenant; and often in Leviticus it is prescribed as the poor man's sin offering (e.g., Lev. 14:22; cf. Luke 2:24).

79. *Ficus* and *grossus* represent security and fertility, the settled life of the people in the land, in 1 Kgs. 5:5 [= 4:25 RSV]. Correspondingly, the removal of the fig tree represents the laying waste of the land in Hos. 2:14 [= 2:12 RSV].

The Dove (2:13b–14)

> Get up, O my beloved,
> my comely one, and come
> my dove—
> in the chinks of the rock
> in the precipitous cave
> expose your face to me
> let your voice sound in my ears
> for your voice is sweet
> and your face splendid.

The lover's reported voice continues here. Following the repetition of the injunction to "get up," the lover introduces a new epithet for his beloved, calling her "my comely one [*speciosa*]." This endearment is used for her only here in the Song, but she also applies it later to him, when she says that "his comeliness is like Lebanon's" (5:15). The word is, scripturally, most often a word used to denote the sexual attractiveness of some particular woman (Abigail in 1 Sam. 25:3; Judith in Jdt. 11:23; Job's daughters in Job 42:15); but it is also used to describe the beauty of Israel as the Lord's beloved (Jer. 6:2; Ezek. 31:9), and this deepens the resonance between the Song's beloved and Israel.[80]

The repetition of "get up" also introduces a shift in the imagery of place, from pastoral to wild. We have moved, quite suddenly, from the cultivated garden to "the chinks of the rock" and "the precipitous cave": the lover asks his beloved to "expose your face" and "let your voice sound" in those wild places, and he asks this in a tone and with a vocabulary that suggests it will be difficult for him to see the beloved's face and hear her voice. The word "chink" (*foramen*) means a narrow opening and often connotes difficulty of ingress or egress: to get from one place to another through a chink is unlikely to be easy. This is the word used in Jesus's likening of the difficulty a camel has in getting through a chink to the difficulty a rich man is likely to have in getting to heaven (Matt. 19:24 || Mark 10:25 || Luke 18:25). The word is used in one other place in the Song (5:4), where it suggests the narrow place of the beloved's vagina as well as a narrow opening in the door ("my delightful man put his hand through the chink / and my belly trembled"; cf. *foramen aspidis* in Isa. 11:8). The word may also indicate a place of safety: the Lord says that he will put Moses in a chink of the rock while he passes by, in order to protect Moses from seeing him directly (Exod. 33:22). In Song 2:14, the "chink" suggests only difficulty: the lover wants the beloved to "expose her face" to him, but he is not sure that she can: she is in a place where it will be difficult for her to

---

80. The noun *species* (Song 5:15) is very frequent elsewhere in scripture and often has a neutral sense, meaning "appearance" or "how something looks"; but it can also sometimes have a positive sense, as when used of Judith's appearance (Jdt. 16:9) or when it is applied to the appearance of the Lord's glory (Exod. 24:17).

do so, a narrow and constrained and uncultivated place. The same implications are present in the mention of "the precipitous cave."

The Little Foxes (2:15)

> Catch for us the foxes—the little foxes—
> who destroy the vineyards
> as our vineyards are flowering."

The lover's reported words certainly extend to the end of 2:14; perhaps they also include this sentence, obscurity-laden as it is. The words are a demand: someone, probably but not certainly the beloved, must "catch for us the foxes—the little foxes— / who destroy the vineyards." While this is among the more obscure verses in the Song, it is also, because of its pithiness and power, among the most frequently quoted and used, though usually without reference to or apparent knowledge of its origin. The immediate context of these words provides no help in assessing who the "foxes" are, why they are spoken of at this point, or what they may be taken to figure. The broader context of the entire Song is not much help either: foxes are mentioned only here.

Elsewhere in scripture foxes are represented in an unremittingly negative light, as also here in the Song. They are agents of destruction or corruption, connected with desolation and ruin.[81] Suppose—a tentative reading—she is continuing to report his words to her. The principal reason internal to the text for assuming this is that her words to him are clearly marked as beginning in the immediately subsequent verse (2:16), and without an indication of transition it seems more reasonable to assume that she continues to report his words to her. On that reading, the words continue and develop the atmosphere of doubt and danger already begun in the immediately preceding words, about the beloved's voice and face "in the chinks of the rock" (2:14). The lover here tells the beloved that all is not well in the blossoming paradise to which he is inviting her. The "vineyards are flowering," certainly (→1:6b); but there are agents of destruction abroad as well, and it is her task to stop them doing their work, to "catch" them.

This reading shows us the beloved (Israel, church, Mary, you yourself) as the Lord's cooperator, someone who has work to do in the world that the Lord needs done. This is certainly true of Israel elsewhere in the Old Testament: she is elected by the Lord for a purpose, which is, in part, to serve as a light to the nations and thereby to bring the world closer to the Lord by soothing ("catch[ing]") those who would deepen the world's damage, and their own, by extending the distance

---

81. Foxes are burned alive in Samson's anti-Philistine stratagem (Judg. 15), roam in desolate places (Ps. 44:20 [= 44:19 RSV]; 63:11 [= 63:10 RSV]; Lam. 5:18; Ezek. 13:4), and are weak (Neh. 3:35 [= 4:3 RSV]). Even they, as by implication the lowest of the animals, have somewhere to live (Matt. 8:20 || Luke 9:58).

between it and the Lord. A standard prophetic image for this work of Israel is the ingathering of the nations to the restored Jerusalem, an outcome dependent on Israel's returning the Lord's kisses. In Luke's Gospel, Jesus calls Herod "that fox" (Luke 13:32), and this belongs to the same sphere of thought. The powers of the world are, or can be, agents "who destroy the vineyards," and the extension of Israel into the church is a means of transmuting those foxes into sheep. The beloved has work to do, and this pregnantly obscure verse calls her to do it.[82]

"The little foxes" are at work in the world outside the church/Israel, but not only there. Their attempted destruction of the vineyards is evident as well in the divisions and conflicts that have always characterized the life of both Israel and the church. Catching those foxes—not only Herod, but also, for Christians, our fellow-baptized—is also part of the church's task. It is her endless work of self-purification, of learning to respond ever more fully to the Lord's embraces, and in that way to make herself less capable of works of destruction.

You too, the reader of the Song, are in part foxlike, wandering in a region of desolation and sometimes turning what was fertile and "flowering" into desert. Your own responses to the Lord's caress are partial and imperfect, withholding as much as giving, absent as much as present, grasping what you want as often as giving it back.[83] Those foxes, the foxes of your destructively concupiscent desires, also need to be caught, groomed, domesticated, made less vulpine and more ovine. That is the work of penitence and penance, a work that, when seriously undertaken, prevents you from thinking of "the little foxes" as if you were not among their number. Christians begin and end this fox-catching work by making their own Paul's confession that he is the first, or greatest, among sinners (1 Tim. 1:15).

A Marian reading also presses itself forward. Mary, considered as the Lord's beloved, is his fullest cooperator. She accepts the work given her to do, which is the bearing of Jesus in her womb; and in doing so she opens herself fully, physically and mentally and spiritually, to the Lord. She is the one who has, as the Lord asked of her in Song 2:14, exposed her face to him and let her voice sound in his ears, most especially with her *fiat mihi*. As a result, Jesus is conceived and born and undertakes his work of atonement and redemption, and it is by this means that "the little foxes" are, finally, caught and the world turned again, proleptically,

82. Most premodern Christian commentators identify the "foxes" with heretics or Jews. See the passages collected and translated in J. Robert Wright, ed., *Proverbs, Ecclesiastes, Song of Solomon*, Ancient Christian Commentaries, Old Testament 9 (Downers Grove, IL: InterVarsity, 2005), 322–24. The latter identification provides a clear instance of the inferiority of premodern commentary to what is possible for us: the indissoluble intimacy between the Jewish people and the Christian people was less evident to (for example) Bede and Gregory of Elvira than it is to us.

83. I draw upon Origen, *Homeliae in canticum canticorum* (Homilies on the Song of Songs) 4.3.1–34 (Lawson 1956: 254–63; French and Latin in *Origène: Commentaire sur le Cantique des Cantiques*, ed. and trans. Luc Brésard, Henri Crouzel, Marel Borret, Sources Chrétiennes 376 [Paris: Cerf, 1992], 720–39). Origen is especially comprehensive here in his collection of a catena of scriptural passages about foxes and in his comments upon the senses in which the individual soul might be a fox catcher.

toward its Lord. Mary's response to the lover's injunction to "catch for us the foxes" figures all other responses: that of Israel, of the church, and of you, the Song's contemporary hearer.

He for Her, She for Him #1 (2:16–17)

> My delightful man is for me and I am for him—
> the one who grazes among lilies—
> until the day breathes
> and the shadows flee.
> Turn back, O my delightful man,
> be like a doe or fawn among harts
> on Bether's mountains.

On the dark note about the foxes his direct address to her (reported by her) ends and her voice resumes, again with passion. She does not at first address him directly: in 2:16 she apostrophizes him in the third person. But then she does address him directly, in the vocative case ("turn back, O my delightful man"), urging him to return to her at once. The language here is of delight and desire intermixed: she rejoices in that he is hers and she his in words of confident and languid intimacy; but then, with urgency, she implores his return, wanting the presence again of what has become absent. As happens throughout the Song, relaxed intimacy, delight in presence, shifts suddenly and without explanation to the anguish of absence.

In her initial expression of delight she uses her favorite epithet for him, "my delightful man." This refrain occurs on her lips almost thirty times in the Song, and it carries with it connotations of fully sexual pleasure as well as of more diffuse sensual and emotional pleasure (→1:7; →1:13–14). She goes on to define him more fully as "the one who grazes among lilies" (→1:7), and then, in a phrase repeated twice more in the Song (6:3; 7:11) with some elaboration and embroidery, she says that he "is for me and I am for him" (Kingsmill 2009: 209–11). These are words expressing confidence in an ineradicable intimacy coupled with a deep note of purpose. The beloved is "for him" in at least the senses that she is gift to him, and that her purpose (end, goal) is, exactly, him. Likewise for him: he is "for me," she says, as gift and end. What he wants is her and what she wants is him, exclusively and finally without remainder. The clearest and deepest scriptural echo is in the formula of covenant:

> Behold, I shall gather them from every part of the earth to which I drove them in my wrath and anger and great indignation. And I shall bring them back to this place, and shall make them live there with security. And they will be a people for me and I will be their God. And I will give them a single heart and a single way so that they might fear me always, and that will be good for them and for their children after them. And I will make an everlasting covenant with them and will

not cease from doing good to them, and I will place the fear of me in their hearts so that they will not go away from me. (Jer. 32:37–40)

In this version of the formula, the Lord expresses the certainty of indissolubility that the beloved expresses in Song 2:16.

Her expression of their mutual self-gift is given a sexual overtone by the immediately following formula: "until the day breathes / and the shadows flee." This formula, here spoken by her, is repeated verbatim by him at 4:6. Verbatim repetitions of this sort, when spoken by both partners, are a strong indication of symmetrical reciprocity between the two: what she says of and to him can also be said by him of and to her. The phrase can be paraphrased (with severe loss) to mean simply "until morning," with overtones of "until everything is as it should be." She affirms that she is for him and he for her all night, in sexual embrace (by implication), and also forever. The "shadows" are those of death as well as those of night; they also figure in part and imperfectly what will be found more fully in the life of the world to come.[84]

Then she urges him to "turn back," showing as she does that he has gone away, as he does again and again in the Song. Presence and intimacy are always shadowed by absence and loss, and the former almost always directly turns into the latter. When he is absent she wants his presence (recall the elements of lament in 1:1–6), and here she directly says so. As in 2:8–9 she delightedly anticipated his "leaping" and "skipping" approach, "like a doe or a fawn among harts," so here she uses the same phrase to urge him back.

She mentions here a place, "Bether's mountains"; this is the only mention of this place in the Song, and it is mentioned (in this form) only once more in the whole of scripture, where it is called one of the cities (or possibly villages) of the mountainous regions (Josh. 15:59).

The formula of ineradicable intimacy in Song 2:16 expresses one aspect of the doctrine of election: the aspect of certainty. She, the beloved, the Lord's Israel-church, knows who she is and rests secure in the indissolubility of her having been chosen as the beloved, the one whom the Lord wants. This is not incompatible with the agony of separation: the visible church here below, like Solomon in his late idolatry and the people of Israel in their wanderings, may forget who she is, obscuring herself to herself by sin, and in that way also forget the certainty of her election, the certainty that she will be taken again into the Lord's bed there to be caressed.

The question of separation is theologically difficult. One impulse is to say that the Lord does not separate himself from us and that all separation is a result of our movements away from him. This must at some level be true: the Lord is not

---

84. *Umbrae* (→2:3b) is used of death in Ps. 23:4. It is characteristic of the cycle of life in Wis. 2:5 and Isa. 9:1 [= 9:2 RSV] and is figurative of something better and more complete in Heb. 8:5. It is in this last sense that John Henry Newman used the term in his epitaph: *Ex umbris et imaginibus in veritatem.*

capricious, not a human lover who plays hard to get; he does not need to stimulate our desire by withdrawing himself from us, and his desire for us is sufficiently passionate that he has no reason for removing himself from us. But against this it must be said that the Song here depicts separation as the result of the lover's action, not the beloved's. And it is a common theme in scripture that the Lord withdraws: Jesus, after all, ascends rather than remain before the apostles' gaze. I should like, with uneasiness and uncertainty, to read such language as epistemic rather than ontological: the Lord's withdrawal is like his walking in the garden in the cool of the day (Gen. 3:8): a reasonable way of talking, a mode of seeming, but not something the Lord actually does. Before his incarnation, the Lord walked nowhere and had no feet. So also, I suggest, the Lord never withdraws from us, whether we as individuals or we as Israel-church. The pedagogy of suffering produced by apparent withdrawal is real and importantly formative; as children are formed by their parents' disappointment at their misconduct, so we are formed by the Lord's apparent withdrawal of himself from us. But that withdrawal is always apparent, which does not at all reduce its felt reality.[85]

The Song's expression of the double certainty of election—the certainty, that is, of the beloved's own continued desirability to the Lord and of the indissolubility of their mutual love—is among the strongest in scripture, and the strength of this certainty is one of the reasons that prompted the church gradually to come to see the Song's beloved as a figure for Mary. Mary's response to the Lord's choice of her is simple: *fiat mihi*; and she stands after that acceptance as the paradigm of one who can say with certainty that she is for him, for her son, and therefore and thereby for the triune Lord, and that he is for her.

The Lord is also for you and you are for him. You are unlikely to have certainty of that fact; but permitting the certainty of the Song's beloved about her own election and desirability to enter with increasing depth into yours may, over time, permit you to see with greater clarity that the Lord does and will do nothing other than batter your heart with his solicitation of you. But not only this. What the Song has to say about the mutual love of lover and beloved provides the archetype and figure of all monogamous desire: it shows what it means to find the one who gives himself (herself) exclusively and without remainder to you in such a way that everything about you finds fulfillment in your lover and that each of you needs nothing but the love of the other. Adulterous dalliance on this ideal-typical view is not only renounced but impossible. None of this is, of course, possible here below among human lovers; our restlessness can find monogamous rest only in the Lord.[86] But our desires for one another are figured by and participate in that love for the Lord, a love that is not one way but rather reciprocal and reciprocated.

85. Discussion with R. R. Reno has been helpful in formulating these points. He would not agree with what I say here, however.

86. Echoing Augustine: *et inquietum est cor nostrum donec requiescat in te* in *Confessiones* 1.1.1 (Latin in James J. O'Donnell, *Augustine: Confessions* [Oxford: Clarendon, 1992], 1.3; English in Henry Chadwick, trans., *Saint Augustine: Confessions* [Oxford: Oxford University Press, 1991], 3).

Your own human loves can gradually be transfigured by this knowledge. They can be moved, that is, though always imperfectly, toward the vision of love's security and love's passion given in these verses of the Song.

She Seeks Him in the City (3:1–2)

> In my bed—night by night—
> I sought him—the man in whom my soul delights.
> I sought and did not find him.
> I will get up and walk around the city
> through the streets and the squares
> I will seek the man in whom my soul delights.
> I sought and did not find him.

Immediately after exhorting her lover to "turn back," she begins to lament his absence. There is nothing in 3:1 to indicate to whom she speaks. In the immediately preceding verse (2:17) she has been talking directly to her lover ("turn back, O my delightful man"), but here she speaks not to him but about him, in the third person ("I sought him . . . did not find"). The words can be read as a dream-soliloquy or reverie on her part, a story told to herself. If that reading is adopted, the transition from 2:17 to 3:1 is from a call of direct address to her man, a plea to him that he should not leave, to an awareness that he has left and is no longer there to be spoken to. All she can then do is lament to herself his absence and eventually (in 3:4) describe to herself his renewed presence.

The place she would like him to be is "in my bed," but he is, "night by night," not there. Not being there, he cannot kiss her and caress her and make love to her. And this she laments. Her bed is where he belongs, as her lover. Their bed has already been mentioned, described in loving detail (1:16–17), and will soon be mentioned again, in connection with Solomon (3:7). Here it is her bed only, a lonely bed. From it, or perhaps in it, she seeks him and fails to find him. Her lament, "I sought and did not find him," is repeated twice, once almost immediately (3:2) and once much later (5:6); it is to this point the most explicit statement of the theme of separation. They have been exchanging endearments; she has eagerly expected his arrival; but he has gone away and now he seems beyond her reach.

She does not find him in her bed, and so she decides to look for him in the city, declaring her resolution in the future tense ("I will get up . . . I will seek"), still, perhaps, in dream-soliloquy. She will walk "through the streets and the squares" in search of him. There too, she reports, she does not (at first) find him. Here is the first mention of the "city" in the Song, and its only use of urban vocabulary ("streets . . . squares"). The "city" is mentioned once more later in the Song (5:7), and in that context too, as also here, as the place in which the beloved wanders in search of her lover. Earlier, the Song has used pastoral and wilderness vocabulary, with the former dominant and treated positively. When the city appears, it does so as a place even more desolate than the wilderness. It is a place of separation and search and grief, certainly; but it is also a place of danger.

Our love affairs are desolate and desolating things. They always involve separation and loss, whether from betrayal or forgetfulness or sickness or death. Every marriage ends in one of those ways. The beloved's lament for her separation from her lover is therefore immediately familiar. That kind of lament belongs, too, to Israel's and the church's love affair with the Lord. The Psalms are full of laments for the Lord's absence, as is Jewish and Christian literature. Why does not the Lord act for us? Why will he not show us his face? Why is he not there with us, in our beds, embracing us, by our sides in the paradisial country he has made? Why, instead, must we weep for our loneliness? Job's laments are the classic case, unsurpassed in intensity: "My days pass more rapidly than a weaver's shuttle / consumed without hope" (Job 7:6).

The Song provides no answer to these questions, but it shows their structure and their unavoidability. These are laments that Israel, the church, and every Christian must continue to make their own. To seek the Lord, as the beloved begins to do here, is a task that ends only with the vision of the Lord after death; and the verb the beloved uses here for the seeking (*quaerere*) occurs dozens of times in scripture, most commonly in connection with the Lord: "Seek the Lord and live!" (*quaerite dominum et vivite* in Amos 5:6; cf. Isa. 55:6; 1 Chr. 16:10; Zech. 8:21). Seeking, however, goes always with lament for absence, as the Song makes abundantly clear.

The Watchmen (3:3)

> The watchmen found me
> they who walk around the city.
> "Have you seen the man in whom my soul delights?"

In the city, the place of danger, the beloved does not at first find her lover, but she is found. The "watchmen" the beloved encounters as she searches "the city" for her lover are presumably the same as the "guards" of 5:7, although the Latin words are different (*vigil* and *custos*, respectively). Their identity is shown by the Song using the same identifying phrase ("who walk around the city") for both groups. Neither "watchman" nor "guard" occurs very frequently elsewhere in scripture, though the few instances there are support, without much developing, the Song's usage. "Watchmen"/"guards" protect places (city walls, city gates, particular rooms, jails) and, by metaphorical extension, also themselves and their virtues or vices.[87] It is

---

87. *Vigil* (as a noun denoting a person) scarcely occurs in scripture outside the Song, except for a cluster of uses in Dan. 4, where it denotes an angel. *Custos* is more common, both as guardian of a place (Isa. 21:11–12; Neh. 3:29; Acts 16:27) and in extended metaphorical senses (Gen. 4:9; Prov. 16:17).

clearly the former sense that the Song has in mind. It is interesting too that both the "watchmen" and the beloved are described as "walk[ing] around the city": they both wander in the same place, a place where the Lord is not, a *regio egestatis*.

The beloved questions the watchmen: "Have you seen the man in whom my soul delights?" And that is all we learn about them at this point. They say nothing, and she passes them by. In the similar later scene (5:6–7) of urban separation and desolation, the "guards" do something more. She says there that "those who care for the ramparts— / they beat me and wounded me / and took my cloak from me." The Song has nothing further of an explicit nature to say about this act of violence. It is, it appears, proper to the "guards" in their function as guards and caretakers of the city to do violence to the beloved just because she is wandering the city in search of her lover. Here she asks them directly whether they have seen him, and gets no reply; in 5:7 she does not ask them, and is simply beaten.[88]

The Song partakes here, in a particularly direct and uncompromising way, of scriptural and traditional ambivalence about the city. Jesus dies outside Jerusalem, having been rejected by it and its authorities, Roman and Jewish;[89] the cities of Babylon and Assyria are places of exile and vice; and Jerusalem's close association with the monarchy makes of it an ambiguous place too. It is not that cities are always places far from or opposed to the Lord, either in scripture or tradition. Zion is the beacon for the nations, the place to which the nations will be drawn as a magnetized needle to the north (Ps. 9:12–15 [= 9:11–14 RSV]; Isa. 2:3); Babylon falls, but the New Jerusalem descends from heaven as the perfect city (Rev. 18–22). Augustine, in the *City of God* and elsewhere, enshrines and canonizes for Catholic Christianity the two-faced aspect of the city as belonging on the one hand to the Lord and on the other to humans.[90] For the Song, however, there is not much ambivalence. It represents, almost without exception or reservation, the negative evaluation of the city.[91] The city is a place of violence and loss, to which the proper response is mourning.[92]

88. Claudel 1948: 91–95 represents another deeply rooted ecclesial tradition about the watchmen, which is that they are the senses, and the city they guard is the soul.

89. In the Song's account of the beloved's wounding by the city's protectors in 5:7 there are echoes of the words scripture uses to depict Christ's passion. The beloved's beating uses the same verb as do Matthew's and Mark's accounts of the Roman soldiers striking Jesus's head with a reed (Matt. 27:30 ‖ Mark 15:19). The quotation of Zech. 13:7 by Jesus after the Last Supper (Matt. 26:31 ‖ Mark 14:27) uses the same verb.

90. Augustine, *De catechizandis rudibus* (Catechizing the Uninstructed) 19.31 (Latin and Italian in Carlo Carena et al., ed. and trans., *Sant'Agostino: Morale e Ascetismo Cristiano*, Opere di Sant'Agostino 7/2 [Rome: Città Nuova, 2001], 248–50).

91. But see Ellen F. Davis, *Proverbs, Ecclesiastes, and the Song of Songs* (Louisville: Westminster John Knox, 2000), on the theme of the reconciliation between city and country in the Song. For a brief study of the city theme in Christian theology, see Paul J. Griffiths, "Christians and the Church," in *Oxford Handbook of Theological Ethics*, ed. Gilbert Meilaender and Bill Werpehowski (Oxford: Oxford University Press, 2005), 398–412.

92. See Gillian Rose, *Mourning Becomes the Law: Philosophy and Representation* (Cambridge: Cambridge University Press, 1996), on the mourning appropriate to the city; and idem, *Paradiso* (London: Menard, 1999), for some suggestive comments on the Song.

A Marian reading of this tale of separation and wandering and violence is close to hand. Jesus is crucified outside the city by its "watchmen," who were then the soldiers of Rome. His mother is separated from him by his death, and she wanders, metaphorically, in grief, assaulted by the violence of the city and its rulers. Her mourning at that separation, city-bound and city-centered as it is, figures yours at your inevitable separations from your lover. And your grief at those separations, unavoidable as they are, can find consolation in her eventual meeting with her resurrected son, a meeting about to be figured in the Song.

Her Mother's House #1 (3:4)

> Soon after I had passed them by
> I found the man in whom my soul delights.
> I held him and would not let him go
> until I could lead him into my mother's house
> into the bedroom of my genetrix.

"Soon after" she has passed the watchmen by, their answer to her question unstated in the Song (the city's watchmen are not equipped, according to the Song's grammar, to answer questions of that sort; they have no access to such knowledge), she finds "the man in whom my soul delights," though where is not said. Perhaps the "soon after" suggests that she finds him while still in the city. In any case, she holds him fast, refusing to let him go until she can "lead him into my mother's house / into the bedroom of my genetrix." Why does she want to do this? The beloved's mother is mentioned frequently in the Song (1:6; 3:4; 6:9; 8:1–2, 5), even though without making an appearance in it or speaking in her own voice. The beloved invokes her own mother four times, and on three of those occasions (3:4; 8:1–2) she does so in speaking to her lover. Her mother's house and more particularly her "bedroom" are places she wants to take him, as we read here; and later (8:1–2) she wishes that her lover could be her brother, joining her in "sucking my mother's breasts" so that she might "kiss" him in public without shame or opprobrium. There she says to him, "I will seize you and lead you into my mother's house," there to make love to him. Here, at 3:4, there is, in parallel with the beloved's mention of her "mother," her use of the word "genetrix"—a synonym for "mother," meaning simply the woman who gave her, the beloved, birth. "Genetrix" occurs nowhere in scripture outside the Song; within the Song it occurs thrice: 3:4; 6:9; 8:5. In the latter two places the lover uses the word in addressing her. In 6:9 it is found at the end of his second hymn of praise to the beauty of her body, where he says that the beloved is his "dove," his "only one," "her mother's only one / set apart by her genetrix." And in 8:5, in one of the Song's interpretive cruxes, he says to her, "Under an apple tree I enlivened you / there your mother gave you birth / there your genetrix gave you birth." This is a rich stew of tropes.

What more may be said about the mother imagined by the beloved? Where and what is her house? The surface of the Song's text provides no further evidence, but a little thought about the matter in the context of scripture as a whole yields a first answer: the beloved's mother is Eve, the *mater . . . cunctarum viventium* ("mother of all the living"), as she is described in Gen. 3:20. This reading is supported by another look at what the lover says to the beloved about her mother, her genetrix. He says that she, the beloved, has a unique relation—she is the "only one," "set apart" (6:9)—to her mother; and that she, the beloved, was birthed "under an apple tree" (*sub arbore malo*; 8:5). This phrase can as well be rendered "under an evil tree": the neuter Latin word *malum* is either an adjective meaning "evil, disastrous, calamitous" or a noun designating a seeded fruit of some sort (a pomegranate, perhaps). In either case, the phrase at once conjures to the scripturally literate the story in Gen. 2–3 of the Lord's command not to eat the fruit of a certain tree, of Eve's tempting by the serpent, of her decision to disobey the Lord's command and to persuade Adam to do the same, and of the consequent calamities.

This conjunction of signs supports rather strongly the view that the Song's text comports well with reading the beloved's mother as Eve. Suppose we do: vistas of interpretive possibility then open. The beloved, who is Israel-church-Mary, with the third of these three as the deepest presence in the Song, seeks Eve's bedchamber as a place to make love with her lover in order to recapitulate and reverse the events that made Eve the mother of all the living. She is that because of the fall. The fruit was taken and eaten in the garden, and at once Eve and Adam knew their nakedness, which is a synecdoche for knowing the difference between good and evil. Then they are cursed and banished, and among the curses is that Eve will suffer in having children. We may add, though scripture does not explicitly say so, that the curse includes the very having of children, not just that parturition is painful. There were no children before the fall, and no need of them: only with and because of death are children necessary, and so it is with mortality that procreation comes, and along with it the pain of childbirth.[93] The curse embraces all three. It is not a curse *simpliciter*, of course, any more than the fall is only a bad thing. With the curse came blessings, which is another way of saying that the Lord does not punish our transgressions but rather blesses them and in doing so transfigures them by grace toward what they should have been all along. Parenthood, while a dreadful thing for both parents and children,[94] is also a blessing for both to the extent that it is transfigured. It is usually not much transfigured.

93. The Christian tradition is divided on the question of whether there could have been offspring born to Adam and Eve had the fall not occurred. The position I take here is strongly suggested by the link between mortality and natality: if one, then the other; without the former, no need for the latter. Gen. 1:28 may be taken to speak against this view; but a figural reading of that verse is possible.

94. No one has surpassed Philip Larkin in clarity of Augustinian perception about this (not that Larkin was anything close to being explicitly Christian and not, probably, that he would have

The beloved is eager to take her lover to her mother's house, and into her mother's bedroom. This is because, reading *ad litteram*, those are places of safety and privacy, both essential for her purposes. She has just found him in the city's streets, and that is a place neither safe nor private. She cannot be sure of keeping him with her there, and she cannot there take him to bed. Hence her mother's house and bed, good for both purposes. Not only this: she also imagines that if she and her lover were brothers—that is, both living in their mother's house—she could embrace him in public without shame or fear. It is in this connection that she imagines them both "sucking my mother's breasts" (8:1). The image of familial intimacy, the closeness of siblings, is overlaid with tropes of strictly sexual desire. She, the beloved Israel-church, seeks every kind of intimacy with the Lord (as does each of us, whether knowingly or not), familial and sexual, familial overlaid by sexual, familial and sexual intertwined.

And so "the bedroom of my genetrix," as the beloved describes it, is the place where that threefold curse is laid and made inseparable from the fabric of all our lives. In wanting to take her lover there in order to make love to him[95] the beloved redoes and undoes what Eve did "under an apple tree." As Israel-church she opens herself eagerly to the Lord's caress, and becomes pregnant by him with the blessing of salvation for the world. Her pregnancy brings into the world the tribe of the chosen, the set apart: she has herself been "set apart by her genetrix" (6:9), which is the people of Israel. That people also, and consequently, brings into the world the church, which is the universal people of the Lord, offering Judaism to the Gentiles. And if we consider the beloved as Mary, in whom the people of Israel and the church are most intensely and fully present, then her eagerness to make love to the Lord, her beloved, in her mother's bedchamber, is to be understood most fully by her willingness to accept the Lord into her womb, both as lover in the figure of the Holy Spirit (embroidering upon Luke 2:32) and as son in the figure of Jesus, the Lord incarnate. In that pregnancy and rebirth, Eve's work is finally recapitulated and reversed. This is why the church so often calls Mary the second Eve and Jesus the second Adam.

This ecclesial/Marian reading of the presence of the beloved's mother in the Song does not at all submerge or overwrite the surface meaning of the text. That remains: we have a young woman who speaks of her mother's house and bedroom as a place of safety and security, a place where she might take her lover; also a young woman who acknowledges her fear that open displays of affection for her lover (the desired public kiss of 8:1) will compromise and threaten her by wishing that she and her lover might be seen by the world as brother and sister and thus

identified what he wrote here as Augustinian): "They fuck you up, your mum and dad / They may not mean to, but they do / They fill you with the faults they had / And add some extra, just for you"; from "This Be the Verse" in Philip Larkin, *Collected Poems*, ed. Anthony Thwaite (London: Faber & Faber, 2003), 142. This is not the whole story, but it is right and true so far as it goes. To deny it is sentimentality.

95. That this is what she wants to do with him there is clear enough in →8:2.

able to exchange kisses without such compromise and threat. That young woman, the Song's beloved, is not erased by reading her as Israel, church, and Mary. Her figure and her particular beauty—her "hair like a flock of nanny goats / coming down from Gilead" (6:5), for example—remain. They are what the Song is in the first instance about. But they are deepened and made translucent to the text of scripture and tradition by understanding her and her beauty and desire for what they also are, which are figures for the Lord's truest beloveds. This figural reading has, in addition to the benefit of treating the Song as scripture, that of permitting readings that clarify details in the Song that would otherwise remain utterly obscure. What, after all, can be said about the beloved's "genetrix" by those who wish to read the Song only within the limits of what can be read from the surface of its text?

The shifts of tone and scene in the verses that run from 2:9 to 3:4 are again deeply disconcerting. There is the lover's approach and then his departure, unexplained; there is the proposed pastoral idyll interwoven with the barren rocks and the destructive foxes; there is her lament for his absence and her odyssey through the city, there suddenly and inexplicably to find her lover again; and there is her unexplained desire to take him to her mother's house, and not only her house but also her "bedroom." The difference in tone between the pastoral language of 2:10–13 and the urban language of 3:1–3 is striking: the blooming and fertile land is the place for love's carefree caresses, while the streets of the city are the place of separation and searching. It is true that she does find him there, in the city, and holds him fast; but even that is almost desperate ("I held him and would not let him go"), carrying with it the suggestion that if she did not hold on to him he would once again leave and she would again be wandering the city alone, with only the watchmen to consult (their mercies are not always tender, as we see in 5:7). Almost everything else is puzzling and disconcerting. The Song's reader must look for help, first elsewhere in the Song and then elsewhere in scripture.

The lover's double plea to the beloved that she should "get up . . . and come" in 2:10–14 juxtaposes the Song's linked themes of hope and despair. The first plea is confident: he thinks she can and will come to him, and so his words are pastoral and sunny and without tension. The second plea is tense: he doubts that she will or can come to him, and so his words are dry and dubious, rock ribbed and difficulty laden. The garden becomes barren and dry; the flowers and figs shift into a precipitous cave. This dialectic is fundamental to the Lord's love for and cajoling of Israel and the church, as it is to his sweet-talking of each of us, and is illustrated with beautiful intensity in this brief call of lover to beloved. You, as hearer of the Song, can see your own call in the double tone of what the Lord says to his beloved: he is sure and not sure of you, confident in your delighted acceptance of his bounty and at the same time aware that you are in a narrow and barren place from which you will find it immensely difficult to show him your face.

Second Adjuration (3:5)

> O daughters of Jerusalem—I adjure you
> by the does and hinds of the fields
> not to enliven or awaken this delightful woman
> until she wishes.

The lover's voice now intervenes again, repeating verbatim the adjuration formula given for the first time at →2:7. Here, as there, the formula serves as a structural marker: a section of the Song has come to an end and a new one is about to begin. The beloved's dithyramb that has run from 2:8 (immediately after the first occurrence of the adjuration formula) to 3:4 (including her lengthy report of the lover's words to her in 2:10–15) is now ended, and a new, and if anything more unfathomable, sequence is about to begin. It is worth noting again that the adjuration formula carries with it the implication that the beloved sleeps, which provides some support for reading the whole of 2:8–3:4 as a dream-soliloquy.

First Question: What Is This? (3:6)

> What is this ascending through the desert
> like a wisp of smoke
> spiced with frankincense and myrrh
> and all the perfumer's powders?

The Song's next sequence, following the second occurrence of the adjuration formula, begins with a question. Who asks it? The text provides no immediate or decisive indication. But it is usually the case in the Song that questions are spoken by the daughters of Jerusalem (the only clear exceptions are the beloved's self-questioning in 5:3 and her rhetorical questioning of her lover in 8:1). In 5:9 and 8:5, for example, as here in 3:6, a question follows immediately upon a variant of the adjuration formula, which is always explicitly addressed to the daughters; and in both those places, as here, you, as the Song's hearer, are likely to assume that it is the daughters who ask the question. They, after all, have just been addressed. In 3:11 and 5:16, a speech follows the question; and it concludes with an explicit mention of the daughters as addressee. The questions of 6:1 and 6:10 too, the latter closely parallel to the one under consideration here, are also most naturally, given their context, attributed to the daughters: each is preceded by a mention of the daughters, which prompts the hearer to think that the daughters speak in response. All these cues, internal to the structure of the Song, dispose the hearer who has heard the Song more than once to judge that it is the daughters who ask, "What is this ascending through the desert?" But it should also be clear that the first-time hearer of the Song will here be jarred and puzzled by the rapid shifts of

speaker and scene from 3:4 to 3:5 and then again from 3:5 to 3:6. The speed of
the shift is disconcerting, almost hallucinatory; and the frequency of such shifts is
among the principal reasons for the intensity of the Song's effect upon its hearers.

The question of 3:6 itself finds an approximate parallel in 6:10 and 8:5. Here,
in 3:6, it is asked of something neuter (*hoc*), while in both those cases it is asked
of someone feminine (*ista*). And here the thing whose identity is questioned
ascends "through the desert" (*per desertum*), while in 8:5, she, whoever she is,
goes up "from the desert" (*de deserto*). The desert is not otherwise mentioned in
the Song, though as we have seen (→2:14), there is certainly wilderness language
that takes the Song's hearer at least to the desert's edges.

Elsewhere in scripture, the desert is typically a place traveled through on the
way to somewhere else. The paradigm case is the wandering of the people of Israel
through the desert on the way to the land of promise. Jeremiah 2:6 resonates with
Song 3:6 and provides the deep scriptural background for the Song's language
here (Jeremiah is contrasting the ancestors at the time of the desert wanderings
with the corrupt, decadent, and ever-complaining people of his time; cf. Deut.
8:2 for wanderings *per desertum*):

> They did not say, "Where is the Lord
> who brought us up [*ascendere nos fecit*] from the land of Egypt
> who led us through the desert [*per desertum*]
> through an uninhabitable and trackless land
> through a land of drought and darkness
> through a land in which no one walks
> and in which no one lives?" (Jer. 2:6)

To go through the desert is to undergo hardship as prelude to enjoying a promised good. The trope is purgatorial and thus expectant; this has close affinity with
and is deepened by the scriptural accounts of Elijah (1 Kgs. 19), John the Baptist
(Matt. 3:1–5 || Mark 1:2–8 || Luke 3:2–19), and Jesus (Matt. 4:1–11 || Luke
4:1–13) in the desert.

The trope of going up or ascending is often used in scripture to describe how
people—both Israelite and Gentile—get to Jerusalem. To get to that place one
always ascends, not because it has a higher elevation than all other places, but
because it is more important than every other place, a place whose elevation in the
Lord's eyes means that one can only go up to it. The English use the same metaphor
for Oxford: one always goes up to Oxford to study and then comes down from it
when one leaves, and not because it is topographically the highest point in England.
Jerusalem is gone up to because it is where the Lord lives, and that is by definition
always up, to be ascended to (Obad. 21; Isa. 2:3; Matt. 20:17 and parallels; Luke
2:42; 18:31; John 5:1). The cry of the people of Israel goes up (*ascendere*) to the
Lord (Exod. 2:23) in just the same way that the people go up out of Egypt and in
the same way that the Lord's temple in Jerusalem is a place to which one goes up

(2 Kgs. 23:2). And, according to the doctrine of the church, Jesus ascends to heaven forty days after Easter (John 20:17; Eph. 4:8). There is another scriptural resonance: something coming through or from the desert to the city may be a message from the Lord, something important to hear and understand. Isaiah, for example, speaks of a vision of the fall of Babylon coming to him *de deserto* ("from the desert") (Isa. 21:1). To ask, then, "what is this ascending through the desert?" is to ask about something on its way to the Lord, or to a place appointed by the Lord, something in transit through suffering to bliss, something being purged and prepared.

The first trope used to describe the approaching thing is "wisp of smoke." "Wisp" (*virgula*) occurs only here in the corpus of scripture, but "smoke" is commonly found elsewhere in that corpus, where it has three ranges of meaning. The first has to do with the transience of all things here below: the entire created order, including us, is like smoke before the Lord, soon to dissipate (Ps. 36:20 [= 37:20 RSV] [the *peccatores* will vanish like smoke]; 68:3 [= 68:2 RSV]; Isa. 51:6). The second is as a marker for the presence of the Lord: Sinai smokes when the Lord is on it (Exod. 19:18), and the temple fills with smoke when the Lord is there (Isa. 6:4). And the third is connected with sacrifices pleasing to the Lord: their smoke rises to him (Rev. 8:4; Josh. 8:20–21 [sacrifice of the entire city of Ai, with its population]). The approaching presence is then to be welcomed rather than understood as a threat: the Lord is present in and with it.

The wisp of smoke is "spiced with frankincense and myrrh." To be "spiced" is to smell good, to be prepared for love (→1:2–3a; →1:13). "Myrrh" occurs frequently in the Song. "Frankincense," by contrast, occurs only here and at 4:6. In scripture generally, frankincense makes whatever it is added to sweetly aromatic and therefore appropriate as an offering to the Lord (Lev. 2:1; 6:15; 24:7). It is to be brought in to Zion by the nations exactly as such (Jer. 17:26; 41:5; cf. Matt. 2:11, where the magi offer *tus* to the infant Jesus). The "perfumer" and his "powders" are mentioned only here in the Song and rarely elsewhere in scripture; the connotations, once again, are of sensory delight and care in preparation, all belonging to what is properly offered to the Lord.[96]

Solomon's Bed (3:7–8)

> See Solomon's bed—
> sixty strong men surround it
> from Israel's strongest
> each holding a sword
> supremely skilled in war
> each one's weapon on his thigh
> against the terrors of the night.

96. Strikingly, the memory of the dead and saintly Josiah is said in Sir. 49:1 to be like a blending of the smells *facta opere pigmentarii* ("made by the perfumer's work").

Something mysterious and beautiful approaches through the desert: so the daughters' question (if it is theirs) of 3:6 tells you. That question is implicitly answered in these verses with a description of "Solomon's bed," which is to be further identified as his "litter" in 3:9.[97] The impressionistically vivid description of King Solomon's bed/litter given here contains no explicit indication of whose voice speaks it. Its addressee is mentioned: the "daughters of Jerusalem/Zion" in 3:10–11. Perhaps it is the lover who speaks these words: he has adjured the daughters in 3:5; they question him in 3:6; and he responds in 3:7–11. But that is a tentative and speculative reading. What matters here is not so much the speaker, but rather the effect upon you, the hearer, of the atmosphere conjured in the question and response of 3:6 and 3:7–11.

The lover, if it is he, enjoins the daughters to go and look at "Solomon's bed," together with its retinue, which is described in strongly martial terms. "Sixty strong men surround it": there are also "sixty queens" (6:8) whose beauty the beloved's is said to exceed, but otherwise the number has no strong symbolic significance in scripture. It serves to indicate a large, but not vast, group of people. The retinue surrounding the bed is prepared for war: "each holding a sword . . . each one's weapon on his thigh." These are standard scriptural images of military readiness (Exod. 32:27; Ps. 45:4 [= 45:3 RSV]; Ezek. 21:18 [= 21:13 RSV]). The soldiers and their weapons are there "against the terrors of the night," a phrase not found elsewhere in the Song, but pregnantly present in Ps. 91:5, where those who take refuge in the Lord are said thereby to be liberated from "the terrors of the night" as well as from other evils and agonies. Solomon's retinue protects therefore—or is prepared to protect, garbed and caparisoned to protect—against what hope and trust in the Lord also protects against.

"Solomon's bed," therefore, "ascending through the desert" (3:6), carries with it the promise of the security and delight of the Lord's presence. To approach it, as the lover exhorts the daughters to do ("see"), is to approach the presence of the Lord, and if the lover is to be assimilated to Solomon—we have already seen reason to both affirm and deny such assimilation, noting the resonances in the Song between the two of them while also denying their simple identity—then the thought that the lover is the Lord and the beloved his Israel-church is deepened and given some new grace notes. Seeking and finding the Lord's embraces on his bed, seeking to be kissed and ravished by him, is to find not only ecstatic bliss but also the passion of security beyond threat. "The terrors of the night" thereby get transformed into the night's delights.

The "bed" (*lectulus*) has been mentioned twice before in the Song. The beloved has rhapsodized about the couple's "flowerful bed" (1:16) and has reported that she sought her lover "in my bed—night by night" (3:1). The "bed" in those places, and by implication also here, is a marriage bed, a place for lovemaking. But that

97. For the connection between the question of 3:6 and the description of Solomon's bed/litter, see Robert W. Jenson, *Song of Songs* (Louisville: Westminster John Knox, 2005), 40–43.

is not all. It is also a figure for the body of Mary-church. In Mary's body of flesh, Jesus's fleshly body was carried; from it, he emerged into the world; and upon it he sat as a child, to suck from his mother's breasts. There is here one of the roots of the title *sedes sapientiae* ("seat of wisdom") given to Mary by the Western church: she is Wisdom's (Jesus's) seat because he sits on her lap and was carried on her hip. These themes are deep in the fabric of Christian art, and these verses of the Song are both consonant with and illuminating of them.[98] It is especially striking that reading the Song in this way requires attention to the Song's beloved as at once Jesus's mother and his lover, his Israel-church. He, the lover-Lord, courts her and wants her and depicts her body as an object of desire; but he is also conceived in her, carried by her, born from her, nourished by her. This is a paradox only if you think that scripture should mean just one thing; one way of exercising such a preference is to prefer allegorical to figural reading, for then you are likely to see the text as a code to be cracked, and its tropes as corresponding one-to-one to some set of objects out there in the world. Those who hold such a view will want to constrain and reduce the gorgeous complexity of scripture: if the beloved allegorizes Mary, they will think, she cannot also allegorize the church; if she is the Lord's lover, how can she also be his mother? But the truth is that scripture has many, indeed endless, meanings. The Song's beloved can perfectly well figure the Lord's lover, his Israel-church, as well as his mother, whom he also loves. Indeed, this must be so if, as it is Christian doctrine to say, the church participates in Mary: what the Lord conceives in Mary is the Lord himself, and from this it follows at once that the marriage bed and the birthing bed are intimate with one another. "Solomon's bed" is both; and the woman he makes love to is the woman who bears him.

The same is true of you, in secondary and participated sense. As a member of Christ's body by baptism (if you are), you have been brought to birth in Christ. In that sense you are a child of the church. But exactly as that, exactly as one conceived and brought into being by the Lord's passion for you, you are the one the Lord wants to kiss with his "mouth's kiss" (1:2).

98. For this interpretation of Solomon's bed/litter I draw upon Honorius Augustodunensis, *Sigillum Beatae Mariae* (Seal of Blessed Mary), esp. 3.6 (English in *The Seal of Blessed Mary*, trans. Amelia Carr [Toronto: Peregrine, 1991], 63–64). For extended discussion and summary of this work, see Rachel Fulton, *From Judgment to Passion: Devotion to Christ and the Virgin Mary, 800–1200* (New York: Columbia University Press, 2002); for more technical considerations, see Valerie Flint, "The Commentaries of Honorius Augustodunensis on the Song of Songs," *Revue Bénédictine* 84 (1974): 196–211. The only visual representation I have seen of Solomon's bed as Mary's body is reproduced and discussed in Kalliroe Linardou, "The Couch of Solomon, a Monk, a Byzantine Lady, and the Song of Songs," in *The Church and Mary*, ed. R. N. Swanson (Woodbridge, Suffolk: Boydell, 2004), 73–85, which is an analysis of two copies of an illuminated twelfth-century Greek manuscript of sermons on the life of Mary by the Byzantine monk James of Kokkinabaphos. For him, "the Couch [i.e., the *lectulus* or *ferculum*] prefigured primarily the all-holy Mother of God" (p. 76). Cf. Rupert of Deutz: "Et quis ille lectus est, nisi uterus tuus, dilecta dilecti, uterus virginalis" (*Commentaria in Canticum Canticorum* [Commentary on the Song] on Song 3:7 [Deutz and Deutz 2005: 272]).

Solomon's Litter (3:9–10a)

> King Solomon made himself a litter
> from Lebanese trees—
> its pillars he made of silver
> its seat of gold
> its step of purple
> its middle ebony-inlaid.

Solomon's "bed," in the immediately preceding verses, is also his "litter." Here it is described in luxurious terms—silver pillars, golden seat, purple step, "middle" (probably to be understood as "floor") "ebony-inlaid," the whole made of "Lebanese trees." The connotations are of kingly power, but also, and more profoundly, of the presence of the Lord. The vocabulary used for the litter is unambiguously and consistently positive when it occurs elsewhere in the Song. Lebanon, where the timber for the litter's construction comes from, is mentioned six times in the Song, second in frequency only to Jerusalem among place-names; and it is always a good place. The beloved is urged to come up therefrom (4:8), her clothes smell like Lebanon (4:11), the garden's living waters flow from Lebanon (4:15), and the beloved's nose is like the Damascus-facing tower of Lebanon (7:5). To say that Solomon's litter is made "from Lebanese trees" is therefore to say that is it made of the best possible wood, the most beautiful and most fragrant.[99] Similarly with "silver," "gold," and "purple": these words resonate elsewhere in the Song with beauty and richness (5:14–15; 7:6; 8:9). "Ebony" is the exception: it occurs only here in the Song, as also do the words for the parts of the litter ("seat," "step," "middle").

Elsewhere in scripture, the collocation of terms used to describe Solomon's litter here in the Song is found in most concentrated form in the descriptions in the book of Exodus of the ark of the covenant's construction and ornamentation. The veil of the ark, for example, is to be hung upon "four gold-plated columns of acacia wood, which shall have golden hooks and stand on silver pedestals" (Exod. 26:32; cf. 27:1 and passim). "Purple," as well as being a royal color in scripture (1 Macc. 10:62; Mark 15:17–20 [Jesus prepared for crucifixion]), is one of the colors of which both the ark's veil (Exod. 26–27) and the ephod (28:15; 39:5), the high priest's vestment, are to be made.

The description of Solomon's bed coming up through the desert and attended by its military guard evokes the Lord of Hosts coming armed to meet and ravish his lover. The description of his litter, in all its seductive gorgeousness, evokes the very presence of the Lord, being carried by the faithful in his ark toward the consummation of his love for his Israel and his church—approaching too the annunciation of his conception in the womb of his ecclesial daughter, Mary; and,

---

99. Cf. the scriptural connection between cedar trees and Lebanon in →1:17. See J. Cheryl Exum, *Song of Songs: A Commentary* (Louisville: Westminster John Knox, 2005), 170–71, on the symbolic connotations of Lebanon.

of course, approaching you, the Song's hearer, as someone he hopes very much to bed, to wrap in his warm embrace. A scripturally serious reading of these verses of the Song cannot avoid the resonances with the protective and seductive power of the Lord (he who transforms the night from a time of terror to a time for love), as well as those with the concentrated presence of the Lord in his litter/ark. The name "Solomon" serves as the mediating symbol here, but the approaching presence mentioned is that of the Lord himself.

These meanings are evident as soon as the Song is read as a book of scripture; the Marian meaning is not, however: perceiving it requires catechesis in the dogmatic teaching of the church, which is not to say that Mary's presence in the text is any less real than the church's and Israel's and yours. The reading just given of 3:7–8, according to which the "bed" is certainly a bed, bearing Solomon to his wedding, but also a figure for Mary's body, carrying Jesus to his birth, applies to the verses under consideration here as well and is deepened by the presence in them of temple tropes, and especially of those having to do with the ark of the covenant.[100] The flesh of Mary, bearing within it the flesh of Christ, has the ark, bearing within it the Lord's presence, as its first and best figure.

Solomon's Wedding (3:10b–11)

> O daughters of Jerusalem
> O daughters of Zion
> go out and see King Solomon
> diademed as his mother crowned him
> on the day of his wedding
> on the day of his heart's joy.

The surface of the text remains, however, neither erased nor called into question by these deeper meanings. In 3:11 we hear the lover urging the daughters to "go out and see King Solomon" prepared for his wedding, "diademed as his mother crowned him." The "diadem" and the "crown" are not mentioned elsewhere in the Song, though they clearly resonate most strongly with the clusters of royal tropes in the Song's first and last chapters (1:4, 12; 7:6; 8:11–12). In scripture as a whole, the "diadem" may be an ornament of both priest and king. When Aaron is dressed, vested for the Lord's service, his ornaments include a diadem made of purest gold with the inscription *sanctum Domino* ("holy to the Lord") incised upon it (Exod. 39:27–30; cf. Lev. 8:9; Exod. 29:6).[101] And kings and queens

---

100. On the application of temple imagery to the church, see *Lumen Gentium* 6 (Latin and English in Tanner 1990: 851–52).

101. George Herbert's poem "Aaron" plays with this image, beginning: "Holinesse on the head," and then beginning each subsequent verse with a mention of what is in or on the priest's head—profaneness, Christ, and so on; *The English Poems of George Herbert*, ed. Helen Wilcox (Cambridge:

too are frequently said to be given the diadem as a mark of royal office (Joash in 2 Kgs. 11:12; Vashti in Esth. 1:11). The same is true of the language of crowning. For Christians, the paradigm case is that of Jesus, crowned (*coronare*) with thorns (Matt. 27:29 ‖ Mark 15:17). The language of Song 3:11, therefore, depicts a man, Solomon, being consecrated—made holy—for union with his beloved. The consecration is a matter of delight for him: it is "the day of his heart's joy."

The merging and separation and overlapping of the Song's characters reaches a high pitch. The lover (if it is he who speaks) urges the daughters (it is explicitly they who are addressed) to go and see the approach of the king, described as if he figured the Lord approaching in power in his ark/litter/bed. Solomon becomes hazy before and translucent to the Lord, shuddering and dissolving into him. But then, Solomon is limned as one being prepared for marriage, for delightful union with this beloved who is, the Song's scripturally attuned hearers already know, the Lord's Israel-church, his immaculate "only one" (6:9), and therefore each of us, his eager but unclean beloveds, "black but lovely" (1:5) as we inevitably are. Here, the lover in the Song and the king in the Song blur and fade into one: they, as figures for the Lord, show their passionate desire for the beloved; and we, the Song's hearers, have forced upon us again the deeply disquieting truth that the Lord wants us as much as we want him.

There is a difficulty in the concluding verse of this part of the Song, into which I cannot see far; it is the mention of Solomon's "mother," who has "crowned him"—presumably on the day of his coronation as king but possibly also (or instead) as part of the preparation for his wedding. The scriptural-historical Solomon's mother was Bathsheba. I cannot see how to weave her into the Song. If, though, you consider Solomon as a figure for Christ, then the mention of his mother is a mention of Mary, and her crowning of him is with a diadem of flesh as she consents to his incarnation, which is to say his conception in her body.

Her Dove-Eyes #2 (4:1a)

> How beautiful you are, O my beloved,
> how beautiful you are—
> your dove-eyes
> through your veil;

The lover apostrophizes his beloved doubly: "How beautiful you are . . . how beautiful you are." The doubling intensifies the effect on the hearer. There is no indication whatever within the Song of any connection between this renewed address of the lover to his beloved and the immediately preceding description of Solomon's bed and litter. This is among the more vertiginous transitions in the

---

Cambridge University Press, 2007), 600–601. Herbert's use of Exod. 29, with the Song behind and before it, is an excellent instance (and has served as a model) of the way I read scripture.

Song, and it deepens the impression that the Song as a whole, when considered simply in terms of its formal structure, is a sequence of lyric poems—or, perhaps better, a large lyric with many small sublyrics, an anthological Song as well as a superlative one.

The first part of the body praised by the lover is the "eyes," here seen as "doves," veiled. The phrase "dove-eyes" has already been used in →1:15. The "veil" is mentioned thrice in the Song (4:1; →4:3b; 6:7). Here it will suffice to say that likening her "eyes" to "doves" is to liken them to the Lord's Israel-dove, his most beautiful beloved, and to liken them—and by extension her—to something chosen and approved by the Lord. They are veiled because their beauty would otherwise be too radiant: the world, and the gaze of the lover, must be protected from them (→4:9; →6:5).

Following the double apostrophe, the lover begins to specify the particular physical beauties of the beloved. This enterprise continues until the end of 4:5. The lover praises the beloved's body by mentioning and praising seven body parts: eyes, hair, teeth, lips, cheeks, neck, and breasts. Each body part is given at least one epithet to praise and specify the beauties proper to itself. And the order of address to the parts is approximately downward from the top of the head to the breasts. These verses are not the only ones in which the beloved's body is praised. There is another version of the same hymn of praise at 6:5–7, in which what the lover says about the beloved's hair, teeth, eyes, and cheeks in 4:1–5 is repeated largely verbatim, though without mention of the lips, neck, and breasts. And there is a significantly different praise-hymn to the beloved's body in 7:2–6, where her feet, thighs, vulva, belly, breasts, neck, eyes, nose, and head/hair are each described and praised. The order in Song 7 is from the ground up (feet to head), and that list mentions five parts of her body (feet, thighs, vulva, belly, nose) unmentioned in Song 4 and partly repeated in Song 6. Taking all three lists together, we find the lover praising twelve parts of his beloved's body: head/hair, eyes, nose, lips, teeth, cheeks, neck, breasts, belly, vulva, thighs, and feet.

That the beloved's body is hymned in three separate places in the Song is immediately striking to the hearer: the repetition of praise to the head, eyes, breasts, thighs, and so on produces a frisson of delighted desire in the hearer's mind reflective of that expressed by the lover. This is not pornography: definitive of that genre is that its only point is to arouse sexual desire in its hearers, and to do so in a way that precludes the full expression of that desire in the love of another human being. But it is nevertheless clear that among the Song's effects is arousal, and that if it is heard figurally rather than allegorically that effect must remain. We do hear the lover's words of desire for intercourse with his beloved; we do hear his delight in the particularities of her body (and hers in his); and we do hear the back-and-forth modulation between the language of delight and desire found in each of these three body-hymns. We respond accordingly, as we should. But that is not all: the body's delights as depicted in the Song point beyond themselves without erasing themselves.

The relation between delight and desire in the body-hymns is important, and awareness of it on the part of hearers is deepened by the repetition. What the lover says in praise of the beloved's body in 4:1–5 he largely repeats in summary form in 6:5–7 and then elaborates in rather different form in 7:2–6. Each of these body-hymns ends with a strong affirmation of the beloved's unmatched and unique beauty (4:7; 6:8–9; 7:7). In each case too, though with somewhat less clarity in Song 6 than in Song 4 and Song 7, the language of delighted appreciation in the body-hymns transmutes into the franker and more direct language of desire: after her body has been praised and the uniqueness of its beauty affirmed, the lover speaks at once in tones of urgent passion (4:6–13; 7:9–10). Delighted appreciation becomes urgent passion, and this modulation, thrice repeated, is what leaves the strongest impression upon the hearer.[102]

The placement of the body-hymns in the Song is also important to note, even if unlikely to be noted at first or second hearing. The first hymn, with its coda of explicit sexual desire, prepares for the nuptial imagery of the end of Song 4: he calls her "bride" for the first time in 4:8, and the language heightens and deepens until the culmination described in 5:1, the chiastic center of the Song as a whole, in which the couple makes love in the garden. Immediately following that climax, there is another song of separation on her lips (5:2–8), analogous in form to that in →3:1–4; both of those close with the caesura of the adjuration formula, and what then follows (5:10–16) is a praise-hymn to his body and its parts spoken by her. After some exchange between the daughters and the beloved about the delights of the lover (6:1–3), his voice speaks again (6:5–7), with a partial repetition of the body-hymn of 4:1–5. Then, after a question and response by the daughters and (perhaps) the lover (6:10–7:1), there is the third body-hymn (7:2–6), more elaborate and ornate than either of the first two, and less clearly spoken by the lover (→7:2–6 should perhaps be attributed to the daughters of Jerusalem).

Given this brief structural comment, the body-hymns find their meaning deepened. The centerpiece of the Song (5:1), where the couple's desire finds its sexual culmination, now appears as bracketed by them. The first of them prepares for it; there is then a moment of separation; and the second and third body-hymns—with the addition of her praises of his body in Song 5 as a fourth body-hymn—begin the rhythm once again of preparation for the union of intercourse, represented obscurely in the puzzling culmination(s) of Song 8. There is a figure here for the fundamental structure of our relations to the Lord: the passion-fueled approach, the kiss, the ever-more-intimate caress, the joining of bodies in intercourse, the withdrawal, the fall away, the sadness of separation, the renewal of passion, the new approach. . . . One of the sadnesses that human lovers have is that they cannot always be making love: mundane needs and the very nature of the body require that other things be done. A deeper grief for the Lord's lovers is that their greatest

102. Much the same modulation of delight into desire can be heard in the beloved's hymn of praise to her lover's body in →5:10–16.

intimacies with him—the eating of his flesh and the drinking of his blood—are punctuated with withdrawal and separation. There is a rhythm to these matters very like that of the Song's structure, a stammering rhythm of approach and retreat; it is a rhythm most perfectly evident in the order of the Mass, the church's most intimate lovemaking with the Lord. That too, in its inner structure, is ordered around approach and withdrawal. The Mass begins with an approach to the altar of the Lord from which we almost at once withdraw, confessing our sinfulness and asking for mercy; then we approach again, by means of the liturgy of the word, caressed by and bathed in the Lord's speech to us; and then we pause, withdrawing again into preparation for the consecration of the bread and the wine; and as that approaches its high point—surely, now, we are about to have the Lord's body enter ours, with praise and thanksgiving—we must again withdraw, confessing our desolation (*non sum dignus*) at our incapacity to love the Lord and be loved by him. There is a template and a figure for all this in the literary structure of the Song.

The lover praises his beloved's body first as beautiful and second as desirable. The difference is important, even though the distinction between delighted appreciation of beauty and desire for closer physical contact with it is not clear or precise. It is rare for us to be dazzled by beauty—to have *admiratio* for it—without seeking some kind of intimacy with it. Appreciative delight is itself a kind of intimacy, even if not a physical kind. But still, there is a different tone and valence: wanting to kiss a pair of lips or stroke and suck a pair of breasts is not in all respects the same as appreciating their color or shapeliness. It is a commonplace that appreciation of beauty can be heightened by certainty that there will be no physical intimacy with it; and in the converse case, appreciation for and delight in beauty may not survive physical intimacy with it, and will certainly be altered thereby. In the speech under consideration here, the tone is predominantly one of appreciation or delight with only one or two top notes of overt desire, and even those by implication rather than explicitly stated. This is certainly not always the case in the Song: in 1:2–4 she positively pants for his kisses and caresses; in 3:1–4 she is desperate for his presence in her bed; in 4:16–5:1 he urges her toward him and she reciprocates; in 5:4–6 she trembles with desire for him and opens herself to him; in 6:4–5 he is disturbed—even injured, hurt, damaged—by passion for her and by her effects upon him; and in 7:9–10 there is explicit and overt talk of desire for closer physical contact; and so forth. But not here: in 4:1–6 there are no verbs of appetite or desire, no mention of the need for closer contact: everything he says about her body is said to her, directly; and all of it uses the language of the eyes: he tells her how she looks to him, not that he wants to touch or smell or taste her (contrast 7:9–10!). Looking requires some distance, and most of the images conjured in these verses suggest the appreciation of a body from the middle distance. He hymns her to herself, encouraging her to take appreciative pleasure in her own loveliness.

The vocabulary, diction, and mood of delight is an offering rather than an asking. The lover's gaze of appreciation and his verbal rendering of what that gaze

sees offer to the beloved his appreciation of her and, in making that offering, give
to her a state of being she could not have given herself. That is the condition of
being a beloved. This is part of the ordinary dynamic exchange of love: when you
are given the gift of being delighted in, you are made new by it, transfigured in
its light. You become capable, by way of this gift, of offering it to others, of taking delight in them. Becoming a beloved makes possible being a lover, and this
is signaled by the Song's vocabulary of delight, which is especially clear in 4:1–6.
When the language of delight is coupled with that of desire, as it is elsewhere in
the Song, offering is supplemented by demand. That too is a gift, but one of a
very different kind: its acceptance requires that the beloved fully accept her new
status exactly by returning it, by delighting in, and then by urgently demanding
responsive intimacy with the one who gave it to her. But that move is not made
in these verses.

The Song's lover figures the Lord, and so his gift to the beloved of her condition as beloved is exactly the gift he gives to you, the Song's hearer. You can see
this with greatest clarity, and allow it to work on you with most effect, if you
discipline yourself in your reading toward an understanding that you participate
in the Song's beloved: that her constitution as a beloved is also yours, and that
you, like her, are made capable of being a lover in your turn by the Lord's gaze of
appreciative delight directed at you. This is, first and last, a matter of theology,
of thinking responsively in relation to the words the Lord has given us to speak of
himself (specifically in this case the words of 4:1–6); but such responsive thinking
configures, if you let it, not only your thoughts about the Lord and yourself, but
also your thoughts about yourself and your human lovers. While the theology is
primary, the Lord's love being strictly prevenient, it is not the only thing. There
is a world with lovers in it: the Song's lovers are among them, in a world of figs
and myrrh and walled cities and spring-quickened vineyards and errant foxes; you
too are among them, and the gift exchange of the appreciative gaze, the look of
delight, relates you to your lover(s) by means of a set of relations formally (though
not substantively) identical with those that relate the Lord's lovingly delighted
gaze to you. As you gaze with delight upon your lover, you give to him or her a
gift of the same kind that the Lord gives you: the gift of being beloved and thus
enabled to love. And, of course, you receive it back. In all cases—the Lord's gaze
upon you, yours upon your lover, your lover's upon you—the gift is the same, and
the range of its possible failures also the same: all that needs to happen for the
gift of the delighted gaze to fail as gift, to fail at making its recipient a beloved,
is for it to be refused, for its intended recipient to turn her gaze away from her
lover and (most often) toward her mirror in which she can see only herself. That
is the ordinary structure of sin.

The Lord's delighted appreciation of you participates in his delighted appreciation of Mary and of his chosen people, his Israel-church. He looks on them with
special delight, just as he looks on you. The case of Mary is the most illuminating.
Is there something especially delightful about her, some merit or beauty or purity

of will and heart such that the Lord looks with particular appreciation on her? Or is it that she becomes especially delightful to the Lord because she accepts without reservation the gift the Lord offers her? This seems a natural, perhaps unavoidable, way to put the question; we can ask it in that way about the Lord's election of his Israel-church, as well. But in fact the question cannot be answered when put so baldly. That is because it presupposes a separateness and competition between divine and human agency that is not in fact in play. Mary is especially delightful to the Lord, more so than any other woman (*benedicta tu in mulieribus*), but neither solely because of something she has done to make herself so nor solely because of something the Lord has done to ornament her and make her so. Rather, it is the Lord's characteristic way of working to make his blessings for the world—in this case his appreciative delight in its beauties, the beautiful ones who are in it—available to the world by way of particularity. The Lord chooses Mary as the paradigmatic delightful one not because there is something intrinsically delightful or beautiful about her, something of that sort proper to herself. Rather, he needs a *theotokos*, a woman to bear himself; and the world is providentially ordered in such a way as to bring into being a woman immaculate, undamaged by the otherwise universal compulsively self-deranging tendency, to whom exactly that offer can be made. All Mary's beauties are, therefore, sheer gift, as are those of Israel-church. They are none the less real for that. Mary could have refused the gift the angel announced to her, and it is her special beauty and glory not to have done so. But her acceptance of that gift, supervening upon the prevenient gift of her immaculate conception, is not hers over against or independently of the Lord. It is, rather, fully hers and fully the Lord's, at once and noncompetitively. And so the Lord delights in her beauty, her "cheeks like a fragment of pomegranate / through [her] veil" (4:3), her "breasts like two fawns / doe-born twins" (4:5), as hers but also his, hers because his. The same is true of his delight in your beauty; what distinguishes his delight in that from his delight in Mary's is that yours figures and participates in hers, while the reverse is not true.

Her Hair (4:1b)

> your hair like a flock of nanny goats
> coming down from Mount Gilead;

"Hair," to a greater degree than any of the other parts of the body depicted and praised in the Song, can be changed at will, rapidly and frequently: it can be cut off, grown long, augmented artificially, dyed, arranged, ornamented, veiled, displayed, and so on (Chrétien 2005: chap. 9). The same is not true for the breasts or the cheeks or the eyes, not even for those with money to spend on surgical alteration. The ease with which the hair can be altered or removed has contributed to the importance given it as a signifier: Buddhist monks shave their heads; some

Christian ones adopt a tonsure; male Sikhs do not cut their hair; particular arrangements and quantities of hair often signal sexual availability or its absence; and the adornment and treatment of the hair—the use of ornaments for it, the addition or removal of color from it, the alteration of its texture, its use to differentiate men from women and both from children—is always the focus of much cultural time and attention and resource. All this is reflected in the Song's depiction of hair, as well as in the scriptural background to that depiction.[103] There is, however, so far as I can see, no well-developed scriptural grammar of the hair, which means that the commentarial tradition offers a wide range of interpretive possibilities in dealing with the Song's mentions of hair (see Chrétien 2005: 184).

The Song uses a variety of words for the hair: *capillus* ("hair" generically), *coma* ("tress"), and *cincinnus* ("ringlet"). The lover praises the beloved's "hair" twice, in almost-verbatim terms, as "like a flock of nanny goats / coming down from Mount Gilead" (4:1; 6:5). And in his third sequence of praises to her body, he says: "Your head like Carmel / its tresses like purple / the king captured by your ringlets" (7:6), bringing together two of the hair words in successive clauses. He describes his own head and locks of hair as he asks her to open the door to him so that they might make love: "Open to me . . . / for my head is full of dew / and my ringlets of the moisture of the night" (5:2). And she, praising his body to the daughters, says: "His head is of the best gold / ringlets like palm fronds / raven-black" (5:11).

The imagery is in part familiar and suggestive to a contemporary user of English: we can at once see what is meant—or something of what is meant—by likening his ringlets to "palm fronds" (they hang down, they are decorative); and the erotic overtones of his description of his ringlets as "full of night moisture" is clear enough. But some of the imagery does not, for us, carry much meaning on its face. Why does he liken her hair to a "flock of nanny goats"? Why the connection with "Mount Gilead"? What is the meaning of likening her head to "Carmel"?

As to the "nanny goats," not much help is to be had from scripture, where, although they are mentioned frequently, it is only as sacrificial animals (Gen. 15:9; 30:32–35; Lev. 3–5; Num. 15:27; cf. the use of *caprae* skins to protect the tabernacle in Exod. 35–36) or, occasionally, as types of the agile and the swift (2 Sam. 2:18; 1 Chr. 12:9 [= 12:8 RSV]). "Mount Gilead," mentioned only in connection with the beloved's hair in the Song (4:1; 6:5), is elsewhere in scripture a hilly or almost-mountainous area of land east of the Jordan, belonging to the tribes of Gad, Reuben, and Manasseh (Num. 32:33–42; Deut. 3:12–17). The image is of a woman's hair cascading or undulating down her back, as fluid in

103. Hair is arranged and adorned for delight and seduction (Jdt. 16:8; 1 Pet. 3:3). Shaving of the head's hair (*capillus*) is an act of purification (Num. 6:18; Judg. 16:22). On the long hair of women and the short hair of men and its meaning, see 1 Cor. 11:14. Hair is representative of male strength (Judg. 16). And hair is something by which prophets can be lifted toward the Lord (Ezek. 8:3; Dan. 14:36 [= Bel and the Dragon 36 RSV]). See also Mary's wiping of Jesus's feet with her *capilli* in John 12 and parallels.

movement as that of agile animals seen from a distance descending a mountain slope. Mount "Carmel," to which her head with its tresses like purple is likened, is, scripturally, the place of Elijah (1 Kgs. 18) and Elisha (2 Kgs. 2–4), as well as a place of refuge from the authorities (Amos 9:3). Her head, with its tresses, is, given this likeness, a holy place, a place in which, with its luxuriant hair, her lover would like to find refuge. Kings may be captured by the luxuriance of her hair—there is resonance here again with the hazy image of Solomon as her lover; her hair, like "purple," is royally attractive, and the connection is made explicit by the mention of the capture of kings and is implicit in the resonance of this mention of purple with the Song's only other use of the term, in the description of Solomon's bed/litter (3:10).

Her Teeth (4:2)

> your teeth like a flock of shorn sheep
> ascending from the bath
> each pregnant with twins
> not a sterile one among them;

The "teeth" (*dentes*) are mentioned thrice in the Song. Twice, using almost identical words, the lover says to the beloved, "Your teeth [are] like a flock of shorn sheep / ascending from the bath / each pregnant with twins / not a sterile one among them" (4:2; 6:6). And once, when the lover is likening her throat to the best wine, she interjects and says, "Worthy to be sipped by my delightful man / ruminated by his lips and teeth" (7:10).

In the twice-repeated simile of the "teeth" like "shorn sheep," the point is to extol the beauty of the beloved's teeth by describing them with the vocabulary of delight.[104] The sheep to which they are likened are in every respect good: they are clean ("ascending from the bath"), with their true and beautiful shape readily apparent because they are "shorn"; and because both of these things are true, the teeth are, it is implied, radiantly white. They are also well rounded and beautifully shaped, as the trope of pregnancy suggests. The lover likes to look upon her teeth because of all these things. This is almost the only place in scripture where the teeth are depicted as beautiful; generally speaking they are depicted as violent and threatening (they gnash, they devour, they consume—Deut. 32:24; Job 16:9; 41:6 [= 41:14 RSV]; Ps. 3:8 [= 3:7 RSV]; 37:12; Lam. 2:16; Dan. 7:7; Matt. 24:51; Mark 9:18), or as instruments for lament, to be ground along with the weeping and wailing proper to those who suffer.[105] Insofar, then, as

104. I draw in this paragraph, and throughout this discussion of the teeth, upon Chrétien 2005: chap. 3.

105. In addition to Song 4:2 and 6:6, the only other scriptural place in which the *dentes* are depicted as beautiful is Gen. 49:12, describing Judah's teeth.

there is a scriptural grammar of dental beauty, the Song provides it. The idea that each of the beloved's beautifully white teeth is, as it were, rounded with pregnancy, is emphasized by the mention of "twins" (*gemellas*). Her breasts are likened to twins elsewhere in the Song (4:5; 7:4), for obvious reasons; and here too the canon of scripture does not provide much by way of resonant help for understanding this word.[106]

The connection of teeth with "chewing" (*ruminare*) in 7:10 provides another element in the grammar of the teeth. They chew and make digestible and nourishing what would otherwise not be so. The teeth of the body do this with food, obviously; but these are not the only teeth we have, and it is a commonplace of the tradition to say that the text of scripture is a proper object for rumination and mastication (→1:2).[107] This is so because scripture's meaning is not exhaustible: the hearer must return to it again and again in order to get from it all the nourishment it can provide by chewing it over with the teeth of the mind. The beloved's teeth, because of their shapely beauty, are especially well equipped for that kind of rumination: and the Lord's Israel ruminates the Torah ceaselessly with her fertile ("not a sterile one among them") teeth, giving birth as she does so to an ever-deeper understanding of that Torah; the Lord's church does the same with the canon of scripture, masticating it with her baptism-washed ("ascending from the bath") teeth; and Mary, nonfigurally pregnant with the Word, ruminates the words given to her by the announcing angel, pondering them in her heart (Luke 2:19).

It is one thing to contemplate the beloved's teeth as a figure for your own; the comments just made may be of help in understanding what it is to do that. It is another to wish to use your teeth to chew and eat the beloved: "let him eat his best fruits" (5:1), she says to him speaking of herself; and "worthy to be sipped" (7:10), she says of her own throat, offering it to him for just that purpose. The Song encourages both thoughts. In doing so it illuminates one of the fundamental desires of human lovemaking, which is to ingest the beloved, to make her (or him) so fully part of yourself, the lover, that her (or his) physical being can no longer be separated from your own. The figure of the toothsome and lickable beloved in the Song sheds light in two directions at once: toward our physical loves, and toward the eucharistic act of eating.

106. The adjective *gemellas* occurs outside the Song in scripture only at Exod. 36:29, where it describes some doubled features in the construction of the tabernacle. The word *gemini* is used at Gen. 25:24 and 38:27 to describe Jacob and Esau.

107. On ruminating scripture, see Augustine, *De doctrina christiana* 2.6.8 (in *Sant'Agostino: La Dottrina Christiana*, ed. and trans. Vincenzo Tarulli, Opere di Sant'Agostino 8 [Rome: Città Nuova, 1992], 66), in turn discussed in Chrétien 2005: 74–78. For a medieval statement, see Hugh of St. Victor, *Didascalicon: De studio legendi* (Teaching Handbook: The Practice of Reading) 3.10–11 (English in *The Didascalicon of Hugh of St. Victor*, trans. Jerome Taylor [New York: Columbia University Press, 1961], 92–93; Latin in *Hugonis de Sancto Victore Didascalicon de studio legendi*, ed. Charles Buttimer [Washington, DC: Catholic University of America Press, 1939]).

Her Lips (4:3a)

> your lips like a scarlet thread
> and your speech sweet;

The lover turns his praises to her "lips" and "speech," a natural progression from the praise of her "teeth," just discussed. The tropes here—the "scarlet thread" of the lips, especially—appeared in →1:2.

Her Cheeks (4:3b)

> your cheeks like a fragment of pomegranate
> through your veil;

From the teeth to the "lips" to the "cheeks": these words occur again in the Song (6:7; cf. 7:13), almost verbatim, as part of the second body-hymn. The "cheeks" have already been mentioned (→1:10). What is new here in the Song is the mention of the "pomegranate" (*malum punicum*). This fruit has a prominent place in the Song and elsewhere in scripture. When the lover is likening the beloved to a garden (4:12–16), he says, "Your shoots are a paradise of pomegranates" (4:13). Twice (6:11; 7:13), the flowering or budding of the pomegranate is mentioned as a sign of spring, something the couple must go out to look for. And, in the Song's final chapter, the beloved promises to lead her lover into her mother's house there to give him "the pressed juice of my pomegranates" (8:2). In addition to beauty, the surface sense here has to do with fertility. The beloved, as a garden, is budding and shooting and growing: the "paradise" of her fruitfulness is for her lover. This connotation is still clearer when she offers him the "pressed juice" of her pomegranates: this is an offer of her fertility, and perhaps also of her virginity. Pomegranates are beautiful and luscious, beckoning the eye and the mouth, offering delight.

These meanings are deepened and made more complex by observing what is said about pomegranates elsewhere in scripture. They are embroidered upon the high priest's robe (Exod. 28:33; 39:24; Sir. 45:8 [= 45:9 RSV]), carved into the capitals of the pillars of Solomon's house, and used to adorn the temple's pillars (1 Kgs. 7:18, 42; 2 Kgs. 25:17; 2 Chr. 3:16; 4:13; Jer. 52:22–23). Pomegranates are also, as in the Song, mentioned as types of something good to look at and delicious to eat (Num. 20:5; Deut. 8:8; Hag. 2:19).[108] They signal, that is, the presence of the Lord, adorning what is close to that presence and what mediates it to the people

---

108. Gregory of Nyssa, *Homiliae in canticum canticorum* 9 on Song 4:13 (Greek in *Gregorii Nysseni Opera*, vol. 6: *In Canticum Canticorum*, ed. Herman Langerbeck [Leiden: Brill, 1960], 282–84), has an interesting discussion of the pomegranate, emphasizing the difference between its unprepossessing outside and its sweet inside.

of Israel. When the beloved's cheeks are likened to them, they are also likened to something intimate with the glory of the Lord, with the radiance that belongs to the Lord's presence. Her cheeks, pomegranatelike, adorn that glory. The lover's connection of the pomegranate trope with the image of the veil belongs in this context too. Those things especially proximate to the Lord's presence—such as the ark of the covenant (Exod. 36:19; cf. Heb. 6:19–20; 9:1–5) and Moses's face after he has spoken with the Lord on the mountain (Exod. 34–35; cf. 2 Cor. 3:12–18)—must be veiled in order that their radiance, given them exactly by their proximity to and participation in the Lord's radiance, not bedazzle those who see them.[109] To describe the beloved's cheeks as veiled pomegranate fragments, then, is at once to assimilate them to things that have been—and will again be—intimate with the Lord. The radiant beauty of her cheeks is not merely hers, on this reading, but a gift from the Lord, her lover. That is why it is veiled.

The beloved's cheeks—and, by extension, her entire body—receives their blushingly fertile beauty from the Lord who loves them. Her body is given to her as the body of a beloved by his loving her. She is not beautiful in her own right; she receives her beauty when she becomes a beloved, when she is fallen in love with by her lover, when she is in that way given to herself as one who can love because she is loved. That is true too of the Lord's Israel-church: the veiled pomegranate fragments of the cheeks of the people of the Lord have the beauty they have (it is real, but it is always damaged, scarred, pitted, scored by refusal of the lover's kisses) only because, and just to the extent that, the Lord has chosen to love them, to seek them out for kissing. When the church speaks of herself as a sacrament,[110] an outward and visible sign of the grace of the Lord's love, she speaks of her veiled pomegranate cheeks.

Her Neck (4:4)

> your neck like David's tower
> built with battlements
> hung with a thousand shields
> with all the armor of the strong;

The lover turns next to her "neck," already mentioned in →1:10 as a well-fortified and beautifully adorned place to which only he, the lover, has access. The "tower," to which her neck is likened here, is always in scripture a place of strength (Judg. 9:51; 1 Macc. 6:37; Luke 14:28), built against potential attackers. Casting down a tower overcomes the strength of those who built it and may result in the yoking

---

109. "House of the veil" serves as periphrasis for the inner sanctum of the temple (Sir. 50:5). For the Song's theme of veiling, see Jill M. Munro, *Spikenard and Saffron: The Imagery of the Song of Songs* (Sheffield: Sheffield Academic Press, 1995), 52–66.
110. *Lumen Gentium* 1 (Latin and English in Tanner 1990: 849).

of their necks in slavery. The only truly impregnable tower is the name of the Lord: "The name of the Lord is a supremely strong tower: / the just run to it and will be exalted" (*turris fortissima nomen Domini; / ad ipsum currit iustus et exaltabitur*) (Prov. 18:10). The extent to which her neck's towerlike strength is praised is the extent to which it is assimilated to the Lord's strength. He, as her lover, imparts to her, as his beloved, his own strength, and in hymning her neck he praises exactly this. But the grammar of the neck is not exclusively one of strength and status; it is also one of delight. The neck is also, in scripture, a part of the body to be embraced, indicating joy at the presence of the one whose neck you might fall upon in this way (Gen. 33:4; 45:14; 46:29). That too is the lover's attitude to his beloved's neck. These images of the tower of David and the "ivory tower" (→7:5) have long been applied by the church to Mary, and insofar as Mary figures the church and the church participates in her, they also apply to the church. The ivorine tower, incapable of being overthrown by anyone except the Lord, ready for the Lord's ornamentation ("beautiful . . . with necklaces"; 1:10), is the Marian church.[111]

Her Breasts (4:5)

> your two breasts like two fawns
> doe-born twins
> grazing among lilies.

The lover grazes downward, verbally and visually, moving from the beloved's "neck" to her "breasts." The first two lines ("your two breasts like two fawns / doe-born twins") occur verbatim in the third body-hymn, at 7:4. All the tropes in these lines have already been discussed ("breasts" in →1:13; deer in →2:7; "lilies" and "grazing" in →1:7). The application to her—more specifically to her "breasts"—by him of imagery elsewhere used by her of him (she says of or to him that he "grazes among lilies" in 2:16 and 6:3) provides an excellent example of the already mentioned boundary-blurring between the two. What she says of him he often says of her; and what he says of her she often says of him. This free transfer of epithets—not all epithets are thus transferred, but many are—moves you deeper into the creative space of puzzlement, in which it is productively unclear who is addressing whom. When she speaks of and to him as he speaks of and to her, something about the nature of love becomes clearer: each partner wishes to be seen by the other as (s)he sees the other. The application of this ordinary fact about human loves (evident too in a slightly different way in the grammar of friendship) to the

---

111. For an instance of the Catholic magisterial use of such figures for Mary, see *Ineffabilis Deus*, the 1854 bull of Pius IX (Latin and English in *Official Documents Connected with the Definition of the Dogma of the Immaculate Conception* [Baltimore: Murphy, 1855], 39), which mentions the tower of David as one of the types of Mary.

love of the Lord for each of us is arresting: he speaks of us as we speak of him,
and we speak of him as he speaks of us.

Until the Day Breathes (4:6)

> Until the day breathes
> and the shadows flee
> I shall go to the mountain of myrrh
> and to the hill of frankincense.

The lover concludes his first hymn of praise to the beloved's body by repeating a
formula ("until the day breathes / and the shadows flee") already spoken by her
at →2:17. Following the formula are the words, "I shall go to the mountain of
myrrh / and to the hill of frankincense." The two spice words, "myrrh" (→1:13)
and "frankincense" (→3:6), are found together at 3:6 in the daughters' question,
"What is this ascending through the desert / like a wisp of smoke / spiced with
frankincense and myrrh?"

The "mountain" to which the lover indicates his intention of going is mentioned
again, this time in the plural, in the Song's last words: there, the beloved encourages her lover to "escape . . . upon the spice mountains" (8:14). Mountains like
spices, mountains of spices—places, that is, of high, rarefied, and intense beauty
where the Lord disports himself and encourages others to approach him for love.
That the lover concludes his praise of the beloved's body with a mention of these
mountains, and that he connects this with the formula meaning "until morning,"
is a scarcely veiled statement that he intends to spend the night enjoying her
body. Her body, the body of Mary and of the Lord's Israel-church, precisely is the
"mountain of myrrh": he, the Lord, will take his pleasure there because that body
is the one he has chosen and set apart (*electa*; 6:9) for himself. It is, above all, the
body in which he himself, in the person of the Son, takes flesh.

The Immaculata (4:7)

> O my beloved—you are completely beautiful
> and there is no stain in you.

The voice of the lover continues, singing now his desire for the delightful body
of the beloved whose particulars he has just completed praising. The Song's beloved is, her lover says directly to her in the vocative, "completely beautiful /
and there is no stain in" her. The trope of the absence of "stain" (*macula*) is repeated
later, when he calls her "my stainless one" (*immaculata mea*) (5:2). It is a pity
not to translate *immaculata* as "immaculate." But if that is done, there is no way
to preserve in English the verbal connection between the noun *macula* and the

participle *immaculata*. That connection is preserved by choosing stain-stainless-unstained-free from stain. These are the only occurrences of this epithet in the Song, but it occurs very frequently elsewhere in scripture. Most commonly, *maculae* are visible physical defects, whether on the body of an animal or a human being—things such as blindness, lameness, leprosy, or psoriasis. These things are what sacrificial animals and the priests who sacrifice them should be free from (Exod. 12:5; Lev. 1:3; 3:6; 4:3; 9:2; 21:17–23); and they are what Christ, as sacrificial lamb, is supremely and perfectly free from (1 Pet. 1:19). But *maculae* are not only visible defects. They may also be invisible impurities or defilements produced by improper actions of various kinds, such as having sex with an animal or with someone else's spouse (Lev. 18:20–23); and to be immaculate is sometimes glossed as being free from iniquity or wrongdoing of any kind (Job 33:9; cf. 15:14), including, presumably, those kinds of wrongdoing that leave no visible trace. There are also, in scripture, people said to be *immaculatus*: this is said of David, for example (2 Sam. 22:24).

Consider also the following text from Ephesians:

> Men, take delight in your wives as Christ delighted in the church and handed himself over for her so that he might make her holy by cleansing her with a bath of water in the word, with the result that he might present that very church in glory to himself, having no stain or wrinkle or anything of that kind, but rather so that she might be holy and stainless. In this way, men should delight in their own wives as in their own bodies. (Eph. 5:25–28; cf. 1:4)

Much of the Song's vocabulary is here: Christ takes "delight" in the church as the Song's couple takes "delight" in one another; and, most importantly for this discussion, Christ's baptismal cleansing of the church ("with a bath of water in the word") makes her *immaculata* ("stainless") and *non habentem maculam* ("having no stain"). In Ephesians, this is said in connection with a discussion of marriage: Christ's love for and cleansing of the church is figured by and participated in by the (ideal-typical, not of course actual) love of men for their wives. The weaving together in this passage of marriage tropes, baptismal tropes, and the image of stainlessness gives it deep and multiple resonances with the Song as a whole, but especially with the attribution to the Song's beloved of the epithet "stainless" (5:2). This intratextual echo assimilates the Song's beloved directly to the church, embraced with delight as beloved by Christ, washed in water and blood, and thereby made free of all stains. When the Song's lover says to the beloved, "you are completely beautiful / and there is no stain in you," his words are, precisely, figures of Christ's words to the church: he (the Song's lover) is preparing to present his beloved to himself as the *immaculata*—giving her to herself as such by his love for and embrace of her, and in that way giving her as gift also to the world. One way to receive that gift is to read of and ruminate its giving as depicted in the words of the Song.

These verses, properly illuminated by reading them as scriptural words, have application not only to the Lord's Israel-church as such, immaculate and shining, burnished and pure, her lips dripping honeycomb as she opens them to the Lord's kisses, but also to the baptized Christian reader of the Song. In baptism you were made immaculate, stainless: the church preserves this idea in the baptismal liturgy, representing it both verbally and by the dressing of the newly baptized in the unstained white garments proper to those who are immaculate. You have not—I have not—preserved your stainlessness since your baptism: your white garments are by now wrinkled and spotted and deeply (but not ineradicably) stained. But you once were stainless, like the Song's beloved and like the church. And this is not the only application to you: the Lord's praise of the Song's beloved as "completely beautiful" (4:7) and "stainless" (5:2) belongs to his delight in and desire for her; and that delight and desire applies to you too, although of course in a derived and participated way. You can, then, take the words of these verses of the Song to heart as addressed directly to you. Even that is not all. Your own addresses to your beloved and his or hers to you participate in and figure those of the Lord to his beloved. Knowing that, seeing it, illuminates the sheer excess of your own delight in and desire for your beloved. That is as it is in its goodness and beauty (it is of course not only that, but also shattered and corrupt, violent and manipulative) because the Lord's delight in and desire for you is as it is. In this, as in all things, you image, to the extent that you are undamaged, the Lord himself.

The deepest reverberations of the attribution to the Song's beloved of the epithet *immaculata* are neither ecclesial nor individual, but Marian.[112] Or, better put, the ecclesial and individual reverberations of that attribution are what they are because of the Marian ones. She is, according to the doctrine of the church, the paradigmatic and supreme stainless one, and the stainlessness of the church is what it is because it participates in hers. She is without stain in many senses, but most fundamentally because she was conceived without the *maculae*, the stains, shared by us all since Adam. Recall Philip Larkin's poem "This Be the Verse," quoted earlier: Mary's parents, Joachim and Anna, did not damage her as ours did; they did not transmit to her the stains, the *maculae*, of human existence since the fall. As Pope Pius IX put it in the course of the document in which the dogma of the immaculate conception was formulated and promulgated in 1854:

> They [the fathers of the church] testified, too, that the flesh of the Virgin, although derived from Adam, did not contract the stains of Adam, and that on this account the most Blessed Virgin was the tabernacle created by God himself and formed by the Holy Spirit, truly a work in royal purple, adorned and woven with gold. . . . They affirmed that the same Virgin is, and is deservedly, the first and especial work

112. The verse becomes a standard point of reference for Mary's immaculacy among commentators in the Latin-using West after the eleventh century. See, for a typical though rather excitable instance, Rupert of Deutz, *Commentaria in Canticum Canticorum* (Commentary on the Song) on Song 4:7 (Deutz and Deutz 2005: 322–26).

of God, escaping the fiery arrows of the evil one; that she is beautiful by nature and entirely free from every defect; that at her immaculate conception she came into the world all radiant like the dawn. For it was certainly not fitting that this vessel of election should be wounded by the common injuries, since she, differing so much from the others, had only nature in common with them, not sin. In fact, it was quite fitting that, as the Only Begotten has a Father in heaven, whom the Seraphim extol as thrice holy, so he should have a Mother on earth who would never lack the splendor of holiness.[113]

This passage has a number of echoes of the Song, unsignaled by Pius IX, as is typical of patristic, medieval, and magisterial discussion of Mary. She is, writes the Pope, "radiant like the dawn" (cf. 6:10), never lacking "the splendor of holiness" (cf. 2:14; 6:4; 7:7), and, of course, *immaculata* (4:7; 5:2). Definitions of Mary's place in the economy of salvation are typically saturated with imagery from the Song in this way.

The Bride (4:8)

> O bride—come from Lebanon,
> come from Lebanon,
> come in—
> look from the summit of Amana
> from the peaks of Sanir and Hermon
> from lions' lairs
> from leopards' mountains.

The lover continues to speak directly to the beloved, in the vocative and with a tone of urgent desire. But now, it seems, she is absent again. In 4:1–6, the lover and the beloved were, it seemed, face-to-face, he praising her body to her face. But now they are apart—again, the presence-absence dialectic—and he is urging her to come into his presence, exhibiting the same intense desire for this as she had earlier (3:1–4) shown for his presence.

  This verse begins a tense rush toward consummation that finds its culmination in 5:1, a press forward signaled in many ways, but not least in the first occurrence in the Song of explicitly nuptial epithets for her on his lips. He calls her "bride" (*sponsa*) for the first time here, and that word occurs six times in 4:8–5:1, four times combined with "sister" (*soror*). This language does not thereafter recur: it is found only here, at the Song's heart, and this is among the strongest pieces of evidence that in 4:7–5:1 we find the central point of the Song. Song 5:1 lies at the Song's halfway point in terms of word count, and the concentration of spousal

---

113. Author's translation from *Ineffabilis Deus*, as given in *Official Documents Connected with the Definition of the Dogma of the Immaculate Conception* (Baltimore: Murphy, 1855), 44–45.

and nuptial imagery immediately before it focuses attention on that point as the place where the lover and his beloved's sexual consummation of their love is most explicitly depicted.

The combination of sibling talk with spousal talk ("sister-bride") seems at first odd. The two are ordinarily incompatible: the levitical marriage regulations are explicit in forbidding marriage and sexual intercourse between brother and sister (Lev. 18), and they have a more extended understanding of who qualifies as a sister than does (for example) US civil law. One way to read the lover's linking of the two languages in calling the beloved his "sister-bride" is to say that he is claiming every possible kind of intimacy with her: not only is she his beloved, the person he is about to make love with; she is also his sister, the one with whom he shares a mother and father and with whom he has grown up and shared the intimacies of the household. There is supportive evidence for this reading elsewhere in the Song. She mentions her "mother's sons" (1:6)—her brothers, that is—in close connection with him, her lover; and she expresses the quixotic hope that someone might be able to give him to her as a brother (8:1), so that she might kiss him in public without scandal. So she too uses spousal, nuptial, sexual, and sibling language to and about him. She too, though less explicitly than he, links the two kinds of intimacy, familial and sexual, and lays claim to both of them with him.[114]

The bride, or wife, who is, or is called, a sister is found elsewhere in scripture. Twice in Genesis there is a story about Abraham and Sara in which he persuades her to present herself as his "sister" (*soror*) rather than his "wife" (*uxor*) in order to avoid the trouble that might result for him if she, a beautiful and desirable woman, is known to be his wife. Perhaps he will be killed, he says to Sara, so that someone else might freely take her as wife. Presenting her as his sister will avoid this, though it leaves open the possibility that other men will feel free to take her to bed, or to try to, because they think she has no husband. In both sister-wife stories, one set in Egypt (Gen. 12:10–20) and the other in Gerar (Gen. 20), the ruse works in that the kings of both places, eager for sex with Sara, take her into their houses and beds. The Lord, however, intervenes, and neither Pharaoh nor Gerar's king, Abimelech, have sex with her. When they learn that she is in fact Abraham's wife, they return her to him with remonstration at the deceit practiced upon them. In the story about Gerar and Abimelech, Abraham responds to the question of why he has done this by saying that Sara is certainly his wife, his *uxor*, but also his *soror*, the daughter of his father though not of his mother, and that therefore he has not lied to Abimelech.[115] The connection of sororal imagery with bridal imagery in this part of the Song evokes all these resonances.

114. On the combination of sororal and bridal images in the Song, see John Paul II, *Man and Woman He Created Them: A Theology of the Body*, trans. Michael Waldstein (Boston: Pauline Books, 2006), 560–68.

115. Abraham's father is Terah (Gen. 11:27), and we are not told his mother's name. Sarah's father and mother are not named, and the only hint that she has the same father as Abraham is in the Gerar story. Compare the sister-wife story about Isaac and Rebecca in Gen. 26:6–11: there

Spousal imagery for the relationship between the Lord and Israel is also common in scripture. For example: "Just as a young man takes a virgin as wife, / so shall your sons take you; / and as a husband rejoices in his wife, / so will God rejoice in you" (Isa. 62:5; cf. Hos. 2:22 [= 2:20 RSV]). The "you" in Isa. 62:5 is Zion/Jerusalem, who is the spouse not only of the Lord but also of the people of Israel, and therefore doubly married.[116] This figure of the double marriage is rich and easily developed: Christians, members of the body of Christ by baptism, are married to (intimate with, wrapped in the arms of, kissed by) their mother-spouse, the church; they are also embraced by Mary, the one who is espoused and embraced by the Lord so that she can bear and give birth to himself; and so, in this figural sense, they are also her spouses. Following the image from Isaiah, the Lord betroths and espouses both his peoples (Israel-church) collectively and severally; the Song's beloved serves as figure for both, figuring in her beauty and desirability both those of Jerusalem-church as a whole and those of each Jew and each Christian as members of those wholes. Mary is the mediating figure for all this: the Jewish mother made pregnant by the Lord sublimes and condenses Israel in her acceptance of the Lord's embrace; and she serves as the hinge, the open door, into the spousal condition of the church. She also, and because of all this, is the one in whom all those individual—mine, yours—returns of the Lord's spousal embrace subsist.

There is a cluster of place-names in 4:8: "Lebanon," "Amana," "Sanir," and "Hermon." Except for "Lebanon" (→3:9–10a), each of these occurs only here in the Song, and "Amana" finds here its only occurrence in the canon of scripture. "Sanir" and "Hermon" are found quite frequently elsewhere in scripture. Sometimes, as here, the two are paired or even identified (Deut. 3:9; 1 Chr. 5:23); and one or the other or both are linked with Bashan (Josh. 12:5; 13:11; 1 Chr. 5:23), the Transjordan, the territory of Manasseh, the Amorites (Deut. 3:9), or the Hivites (Josh. 11:3). It is doubtful that an entirely consistent geographic or political picture can be derived from these scriptural mentions of "Sanir" and "Hermon," but scripture is consistent in depicting them as mountains close to or in Lebanon (Josh. 11:17; 13:5) and as being, therefore, at the northern edge of the promised land. There are also occasional scriptural connections drawn between "Sanir" or "Hermon" and the cypress tree (Ezek. 27:5; Sir. 24:13), elsewhere often connected with "Lebanon."

These peaks, places of distant beauty, are connected here in the Song with "lions' lairs" and identified as "leopards' mountains." These animals are mentioned only here in the Song, but frequently elsewhere in scripture. The "lion" is a scriptural symbol of power and especially royal authority; it is in that connection that it is carved among the decorations of the Solomonic temple (1 Kgs.

---

too the place is Gerar and the local king Abimelech. Compare also the story of Amnon's rape of Tamar, his sister, in 2 Sam. 13.

116. The figure of Jerusalem as the Lord's spouse is extended into the future in Rev. 21, where the New Jerusalem descends as such.

7:28–36) and beside the armrests of Solomon's ivory throne (1 Kgs. 10:19–20). It is also a symbol of danger and uncontrollable hunger: the lion ravens for its prey (Ps. 7:3 [= 7:2 RSV]; Sir. 27:10; Zech. 11:3).[117] "Leopards," scripturally speaking, are also beasts of prey (Sir. 28:23; Isa. 11:6; Jer. 5:6); but they do not appear to have any of the leonine connotations of royal power, and they are without connection to the symbolism of the temple. They are often mentioned together with "lions."

When the lover calls his beloved to "come from Lebanon" and "look from the summit of Amana," then, he is calling to her to look for him from a distant, beautiful, and dangerous place and to come from there to a more familiar, closer, more ordered, and less threatening place. She, her body just delineated and caressed with words of delight (4:1–6), is absent, and needs to become present. Here, as so often, the Song jarringly confronts its hearers with the dialectical tension between presence and absence. She is here, close to him; and then, suddenly, far away, her presence needing to be invoked. The Lord is as troubled by his beloved's absence as she is by his: he calls her—Mary, his Israel-church, and you—to him with as much insistence as she searches for him.

The Sister-Bride (4:9–10)

> O my sister-bride—you have wounded my heart
> you have wounded my heart with one of your eyes
> with one of the necklaces of your torque.
> O my sister-bride—how beautiful are your loves
> your loves are better than wine
> and the scent of your ointments is above all spices.

The stainless immaculate one has come from the north ("from the peaks of Sanir and Hermon"; 4:8), from the dangerous and wild places ("from lions' lairs / from leopards' mountains"; 4:8), where the land has not been tamed and cultivated. These are places where the traveler can be attacked by beasts or can starve or die of thirst. That he can call her from such a place is among the Song's indications that the beloved is not merely beautiful and desirable, but also dangerous. That theme is underscored by the introduction of the language of wounding here: "you have wounded my heart," a refrain repeated here, like a tocsin. She has wounded him, cut him, made him bleed; and she has done so with her eyes, and with the ornaments of her body, "with one of the necklaces of [her] torque" (→1:10–11). Wounding is mentioned explicitly only here in the Song; but the thoughts that love is a wound and that the beloved can wound her lover and the lover his beloved

117. Cf. Isa. 65:25, where the lion becomes (eschatologically) vegetarian, and Judg. 14, where Samson's lion-killing shows the victory of those gifted by the Lord over the power of kings.

are clichés of love poetry everywhere, ancient and modern.[118] In the Song, the pain of love and its wounds are depicted mostly by way of the tropes of absence, separation, searching, and loss (3:1–4; 5:6–8); here, the depiction is more pointed and more agonizing. It is exactly the ornaments in which the lover delights—her "torque," decorating her elegantly columnar neck, beckoning his eyes, placed there as ornament by him (1:10)—that cut him; and it is precisely her eyes, those eyes like doves, whose gaze draws him into themselves (1:15), that lacerate his heart. The wound here is not that of absence's pain: she is on her way to him, and he is just about, in the immediately following verses, to praise her beauty. Rather, the wound is a concomitant, or even an ingredient, of love: love cannot exist without it. The lover, in loving his beloved into existence as a beloved who can return his love, wounds both himself and her.

Love's wounds are obvious enough for human lovers: we understand them too well. They do not belong only, or even especially, to failed loves, loves darkened by betrayal, or loves offered but not returned. Those wounds are not love's wounds, but rather the wounds produced by love's absence or loss. Those absences and losses are themselves almost inevitable, but the wounds spoken of here belong exactly to human love, love reciprocated and exchanged, not to its decay or loss. As the lover caresses his beloved's hair and gazes into her eyes and murmurs the sweet nothings of delight and desire into her ear he wounds her by provoking in her an intensity of delight and desire that she knows, viscerally and bone-deep, he cannot satisfy. He, in desiring and delighting in her, knows the same about her. What she provokes in him exceeds what she can give him: the gift of being a lover provided by being beloved is so far in excess of what its giver and recipient are that the gift is both ludicrous (hence the laughable behavior of those in love) and agonizing at the same time.

This wound is not avoidable. Stoics try to avoid it by refusing love, but that is not possible: it is like the attempt to remove a limb's pain by amputating it, an attempt that produces only the more intense and utterly incurable pain of the phantom limb. Hedonists try to avoid it by increasing the intensity with which they pursue love's physical and emotional satisfactions (multiplying lovers, deifying a particular lover, seeking love's intensification by baroque artifice and the delusions of technique—Sade is the best literary instance of this tactic), but that is a game of diminishing returns that ends in the incapacity for love. The wound has to be embraced and understood. Christians can do this because we know what love's wounds figure. When you say, with the Song's lover, "you have wounded my heart with one of your eyes / with one of the necklaces of your torque," you know that the unavoidability of that wound figures and participates in the wounded mutual love of the Lord for his Israel-church, and of the Lord for Mary *theotokos*, the one who conceived and gave birth to himself. Those wounds are real and unavoidable;

---

118. On the theme of the wound in Christian theology generally, see especially Rowan Williams, *The Wound of Knowledge* (London: Darton, Longman & Todd, 1979).

but they carry with them a promise of eventual healing. Christ's wounds on the cross; Mary wounded by knowing that her son will die before her and seeing that happen, holding her dead son on her lap; the wounds inflicted on the Lord's Israel-church by the world (the martyrs, the Holocaust, the endlessly imaginative means of dealing death and shedding blood, all of them distorted loves)—the wounds of human loves, of the two lovers in the Song, figure all these, and the knowledge that this is so, while bringing its own wounds with it, transfigures, without removing, the heart-wounding glance of the loving eye (→5:3–7).

The verses under consideration here move at once from wound to beauty: "O my sister-bride—how beautiful are your loves / your loves are better than wine." These are words already spoken: in →1:2 the beloved has said exactly this to her lover, and now he says it to her. His immediately following words to her, "the scent of your ointments is above all spices," are also closely paralleled in what he has said to her in →1:3a. This is one more example of the Song's depiction of the lover and his beloved as in part exchangeable. They exchange not only caresses, but also words, passing them back and forth: that what she says to him can also be said by him to her suggests mutual interpenetration at the verbal as well as at the physical level. The lovers are assimilated one to another, and it begins not to matter who says what. Ownership, like separateness, dissolves in intimacy's sweet acids. This too is a familiar feature of human love: who has not, in bed, ceased to be sure whether that leg, that arm, those lips, that tongue, are yours or your lover's? This dissolution of separateness figures and finds its fulfillment in the intimacies that connect the people of the Lord's Israel-church one to another.

Honey and Milk (4:11)

> O bride—your lips drip honeycomb
> honey and milk are under your tongue
> the scent of your clothes is like that of Lebanon.

He speaks of the sweet taste of her "lips" and "tongue" and the sweet smell of her "clothes"—and, by implication, of the body clothed by them.[119] The "tongue" is mentioned only here in the Song; the "lips," by contrast, are mentioned frequently (→1:2; →2:3b on "throat"; →3:9 on "Lebanon").

Her mouth drips with sweetness, to be tasted by him; and the mention of "honey" (*mel*) and "honeycomb" (*favus*) in connection with "lips" and "tongue" draws upon a broad and deep fund of scriptural mentions of honey, often together with milk. Most obviously, the land promised to Israel flows with milk and honey (Exod. 3:8, 17; 13:5), and her lips and tongue and throat, in being said likewise

---

119. For the sweet smell of the garments of the Davidic king, see Ps. 45:9 [= 45:8 RSV]. The verbal resonances are close; it is once again interesting to note that a description of the Lord's male beloved, in this case the king, can be so easily applied to the Lord's female beloved here in the Song.

to do so, are assimilated to the land of promise in which all such good things are freely given and freely available for the taking. "Honey" and "honeycomb" often stand in scripture for something freely and serendipitously available to which no human work has contributed and that is sweet to the point of intoxication. Samson finds honeycomb in the carcass of the lion he has slaughtered (Judg. 14:8–9); Jonathan, walking through the woods on the way to a battle, eats of the honey dripping from the trees, and his eyes begin to shine as a result (1 Sam. 14:27); and the prophetic scroll tastes like honey to Ezekiel's lips (Ezek. 3:3; Rev. 10:9–10).

The beloved's honeyed throat and tongue are a delightful gift in all these ways, "worthy to be sipped" (Song 7:10) by her lover and given to him as something to whose existence and nature he made no contribution. The explicitly sexual meaning of the throat-tongue-lips-honey-honeycomb complex of words is also found in scripture outside the Song, but rarely and only with a negative meaning. Consider: "Honeycomb drips from a prostitute's lips / and her throat is smoother than oil" (Prov. 5:3). This is very close, verbally and conceptually, to the lover describing the beloved's throat as "supremely smooth / and completely desirable" (5:16), but with the valence reversed.[120] In both cases, the urge is for close contact, contact that permits touch and taste.

The Closed Garden (4:12)

> A closed garden is my sister-bride
> a closed garden
> a sealed spring.

The lover continues to use nuptial language, but here he shifts from direct address to his "sister-bride" to speech about her: perhaps in soliloquy, he describes her as "a closed garden / a sealed spring," reverting to the language of delight rather than that of desire.

If a "garden" is "closed" and a "spring" "sealed," the good things they contain (plants, trees, fruits, flowers, life-giving waters) are kept from the world, privatized, shut in, incarcerated (cf. Isa. 29:11). The verbs used here (*concludere, signare*) are, in scripture, mostly used in this sense: those "closed" in prison need release (Job 16:11; Jer. 19:9; Acts 22:19 [Paul]); a letter "sealed" with the king's seal awaits opening (Neh. 10:2; Esth. 3:12; 8:8; Jer. 32:11; Rev. 5:1); a prophetic oracle, even if given publicly, is a "sealed" book for those without ears to hear and eyes to read. When the lover describes the beloved in these terms, she is depicted as someone whose gifts and delights have yet to be opened up, permitted to blossom and flow freely and thus to bless both him, her lover, and the world, which is also eager

120. There is no echo in the Song of the most common scriptural understanding of the tongue, which is an organ of speech capable of speaking truth or lies, of praising or cursing the Lord (Exod. 4:10; 2 Sam. 23:2; Job 6:30; Prov. 18:21).

for the removal of the barriers that keep her from the public eye. She is a letter waiting to be read, a book waiting to be opened.

Another range of scriptural meanings for "sealed" should be kept in mind even though it forms a distant ground bass to the dominant melody of the closed-in/ immured meaning. In this second sense, to say something is "sealed" can also mean that it is marked, identified, branded. It is in this sense that Paul writes of the Corinthians as the seal—the identifying mark, the proof-text—of his status as an apostle (1 Cor. 9:2); it is also in this sense that John can write of the elect being "sealed," marked with the seal of the living God (Rev. 7:1–9; cf. Ezek. 28:12; Hag. 2:23; Rom. 4:11). The beloved may be thought of as "sealed" in this sense too; but because of the parallelism between "closed" and "sealed," this must be a secondary meaning.

The "garden" (which is "closed") and the "spring" (which is "sealed") are both tropes of beauty and fertility, the former belonging to the sphere of the cultivated and the latter to the sphere of the natural. Gardens are always made by and for someone; springs are found, gushing forth without human work. The beloved can be understood as belonging to both realms. The cultivated garden is mentioned six times in the Song: twice in these verses and once immediately following them (5:1), where the beloved is likened to a garden prepared for growth—prepared, that is, for sex; once (6:2) when she says to the daughters that her "delightful man has gone down into his garden," which is likely another reference to the garden of her body; once when he says, obscurely, that he has gone "down into the nut garden" (6:11); and once still more obscurely, when there is mention of the "one who inhabits the gardens" (→8:13). All these references are either centered upon the Song's crux (4:12–5:1) or flow from the events described in that crux. There is no mention of the "garden" before 4:12: in the Song, talk of gardens goes closely with talk of brides, and the garden is the fundamental trope for the site of sexual intercourse—"site" in the sense of the body of the beloved and in the sense of place where they make love. To call the beloved a "garden" is, for the Song, to depict her as a sexual partner; and to speak of the lover as going to his "garden" is to speak of him as going to her, making love with her. As cultivated—as a "garden"—she is ready for him, made beautiful for him, ornamented and decorated for him. Images of the cultivated order, the beauties of the gardens and vineyards in which the couple wanders, occur predominantly in the Song's second part (6:2–3, 11–12; 7:12–14; 8:11–13), and that is because the couple can be shown to wander in the gardens of sexual delight only after they have been depicted as lovers, after her "closed garden" and "sealed spring" have been opened so that she can flow into and with him.[121]

---

121. On the "closed garden" and "sealed spring" in their nuptial meaning, see John Paul II, *Man and Woman He Created Them: A Theology of the Body*, trans. Michael Waldstein (Boston: Pauline Books, 2006), 568–73. Augustine quotes these phrases many times, and almost always with reference to the church understood as paradise; see *De civitate dei* 13.21 (Latin at www.augustinus.it/latino/cdd/index.htm; English in Henry Bettenson, trans., *St. Augustine: Concerning the City of God against the Pagans* [London: Penguin, 1984], 534–35).

The sister-bride who is the closed garden can be understood more fully by considering what is said of gardens elsewhere in scripture. They are, like her, always cultivated or made, brought into being by divine or human agency, and when human, usually royal. There is a distinction between the *horti* (the word used for the beloved in the Song), the gardens of the world made by people for earthly delight, and *paradisus* or Eden, made by the Lord for the first people. The distinction blurs a little when earthly gardens are likened to the paradisial one; but for the most part it is kept in place and signaled by the verbal difference between *hortus* and *paradisus*. The archetypal garden is paradise/Eden (Gen. 2–3; cf. Ezek. 28:13; 31:8); the promised land as the people of Israel see and enter it is sometimes likened to Eden (Jer. 2:7; Gen. 13:10); and the eschatological restoration of Zion is sometimes depicted by the prophets as the replanting of Eden (Isa. 51:3; cf. Joel 2:3; Ezek. 36:35). A garden, whether *hortus* or *paradisus*, is a place of beauty made for pleasure (1 Kgs. 21:2; 2 Kgs. 21:18, 26; 25:4; Neh. 3:15; Esth. 7:7). There is nothing in it of the wild, the ungoverned, or the threatening. But, like everything else made for and by humans, the garden can be a place in which beauty is made ugly by sin. In paradise this happens; and in a garden Jesus is betrayed by Judas and arrested (John 18–19);[122] it is also in a garden that he is buried, and from that garden tomb raised to life eternal.

The Song's gardenlike sister-bride is, more than anything, like the paradisial garden. She awaits only her lover's—the Lord's—quickening embrace to be made open to the world, to have her "shoots," her "paradise of pomegranates," her "incense-bearing trees," and her "prime ointments" made available to the world (4:13–14). When these embraces occur, when her "springs" of living water flow, the eschatological promise of the replanting of Eden will be fulfilled (Ps. 36:10 [= 36:9 RSV]; Prov. 13:14; 16:22; 18:4; cf. Joel 4:18 [= 3:18 RSV] and Zech. 13:1). The application to the Lord's Israel-church is straightforward enough: his embrace of her is like a new creation, bringing her into being (without the unmerited gift of his grace she neither does nor can exist as his beloved) and then making her fecund and beautiful as a place for the nations and peoples to come to and begin to learn the names of the trees and flowers and fruits growing there. To the extent that they learn these names, they become admirers of—wonderers at—the beauty of the Lord's beloved and, in the end, themselves her habituated lovers. The Lord's garden-beloved becomes in that way the place for the world's recreation.

The Garden's Beauties (4:13–16 [= 4:13–16a RSV])

> Your shoots are a paradise of pomegranates
> with the best fruits—
> henna with spikenard

122. The Synoptics do not call Gethsemane a garden, and John does not call the garden of the betrayal Gethsemane.

> spikenard and saffron
> sweet calamus and cinnamon
> with all the incense-bearing trees—
> myrrh and aloe
> with all the prime ointments.
> The spring of the gardens is a well of living waters
> streaming forcefully from Lebanon.
> North wind get up—
> south wind come—
> blow through my garden—
> let its spices stream!

The lover extends the metaphor of the garden by describing her "shoots" as "a paradise of pomegranates / with the best fruits," and then listing some of the beautiful and fragrant things growing from her considered as garden—"henna with spikenard" and so on.

Concluding the descriptive trope of the garden at the end of 4:15 by describing the waters that sustain its beauty and fertility ("the spring of the gardens is a well of living water"), the lover then shifts to the imperative mood, addressing the north and south winds: "Blow through my garden— / let its spices stream!" The wind is to ruffle and disturb the garden—the beloved—and make its (her) delightfully scented fluids flow. Winds blow[123] and waters stream:[124] the sexual imagery is quite direct and almost explicit, and the Song here approaches its center, in which the lovers bring their love to its consummation.

These verses contain the most concentrated cluster of herb and spice names in the Song. Four of these terms—"saffron" (*crocus*), "sweet calamus" (*fistula*), "cinnamon" (*cinnamomum*), and "aloe" (*aloe*)—occur only here in the Song; the other terms occur frequently (→1:12–14 on "henna," "spikenard," and "myrrh"; →1:3a on "ointment"). "Saffron" occurs nowhere else in scripture; the Latin term (*crocus*) suggests that, for the Latin Song at least, *crocus sativus* is in mind, and probably not only the plant but especially its yellow flowers and the oils derivable therefrom, sweet smelling and beautiful to look at as these are. "Sweet calamus" as a translation for *fistula* is little more than a guess. The Latin word means "hollow tube," and when it occurs elsewhere in scripture, it usually refers to a musical instrument in the form of a hollow tube—perhaps something like a flute (Dan. 3). Only in the Song does it seem to mean some kind of plant. "Sweet calamus"

---

123. Imagery of wind in scripture is most often negative. Winds are violent, destructive, threatening, sent by the Lord as punishment or sign (Sir. 43:21 [= 43:17 RSV]; Ezek. 27:26; 1 Kgs. 18:45; Job 1:19; and often in the Psalms. Cf. Matt. 14:30–32; Mark 4:41; 6:51).

124. On John 7:38 as echoing, perhaps distantly, perhaps closely (there are textual complexities here about the relations between the versions in Hebrew, Greek, and Latin), Song 4:12–15, see Mark W. Elliott, *The Song of Songs and Christology in the Early Church 381–451*, Studien und Texte zu Antike und Christentum 7 (Tübingen: Mohr/Siebeck, 2000), 3–5.

(*calamus aromaticus*) is a possible rendering—a tubelike sweet-smelling plant, rather like sugarcane, but this is really no more than a guess. "Cinnamon" is in Exod. 30:22–28 among the spices used to make the anointing oil and incense; elsewhere in scripture it is mentioned as a generically delightful-smelling substance (Sir. 24:20 [= 24:15 RSV]; Rev. 18:13); and there is one explicitly sexual connection, where cinnamon is used to prepare the bed for lovemaking (Prov. 7:17, together with "aloes" and "myrrh"; see Kingsmill 2009: 57–59). "Aloe" (*aloe*), probably referring to the sweet resin derived from the wood of the *Aquilaria agallocha* tree, is also mentioned a few times in scripture, in connection with gardens (Num. 24:6), with the scenting of the clothes (Ps. 45:9 [= 45:8 RSV]), or the preparation of the bed (Prov. 7:17, together with "cinnamon" and "myrrh"). This concentration of sweet-smelling and good things, pressed down, shaken together, overspilling, is, in these verses, not simply to be admired with the language of delight. Rather, the lover urges it, in imperative voice, to "stream" for him. He wants not only to look at it and smell it, but to be submerged in it, to enter it, and be bathed in it. That too is what the Lord wants from his Israel-church; it is what his assenting servant Mary gave him, responding to the wind of the angelic address with the streaming flow of her *fiat mihi* and the conception and birth that followed hard upon it; and it is what he seeks from you, the Song's hearer.

Lovemaking (5:1 [= 4:16b–5:1 RSV])

> Let my delightful man come into his garden
> and let him eat his best fruits.
> O my sister-bride—I have come into my garden
> I have harvested my myrrh with my spices
> I have eaten honeycomb with honey
> I have drunk wine with my milk
>
> O lovers—eat and drink—
> O dearest ones—be drunk!

This long verse—eight lines of Latin in the New Vulgate—lies at the center of the Song. This is true in word count,[125] in the order of events, and in tone and intensity. The verse includes all three of the Song's speakers: the lover, the beloved, and the daughters. The first two lines—"let my delightful man come into his garden / and let him eat his best fruits"—are the beloved's *fiat mihi*. He has urged her, ordered her, beseeched her, to open herself to him, to let her sweet-smelling juices flow for him, to receive him into her body. Here she says yes ("let my delightful man come"),

125. In Jerome's version, the Song has 213 lines, rendered *per cola et commata*. The line that constitutes 5:1c according to the versification of the New Vulgate ("O my sister-bride—I have come into my garden") is line 107 of Jerome's version—i.e., the midpoint in Jerome's line count.

using again the image of the "garden" and the "fruits." She is his garden, and her body his fruit to pluck and eat and enjoy. Then his voice, using again nuptial language ("O my sister-bride") to address her, using now the perfect tense to describe what has happened. He has entered the garden and "harvested," "eaten," and "drunk" the spicy and sweet things she has offered him: "myrrh" (→1:12–14), "honeycomb with honey" (→4:11), "wine" (→1:2–4), and "milk" (→4:11). He is now, in the full and proper sense, her lover. Then the voice of the daughters, looking on in delight and encouraging them in the imperative mood: "eat and drink / . . . be drunk."

Almost all the tropes in these eight lines have already occurred, and have been discussed in their places, especially the nuptial verses (→4:9–16) immediately preceding and culminating in this one. The only image new to these lines is that of inebriation, being drunk.

To speak of being in love and making love as a form of intoxication is now a cliché of love poetry, but it is rare elsewhere in scripture. Most often, the verb in question (*inebriare*) is used in connection with slaughter and violence: swords become drunk with the blood of the slaughtered and so on (Deut. 32:42; Jdt. 6:4; Isa. 34:5; 49:26). There is also a close connection between drunkenness and fornication (Gen. 9:21; Rev. 17:1–2). But sometimes scriptural uses of the trope of inebriation closely resonate with those in this verse of the Song. The Lord is spoken of as making the inhabitants of the earth drunk with the excess of his delightful gifts (Ps. 36:9 [= 36:8 RSV]; 65:10 [= 65:9 RSV]; Sir. 32:17 [= 32:13 RSV]; Isa. 29:9), and that is very closely consonant with what the daughters say to the lover and his beloved in Song 5:1. This is one more signal that a scripturally attuned hearer of the Song will hear in the daughters' acclamation of the couple's intercourse an acknowledgment that the lover is the Lord and that the mutual intoxication of the lovers is the reciprocal delight of the Lord and his Israel-church.

It is remarkable that the Song draws a veil, as it were, at this high point, at its very center. If it is right to see these words as framing the sexual intercourse of the lovers, then the feel and texture and savor of that intercourse is left undepicted. She urges him on; he retrospectively acknowledges what has happened; but the particulars are undescribed. There are a number of things to say about this.

The first is that descriptions of sexual intercourse tend to occupy a position on a spectrum between the grossly physiologic and the risibly high-toned. At one extreme we have the physiology textbook, whose language is hydraulic and mechanical and which makes the lovers' bodies objects for dispassionate observation—you can imagine the lecturer's laser pointer hovering over this body part or that; at the other there is the purple prose of the bodice-ripper, in which organs and secretions and sensations are depicted, but juiced-up with the language of bad ecstasy so that what's written is either quotidian physical pornography or, worse, the high-emotional kind in which the earth moves. It is difficult to do better: lovemaking is, among humans, something better engaged in than depicted, whether verbally or visually. The Song does not belong on this spectrum. It is reticent, leaving an opening for imagination and memory.

Second, if sexual intercourse, specifically the extended present of orgasm, serves in the Song (inter alia) as a figure for your full embrace by the Lord, an embrace of greater intimacy than which there is none, then the occlusion of its particular sensations and motions coheres well with the difficulty of representing that divine embrace in language. We can anticipate it, linguistically, and note its subsequent effects; but attempts to phenomenologize it, to account for what it seemed like to you at the time to be embraced by the Lord, can be no more than metaphorical-suggestive.[126]

Third: the anticipatory and retrospective frame for the couple's lovemaking is sealed by comment and encouragement from the daughters. Their lovemaking is not only for them; it occurs and has significance within a context wider than the couch-bed they have shared. At the first level, *ad litteram*, their pleasure and delight is communicated to those around them: the daughters are delighted by their delight, just as the guests at a wedding are delighted at the delight shared between bride and groom. That is a mutually resonant and mutually magnifying delight that is not only sentimental (how they love one another), but also physical and procreative (they will soon be lovers and may before long be parents). At the next level, in terms of the Lord and his Israel-church, his preparation of the bride to receive his lovemaking is not only for her and not only for him, but also for the pagan world. That he has chosen her has significance for the enlivening and awakening of the world that will, one day, come in to Zion to share in the amorous blessings already enjoyed by Israel-church. The daughters' delighted comment on the couple's lovemaking figures this. Further yet, your own lovemaking with the Lord is not only yours: you have been prepared for it by the people of the Lord, whether Jewish or Christian, anointed by that people as the Lord's lover. When—and this is the Christian version—the oils of baptism and confirmation stream luxuriously from your head into your eyes, you are being embraced by Jesus: and the congregation acclaims your embrace, a communal acclamation figured by what the daughters say in 5:1 to the couple. And, lastly, when Mary received the Lord's embrace and as a result conceived the Lord in her womb, that too was marked and acclaimed by others: angels, shepherds, magi, and, eventually, the church. In their acclamations can be heard echoes of the daughters' delight.

You can place yourself into the dialogue in these pivotal eight lines. You are the Song's beloved saying to the Lord, your lover, that he should come into your garden—into you as his garden—there to "eat his best fruits." To think of your-self as a garden planted and cultivated by the Lord is to assimilate yourself to the

126. A *locus classicus* is Augustine's description, retrospective and memorial, of the shared vision at Ostia in *Confessiones* 9.10.23–26 (Latin in James J. O'Donnell, *Augustine: Confessions* [Oxford: Clarendon, 1992], 1.113–14; English in Henry Chadwick, trans., *Saint Augustine: Confessions* [Oxford: Oxford University Press, 1991], 170–72). He too does not attempt to depict its phenomenology; he says things about what prepared for it and what followed from it; and he notes its transience, its occurrence *in ictu* ("in a lightning flash"). And no more. The affinity with the Song's depiction of orgasm is deep, and not accidental.

scriptural account of the Lord's Israel-church and to Mary, the figure at the heart of that account. And that is a properly Christian mode of reading these lines. But so reading them is also to do something more: it is to reconfigure your sense of yourself in your particularity. What are the things in you and about you planted by the Lord and delighted in by him? The formal answer is clear: the Lord's good fruits in you are all and only the things about you that are good: your beauty, your words and works of loving-kindness, your intellectual acuity, your moral virtues. Your own fruits, the ones you have planted and cultivated yourself, without the Lord's help, are all those that are bad: your ugliness, your corruption, your vice, your blindness, your violence. These things the Lord will not judge to be his "best fruits" and will not, when he enters your garden (something he does only at your invitation), be able to eat with delight. But this formal answer is not of much help in discerning which things about you are in fact good and which bad. We are not very good at doing that, mistaking often our vices for virtues and our virtues for vices. Introspection is a very blunt instrument. Hence the Song's impassioned invitation to the Lord to do that work: he is the one who is to come into the garden that is you, there to make the appropriate discriminations. You cannot do it: the Lord as your invited lover can. Just as your human lovers give to you your sense of yourself as a beloved, remaking you with a gift you cannot give to yourself and in that way permitting a self-understanding otherwise unavailable, so also the Lord will, if you ask him, do the same with respect to your "best fruits." He will show you what they are by eating them; and what he chooses to eat will often be a surprise. And, so the Song says, when you do ask the Lord into your garden, he will find there much to delight in: "myrrh with . . . spices," "honeycomb with honey," "wine with . . . milk."

Knocking at the Door (5:2)

> I sleep with wakeful heart—
> the voice of my delightful man who is knocking—
> "Open to me, O my sister, my beloved
> my dove, my stainless one—
> for my head is full of dew
> and my ringlets of the moisture of the night."

After the orgasmic culmination of 5:1, voice, place, and tone shift suddenly. She is in bed, speaking to and about herself in the present tense: "I sleep with wakeful heart," she says; and then at once she hears "the voice of my delightful man who is knocking," and reports what she hears. He is urging her, in the imperative mood, to "open" to him, and he follows the request with a flood of endearments, each of which has already been used at least once, and some many times, in the Song ("sister" in →4:8; "dove" in →1:15; "stainless one" in →4:7). This verse contains the first instance of the verb "open" (*aperire*): it occurs twice more in the immediately following verses (5:2, 6), and in each case it has an obvious and explicitly sexual meaning—he wants her to open her body—as well as the surface meaning that he wants her to open the door to her bedroom.

They are apart again. A new lyric begins. The shift here is evidence of the approximately chiastic structure of the Latin Song as it now stands. Immediately before the pivotal eight lines of 5:1, the lover has been addressing his beloved ("a closed garden"; 4:12) and calling to her ("north wind get up!"; 4:16) to come to him and open to him. Here, in 5:2, immediately after the crux, the same occurs again: they are separated and she hears him calling to her, asking her once again to open herself to him.

The Song's chiasmus is evident in this repetition of the separation-and-calling theme: it brackets the delightful consummation of 5:1. The structure is theologically suggestive too. Union has just occurred, but it is transient, maintained for only a moment, immediately preceded and immediately followed by separation. The lyrics of the Song do not provide a clear narrative line—they are, after all, lyrics—and so no narrative explanation is given for the oscillation between presence and absence. Reading the Song as a scriptural book makes the oscillation clear, however: intercourse between the Lord and his Israel-church is always intermittent in this way. That is not because the Lord's love for his people fluctuates, although it may often seem to the people that this is so. It is because the people cannot sustain intimacy's embrace. They (we) withdraw from it because of ignorance and sin; and they (we) must then constantly turn back to it in order to receive it again. The Lord is always "knocking," asking that we open to him. Sometimes we do, fully and willingly, as Mary archetypally did; sometimes we do in part, withholding something, giving the Lord our embraces tentatively, our lips half-open under his; and sometimes we altogether fail to do so, turning our gaze away and averting our bodies and mouths. These rhythms are of course familiar to human lovers: in those loves too there are rhythms of joining and separating, presence and absence, desire and aversion. Those rhythms participate in and are figured by those of the Lord and his loves.

The lover says that his "head is full of dew" and his "ringlets" dripping with "the moisture of the night." The words "dew" (*ros*) and "moisture" (*gutta*) occur only here in the Song, but there are frequent mentions of the head and the hair, both his and hers, and always as part of the vocabulary of delight and desire (→4:1b). The hair is ornamented and arranged to be delightful to the beloved other, and the tropes of wetness here add to this effect. "Dew," in scripture, has some particular resonances that support and deepen the surface erotic meaning. Most frequently, "dew" is spoken of as the Lord's gift (Ps. 133:3; Isa. 45:8), freely given and delightful, ornamenting the ground in the morning and making whatever it touches beautiful ("heavenly" [*caelis ros*] in Dan. 4–5). Its spontaneous descent illustrates and embodies the Lord's gift of knowledge, justice, and wisdom: the Lord gives these as he gives the dew (Prov. 19:12; Exod. 16:13 [manna]; Isa. 26:19

[resurrection]). "Moisture," meaning usually "drops of moisture," is less common in scripture (Wis. 11:22); but it shares in many of the meanings already given for "dew" and sometimes occurs together with it (as a gift from above in Sir. 1:2; 18:8 [= 18:10 RSV]; 24:21 [= 24:30 RSV]). With these scriptural echoes in mind, the description of the lover's hair wet with dew emphasizes his appearance as gift to her: if she opens her door to him, she will be receiving blessings. But it is not clear that she can do it, just as it is not clear that we can. Having been the Lord's beloved, ravished by him, does not mean that we can continue to be.

Doubts (5:3)

> I have stripped off my tunic—
> how can I put it on?
> I have washed my feet—
> how can I make them dirty?

She, in bed, is not sure she wants the blessings of his dew-filled hair and his caressing presence. "I have," she says in soliloquy, debating with herself (reporting these events as though recalling them, again, perhaps, in dream-reverie), "stripped off my tunic / how can I put it on?" She has washed her "feet" for bed, and if she gets up she will make them "dirty" again. She offers here two objections to closer union, objections that stand in deep tension with the passions already described.

The "feet" are the organs in question, and they are not made much of in the Song, being mentioned only here and in 7:2, at the beginning of the lover's third body-hymn: "How beautiful your sandaled feet." Elsewhere in scripture, feet are mentioned hundreds of times (Chrétien 2005: chap. 15): to fall at someone's feet is to venerate them (2 Kgs. 4:37; Matt. 28:9; Mark 5:22; Rev. 22:8); to tread on someone is to dominate them (Josh. 10:24 [cf. Ruth 3:4]; 2 Sam. 22:39; 1 Kgs. 5:17 [= 5:3 RSV]; Matt. 22:44); to wash someone's feet is submissively to love and serve them (Gen. 18:4; 19:2); to speak of someone's feet is to speak of where they are going and where they have come from, of the person in motion toward or away from a proper goal (1 Sam. 2:9; 2 Sam. 22:34; Job 29:6; Ps. 73:2; Prov. 1:15; Eccl. 4:17 [= 5:1 RSV]; Isa. 52:7; Matt. 18:8; Rom. 3:15); and to go unshod may show reverence or penitence (Exod. 3:5; Josh. 5:15; Isa. 20:2). For Christians, feet have a special significance because of two New Testament episodes: the anointing of Jesus's feet with oil and tears by Mary, the sister of Lazarus and Martha (Matt. 26:6–13 || Mark 14:3–9 || Luke 7:36–50 || John 12:1–8), and Jesus's washing of the disciples' feet (John 13:1–20). In these stories, the feet represent the dirtiest part of the body, the part most in need of washing and anointing; and the two washings—of Jesus's feet with ointment (→1:2–3a) and of the disciples' feet with water—show the necessity, for Christians, of revering and serving what is most unclean.

The Song's grammar of the body does not have much to say explicitly about the feet: it is especially notable that nothing is said about the lover's feet (even though there is a good deal about his coming and going, his approaching and leaving). But the resonances between the beloved's thought that her clean feet serve as a reason for not getting up to let her lover in and the foot-washings of the New Testament are suggestive. When the beloved's lover is read as the Lord, and especially as the Lord most intimately known in the flesh as Jesus, her refusal to dirty her feet in approaching him becomes a clear instance of her (and Israel's, and the church's, and our own) tendency to guard her purity from the risk of defilement. She is, she thinks, clean in her bed, safe in her room, thoroughly washed. Her feet, a synecdoche for the person in motion, therefore, she thinks, do not need to take her anywhere: she is where she needs to be. But she is not: her feet, and ours, have only one direction in which they need to move us, and that is toward the Lord's face and embrace. If our feet get dirty on the way to him, he will cleanse them for us, as he did for the disciples. What she needs to do is to get up and get moving, secure in the certainty that the Lord will wash her in making love to her.

There is much movement in the Song: from country to city, from inside to outside, from city back to country. And although the feet are not explicitly mentioned in connection with these comings and goings, they are there in the background. The feet are what take you where you are going, and the wanderings and separations in the Song (especially 3:1–4; 5:3–7; 7:1) play with this *pars pro toto* meaning of the feet. With them, the beloved wanders, separated; thinking of them, she moves both toward her lover and away from him; and he, "leaping among the mountains / skipping over the hills" (2:8), comes to her by foot, and as often departs from her to mysterious places—to "the nut garden" (6:11) and "the spice mountains" (8:14). The participation in all this of the relation between the Lord and his Israel-church should be sufficiently clear not to need belaboring.

Her Belly Trembles (5:4)

> My delightful man put his hand through the chink
> and my belly trembled.

Her objections to getting up to let him in seem flimsy to the Song's hearer, and as soon as her "delightful man" puts "his hand through the chink"—presumably, through the door's narrow opening (→2:14) or perhaps an opening at the window (→2:9)—her "belly tremble[s]."

In addition to this mention of the "belly," the beloved praises her lover's "belly" (*venter*) as "ivory / sapphire-adorned" (5:14), and he likens hers to "a heap of wheat / fortified by lilies" (7:3). Scripturally, the belly has a range of meaning.[127] The first

---

127. "The belly is not an organ but a region of the body of which the exact delimitation varies according to the vocabulary of one or another author" (author's translation of Chrétien 2005: 225); for further analysis, see Chrétien 2005: chap. 11.

is that it is a fecund place, and when the word is used in this sense it is effectively indistinguishable from the womb, the place in which babies are conceived and carried and from which they are born (Gen. 25:23; Deut. 7:13; Mic. 6:7; Luke 11:27 [Mary's *venter* blessed as the region of the body that carried Jesus]; John 3:4). The second is that it is a place of digestion, into which food goes and from which excrement comes (Sir. 36:20 [= 36:18 RSV]; Ezek. 3:3 [the place where the scroll the prophet is ordered to eat is to be digested; cf. Rev. 10:9–10]; 1 Cor. 6:13; Matt. 15:17). And the third, most relevant to understanding the Song's use of the word, is that the belly stands as synecdoche for the body as intensely labile and motile, tremblingly responsive to whatever is offering itself (Ps. 31:10 [= 31:9 RSV]; 22:15 [= 22:14 RSV] ["my heart has become like liquid wax in the midst of my *venter*"]; 44:26 [= 44:25 RSV]; Sir. 51:29 [= 51:21 RSV]; Hab. 3:16). The response may be fearful, lustful, joyful, anticipatory, or what-have-you; but when the person's belly trembles in any of these ways, she is fully engaged, profoundly responsive. This is the meaning present in the beloved's mention of her belly trembling at her lover's approach: she is emotionally and sexually excited, her whole body responsively and tensively attuned to his. There is also, in the Song's use of the word, at least a hint of the fecund-sexual range of meanings. When the lover likens the beloved's belly to a "heap of wheat" (7:3), he is suggesting that her belly is like wheat stacked in sheaves after the harvest, ready to be baked and eaten (Job 5:26); and when she speaks of his belly as ivorine and bedecked with sapphires (Exod. 24:10 [sapphires under the Lord's feet]; Ezek. 1:26; 10:1 [chariot visions]; Rev. 21:19 [the foundations of the New Jerusalem]), or he of hers as lily fortified (→1:7), the connotation is of the delightfully attractive purity of the body prepared for love. When the couple speak of one another's bellies, therefore, they are speaking of one another as ready and eager for love, responsive, attuned, trembling, open, and beautiful.

The beloved's belly figures that of the Lord's Israel-church. It is tremblingly attuned to his approach as she is to the lover's, and her trembling belly carries with it the promise and possibility of conception and birth. This possibility becomes actual in Mary's belly/womb, blessed by Elizabeth and by an unnamed woman in Luke's Gospel as having borne Jesus (Luke 1:42; 11:27; cf. 23:29). The attuned responsiveness of Israel-church culminates here, finds its supreme fruit here.[128] But that is not the end of the belly story. In John's Gospel we find the following passage: "On the last and greatest day of the Festival [of Tabernacles], Jesus stood and exclaimed, 'If someone thirsts, let him, the one who believes in me, come to me and drink. As scripture says, rivers of living water will flow from his belly.' He said this about the Spirit whom those who will have believed in him were to receive" (John 7:38).[129] The suggestiveness of this passage for exegesis of the

---

128. Rupert of Deutz, *Commentaria in Canticum Canticorum* (Commentary on the Song) on Song 5:4 (Deutz and Deutz 2005: 418–26).

129. The word translated "belly" is *venter*. The New Vulgate's Old Testament provides no verbatim equivalent for the words *flumina de ventre eius fluent aquae vivae*, but there are many

Song is that the lovers' bellies participate figuratively in and foreshadow not only Mary's belly as pregnant with the Son, but also the church's belly as delivering the Spirit. Each of the baptized—and the church as a whole—has a belly from which comes streams of living water to give the parched world life and to douse the fires of its self-assertive and self-possessive passions.

The Song's few mentions of the belly open up a rich scriptural field and thereby an even richer theological one. You, as the Song's hearer, may, by attending to the Song as scripture, come to think of your own belly as attuned to the Lord, tremblingly anticipatory of the Lord's love, fertile, delightful, pregnant with blessings for the world, full of living water. This understanding, no more than sketched here, attunes you to Mary as the fullest image of the Song's beloved. But it does not erase the particularity of the bellies of the Song's lovers; those bellies remain as they are: beautifully seductive to one another, ivorine, sapphire ornamented, wheat heaped, trembling with desire.

She Gets Up (5:5)

> I got up so that I might open to my delightful man
> my hands dripping with myrrh
> my fingers full of choicest myrrh
> above the bolt's handle.

When the lover's hand reaches in to her, she responds in spite of her doubts and reservations. She cannot help herself. She gets up so that she "might open to" him—open, that is, both her door and herself—and with her "fingers full of choicest myrrh" moves her hands toward the bolt of the door[130] and opens to him. "Myrrh" (→1:13) is connected scripturally with both sex and death, as well as with the anointing of the ark of the covenant and the body of the Lord Jesus. Her fingers drip with it here; her lover was a sachet of it between her breasts (1:13); and his lips will soon be said to drip with it (5:13); its erotic overtones are overwhelming. That her fingers are dripping with myrrh shows her readiness and eagerness for his lovemaking.

This is the most concentrated instance of hand and finger talk in the Song, heavily laden with erotic imagery. Elsewhere, his hands are praised too, as "lathe-turned gold / violet-full" (5:14). "Lathe-turned gold" carries with it connotations of smoothness and beauty and elegance all at once: his hands are (like the) work

---

echoes and overlaps and resonances (Isa. 44:3; 55:1; 58:11; Ezek. 47:1; cf. "living waters" in →4:15).

130. *Pessulum*, the word translated "bolt," occurs only here in scripture. *Ansa* ("handle") is found elsewhere, but exclusively in discussions of the Solomonic temple's decorations (Exod. 26:5, 10; 36:11, 17). This is one more piece of evidence that the house in which the beloved sleeps is like the Lord's temple, a place to which he returns as if to his own place.

of a master craftsman ("craftsmen's hands" are said to have made "the curves of [her] thighs"; 7:2), working beautifully in response to that work.

Our hands and fingers are instruments for our work and our making; talk of them in scripture is also often talk of what we do and how we do it, of our capacity as agents to shape, form, adorn, and reach out to the hands of others (Chrétien 2005: chap. 13). This range of meanings is evident in scriptural talk about the Lord's hands and fingers too: the *manus Dei* or *digitus Dei* can lie heavily upon the people of Israel as a weight shaping them (1 Sam. 5:11; Job 12:9; 19:21; 1 Pet. 5:6); it can serve as periphrasis for the Lord's agency in general, and for his gift of particular things (Eccl. 2:24), some perceived as good and some as bad; and when the reference is to the "finger" rather than the "hand," some very particular action is usually in play, as when the Lord's finger writes upon the stone tablets (Exod. 31:18; Deut. 9:10) or when the priest is instructed to smear the blood of the sin offering on specific parts of the altar with his finger (Lev. 4). With a similar degree of specificity, Jesus sticks his finger in a deaf man's ear to heal him (Mark 7:33) and uses his finger to write something on the ground when asked by the Pharisees whether an adulterous woman should be stoned (John 8:6). Of like kind too are Thomas's demand to be able to put his finger into Jesus's wounds (John 20:25–27) and the suffering rich man's request of Abraham to have Lazarus "dip the end of his finger in water and cool my tongue" (Luke 16:24).

The grammar of the hands and the fingers in the Song fits into this broader picture. The lovers' hands and fingers perform the very particular actions of reaching out to one another with the promise of caresses—"full of choicest myrrh," ready to anoint the body of the other. Their agency as lovers finds concentrated expression in the ends of their fingers to a degree rivaled only by their lips. In this all lovers participate and can find their use of their hands and fingers in their lovemaking intensified and sanctified by knowing what the Song says about these parts of their bodies.

Absence (5:6)

> I opened to my delightful man,
> but he had turned aside and gone away.
> My soul melted because he had left.
> I sought and did not find him
> I called and he did not respond.

Still recalling, in reverie, she remembers that she has "opened" herself to him. But he is not there: "he had turned aside and gone away." She is anguished ("my soul melted") because he has left. At once, she recalls, she looked for him and called him, but she "did not find him" and "he did not respond." This is a theme the Song has already sounded (3:1–4), and its importance is signaled by the triple verbatim repetition of the words "I sought and did not find him" (3:1, 2; 5:6). Here the theme of seeking and not finding is intensified by reference to the "melting" (*liquefacere*) of her soul, something that has no parallel in 3:1–4. This verb occurs only here in the Song, and rarely elsewhere in scripture. When it does occur, it always connotes loss of solidity and firmness: kingdoms and cities may melt in this sense (Ps. 46:7 [= 46:6 RSV]; 75:4 [= 75:3 RSV]; 147:18), as may confidence or arrogance (Josh. 7:5). Whether the melting is a good thing or a bad depends entirely upon whether what is melted is desirable. In the beloved's case, it is her "soul" that melts, which is the locus of her delight: "the man in whom my soul delights" has been a refrain earlier in the Song (3:1–4), and her soul's melting signals the loss of delight: her "delightful man" is no longer present to her, and in his absence what gave her soul—the faculty of delight—solidity is also absent. She dissolves, and the marks of her dissolution are grief and the quest for reunion and further delight. That quest is at first frustrated: "I sought and did not find him / I called and he did not respond."

The Guards (5:7)

> The guards found me,
> those who walk around the city
> those who care for the ramparts—
> they beat me and wounded me
> and took my cloak from me.

What happens instead, she continues to report, looking back on events now past, is that the "guards found" her, "those who walk around the city" and "who care for the ramparts." The "guards" (*custodes*) have appeared in the Song before, in 3:1–4, there called "watchmen" (*vigiles*): the identifying descriptive phrase, "those who walk around the city," appears verbatim in both places (→3:3). In 3:1–4 she asks these watchmen/guards whether they have seen her lover, the man in whom her soul delights; and while their answer is not given, she reports that "soon after I had passed them by" (3:4) she finds him again. Here, in 5:3–7, the matter is rather more grim: "they beat me," she says, "and wounded me / and took my cloak from me." Here again, the city is the place of desolation, the place where the lover is not and where roam all the dangers of separation and absence. The "guards" are there to preserve the integrity of the city and especially to take care of its "ramparts" (*muros*), a word that occurs later in the Song (8:8–10), where it is used, enigmatically, perhaps on the lips of the beloved, to describe both herself and "our sister" who is "little / and without breasts" (→8:8). The thought, perhaps, bearing both these texts in mind, is that the beloved is the true city and therefore stands over against the false city. Those who guard the streets and ramparts of the false city, therefore, must oppose her, and this they do by beating and wounding her.

The beloved's wound in these verses is not the first to be mentioned in the Song: the lover's heart has already been "wounded" by her eyes (→4:9). The wound is in both cases a love wound, in the former the kind belonging to love's presence, and in the latter the kind belonging to separation from the beloved. Love's separation wounds are everywhere in scripture and tradition: in Israel's exile, in Peter's tears, in Mary's grief for her dead son. The separation wound in which all these participate, around which they circle, is the wound of Christ crucified,[131] a wound given verbal form in the cry of desolation on the cross (Matt. 27:46). The Song's love wounds, heard in the light of knowledge of that wound, are given their deepest possible resonance: hearing them in that way and interpreting through them your own separation wounds, which you have either undergone already or shortly will, adds depth to your understanding of and response to those wounds too. They are no longer uniquely yours, unprecedented and incomprehensible. Such knowledge will not, and should not, lessen their pain; but it can place that pain under the cross's shadow and wash it in the blood dripping from the Lord's side as he hangs dead thereon. The city's "guards" have beaten and wounded the beloved in her separation. They will beat and wound you too.

These verses (5:3–7) pack a great deal into a very few words. She, the beloved, is reluctant to get out of bed for him, reluctant to open herself to him, hugging the warmth and comfort and cleanliness of her solitary bed to herself. But then, overcoming her reluctance, warm and wet now with eagerness for him, dripping with myrrh, she gets up to open her door, happy to embrace him. But he is not there. He does not respond to her call. She cannot find him. She wanders, searching and suffering, and is beaten and wounded. She is desolate. This is love's story in a nutshell for all of us: it is Dido, wounded by Aeneas's departure and weeping and dying in flames for it; it is Jude Fawley, wounded by Sue Bridehead's absence as much as by her presence, separated from his children by murder and suicide, and dying in disappointment; it is King Lear's grief-death, sundered from the daughters he has loved by their murders, suicides, and executions; and it is your own foolish reluctance to love, and your inevitable agonies of separation. All these participate in and figure Mary's separation from her son and her grief at his death on the cross. Love's separation wounds are incised deeply into all our bodies, and the Song's thematization of them permits them, rightly heard, to appear in their livid and bloody glory.

131. There is no verbal echo here, however. The verbs used for the scourging and piercing of Jesus in the Gospel accounts of the crucifixion are different from those used for wounding and beating in 5:7.

Third Adjuration (5:8)

> O daughters of Jerusalem—I adjure you
> if you should find my delightful man
> what should you say to him?
> That I languish with love.

The beloved's voice now speaks, echoing but changing the adjuration formula spoken thrice elsewhere in the Song (2:7; 3:5; 8:4) by the lover to the daughters (→2:7). The beloved, like the lover, adjures the daughters; but unlike the lover's instruction to them not to awaken the beloved, she tells them to carry a message to her lover: "I languish with love" (*amore langueo*; verbatim at 2:5). She is heavy, that is to say, with love's sickness (→2:5), injured by the absence of the lover; she wants them to find him for her and let him know that.

What Is Good about the Lover? (5:9)

> O most beautiful of women
> how is your delightful man better than others
> how is he better than others
> that you so adjure us?

The adjuration formula in 5:8 marks, as it has before, the end of a lyrical sequence describing the couple's coming together (4:9–5:1) and their consequent separation. The new lyric is introduced by the daughters' questioning response to the beloved's adjuration of them: Why should we bother? What is so special about your lover? "How is he better than others / that you so adjure us?" The daughters here do what they do in six of their seven interjections, which is to ask a question as prompt for what is to follow (3:6; 5:9; 6:1, 10; 7:1; 8:5).[132] Their voice also serves here, as often (but not always) elsewhere in the Song, as the voice of the Song's hearers—as your voice. Why, you want to know, does the beloved adjure the daughters to tell her lover that she languishes with love? The daughters voice your question, and in the following verses (5:10–16) the beloved answers it by depicting the delights of his body, cataloging the things that make her lover better than others.

Praising the Lover's Body (5:10–16)

> My delightful man is dazzling and ruddy
> distinguished among thousands—

132. The exception is 5:1, where the daughters encourage, imperatively and in congratulatory tone, the couple's lovemaking.

his head is of the best gold
ringlets like palm fronds
raven-black;
his eyes are like doves'
above rivers of water
milk-washed
beside completely full streams;
his cheeks are like seedbeds of spices
ointment piled up;
his lips are lilies
dripping prime myrrh;
his hands are lathe-turned gold
violet-full;
his belly is ivory
sapphire-adorned;
his legs are marble pillars
founded upon golden pedestals;
his comeliness is like Lebanon's
he is set apart like a cedar;
his throat is supremely smooth
and completely desirable.
Such is my delightful man—that very one is my lover
O daughters of Jerusalem.

In this, her only hymn to her lover's body, the beloved answers the daughters'
question as to why she thinks him better than other men (her lover, by contrast,
as we have seen, praises her body in three separate hymns: 4:1–6; 6:5–7; 7:2–6).
It is because he is so physically beautiful and desirable that he is "distinguished
among thousands." Her praise-hymn begins and ends with a formula of response
to the daughters, and in between (5:11–16) mentions, in the following order, his
"head," "ringlets," "eyes," "cheeks," "lips," "hands," "belly," "legs," and "throat." She also
praises his appearance ("dazzling and ruddy," perhaps indicating his complexion)
and mentions his "comeliness" as a general term of approbation. There is no clear
top-to-bottom or bottom-to-top order here; all the body parts, whether his or hers,
have been mentioned and elaborated before; and a high proportion of the tropes
here have already occurred, as well. The language is throughout of delighted appreciation rather than overt desire, at least until we reach 5:16, where she calls his
"throat" "completely desirable" (→2:3b). In praising his body she uses a mixture of
similes, explicitly likening a part of his body to something (*sicut . . . sicut . . . sicut
. . . ut*), and metaphors, in which the part in question is simply said to be this or
that—"marble pillars" for the "legs," or "lathe-turned gold" for the "hands."

She begins by applying to him, perhaps to his skin, the adjectives "dazzling"
and "ruddy." The first of these, "dazzling" (*candidus*), occurs only here in the Song.

It is, elsewhere in scripture, most often applied to things (teeth [Gen. 49:12], clothes, thrones, clouds [Rev. 14:14], head and hair [1:14]) that dazzle the eye because of their whiteness. It is always a positive term, used of such things as angelic garments and the garments of the transfigured Jesus (Dan. 7:9; Eccl. 9:8; Lam. 4:7; 2 Macc. 11:8; Matt. 28:3; Mark 9:3; 16:5; Acts 10:30; Jas. 2:2). The beloved couples it here with the epithet "ruddy" (*rubicundus*), which also occurs only here in the Song and rarely elsewhere in scripture. When it does occur, it is always to label something red or reddish, sometimes neutrally and sometimes positively (red paint in Wis. 13:14; the bodies of princes in Lam. 4:7; the sky in Matt. 16:2). When she calls her lover both "dazzling" and "ruddy," she combines images of redness and whiteness into a whole that emphasizes the overwhelming beauty and vitality of his face, which is what the world—or the daughters—will see first when they look at him.

She moves then, in her lovingly delighted depiction of his body, from the skin of his face to the beauties of his "head" and his "hair," applying to "head" a metaphor of delight ("of the best gold") and to "hair" a simile of the same ("like palm fronds / raven-black"). "Gold" is precious and beautiful and rare; so also his "head." And the "fronds" dangling from a "palm" tree ornament its shape delightfully, as his "raven-black ringlets" do that of his head. The language is sensual and delighted; you can feel her eagerness to run her fingers through those ringlets and to stroke the dazzlingly ruddy skin of that golden head, and in feeling it you can, and should, have the texture and color and smell of your own lover's hair brought to mind.

"Hair" is a synecdoche more often for female beauty than male in scripture: women arrange and adorn their hair for seduction and for the provision of male delight (Jdt. 16:8; 1 Pet. 3:3; cf. 1 Cor. 11:14 for the difference between male and female hair), but such tropes are not used in scripture outside the Song for male hair and heads (→4:1b; →5:2). When the beloved speaks like this of her lover's head and hair, she uses terms more commonly applied, scripturally speaking, to women. She also uses terms he uses elsewhere in the Song of her: she too has "ringlets," praised in strong terms by him (7:6). There is here an instance of a theme often present in the Song, which is that the endearments and praises they offer one another are reversible and exchangeable. What she says to him he can say to her, and what he says to her she can say to him. The Song's depiction of desire and delight in the body of the other shows considerable fluidity in this way, and this is among the reasons why you, whether your beloved is male or female, can with relative ease see the delights of his or her body refracted and deepened through the Song's praises of both the male and the female body.

From the hair of the head to the "eyes," which are like "doves" or (as here) the eyes of doves (→1:15). Again, there is exchangeability: what is said of her eyes can also be said of his.

Thence to his "cheeks" (→1:10; →4:3b), moving still in downward direction from the eyes. The new element here is the simile of the "seedbeds of spices" (*areolae aromatum*), an expression repeated verbatim at →6:2, where it is a place in the beloved's garden. The only other scriptural occurrence of *areola* ("seedbed") is Ezek. 17:7 in the story of the two eagles and the vine. There the word is used to describe the place where the Lord plants the Israel-vine, and it is contrasted with the transplanting of that vine into exile in Babylon. The "seedbed" is therefore a place in which by divine favor good and beautiful things grow. So also for the lover's cheeks. The fluidity of the Song's tropes is shown by the "seedbeds" serving to explain what his body is like, while in 6:2 they represent what his garden is like, and thus, because his garden is also his beloved, also her body. The same is true of the "ointment," which in →1:3a is attached to the lover's "kisses" and "loves," in 4:10 to her scent, and in 4:14 to the beloved-as-garden.

And so to the "lips" (→1:2; →4:3a), which she likens to myrrh-dripping "lilies" (→1:7–8), thus combining an image of the purely delightful ("lilies") with one of sensual excess ("dripping prime myrrh"). Her hands have already been said to be "dripping with myrrh" (→5:5; →1:13), and so again we have an epithet exchanged between the two of them.

After the "lips" come the "hands," which she describes as of "lathe-turned gold." They reach out, "violet-full," for her. His hands are, that is, full of one of the colors used to weave the tabernacle's curtain and the priest's vestments, colors that signal the intimacy of those who bear them with the Lord.[133] The lover's hands have, therefore, a like intimacy, and in reaching out for her they intend to share that intimacy with her, to stain her body violet with their caresses, and in doing so to make her body violetly holy. The application of this image to the Lord's church is clear and easy: he, as lover, reaches for her, as beloved—again, the theme of the Lord's desire—and as his violet-filled golden "lathe-turned" hands (→5:5) find her, she is marked as his beloved, violet-stained as a public sign of her reconfiguration.

The lover's "belly" is, she says, ivorine and "sapphire-adorned." Both are images of purity and beauty, and they resonate with his later description (7:3) of her belly as "a heap of wheat." The belly is the place, scripturally speaking, of response to the Lord, whether with fear or delight: her "belly" trembles when he reaches for her "through the chink" (→5:4), and when it is both beautiful and adorned, as she here says of his belly, the implication is that the person is prepared for the Lord's caresses.

From "belly" to "legs," which are "marble pillars / founded upon golden pedestals." This is the only mention of the "legs" (*crura*), whether his or hers, in the Song, and the only mention too of "marble" or "pedestals." The only resonance her praise of his legs finds elsewhere in the Song is in her comparison of them

---

133. *Hyacinthus* ("violet") occurs only once in the Song, at 5:14, and it is hard to know how to translate it. It occurs dozens of times elsewhere in scripture, mostly in descriptions of the colors of fabrics to be used for such things as the veil around the tabernacle of the ark or the vestments of the high priest (many times in Exod. 25–39). The color in question appears to be blue-purple, perhaps violet. There are also a few cases in which the word is used, it seems, as the name of a precious stone (Exod. 28:19; 39:12; Rev. 21:20).

to "pillars," which also belong to Solomon's bed (3:10). The tropes are of beauty, solidity, and power. A scriptural echo of importance for Christians is the description in John 19:31 of the Roman soldiers' decision not to break Jesus's legs (*crura*) on the cross because he is already dead (this is the only use of this word in the New Testament). The Song's lover's legs have the stability and beauty of marble, difficult to break; and the echo of the unbrokenness of Jesus's legs is one more inner-scriptural way in which the lover figures the Lord—in this case the incarnate Lord (Chrétien 2005: chap. 14). Otherwise, there is no developed symbolism of the legs in the corpus of scripture: their grammar is not significantly different from that of the feet (→5:3; →7:2).

She follows the description of his legs with a mention of his "comeliness" (*species*), which is a word already used of her (→2:13b) and which is most often in scripture applied to a beautiful woman rather than to a man, though also to Israel, as the Lord's beloved. His "comeliness" is "like Lebanon's"—a place of beauty; Solomon's litter, we have already learned, was made of its woods (→3:9)—and he, she says, is "set apart" (*electus*) like a "cedar" tree, the tree traditionally and scripturally associated with Lebanon, and a tree of distinctive height and appearance. To be "set apart" is to be chosen for special status: the beloved will be said by the daughters to have been similarly "set apart" (→6:9–10), and the word carries with it overtones of covenant privilege: Israel has been set apart by the Lord, as was Mary. Her words about his "comeliness" provide the most concentrated instance yet of the exchangeability of epithets, and in very elevated terms: the lover and the beloved begin to merge.

"Such is my delightful man." You, the Song's attentive hearer, have your passions roused by the beloved's description of her lover, and that in two directions. The Song wants you to share in the beloved's delight in her lover: he is, physically, the ideal lover, the superlatively attractive lover, the lover you should want as yours. The daughters' question should be your question: why should we, why should you, care about this lover? The answer is simple: he is the best—her description of him concludes with superlatives ("supremely . . . completely"). The enumeration and specification of his charms provides the particulars of his unexcelled (and unexcellable, to take only a small step beyond the Song's text) beauty. But it is not just that you, the Song's hearer, begin to share the beloved's desire for the lover; it is also that you begin to see your own lover's beauty and desirability as participatory in those of the Song's lover. The particulars of your lover's desirability, whether male or female (specificity of gender is not to the point here; what the Song's female beloved says about her male lover can with equal ease be applied to your female lover, if you have one, as to your male lover, if you have one), are what they are because they are asymptotically like those of the ideal lover, whose body is eulogized in these words of the Song. Your delight in your lover's body is heightened and deepened by your saturation in the Song's beloved's delight in the body of her lover. This is one of the repeated effects of hearing the Song: transfiguration of your own particular loves.

Where Has the Lover Gone? (6:1)

> O most beautiful of women—
> where has your delightful man departed?
> Where has he turned aside?
> Shall we seek him with you?

The beloved has just praised her lover's body in detail and in that way given an answer to the daughters' first question, about what distinguishes her lover from other men. They respond to this answer first by calling her "most beautiful," a superlative already used of her twice in the Song (1:8; 5:9). This is one among the Song's constant reminders that the beloved, the Lord's Israel-church, has no peer: she is unique in the world, set aside and apart for the Lord's admiration and caresses as no other. She has just praised his body, and now, reciprocally, the daughters acknowledge her unsurpassed beauty.

But the daughters are puzzled. They have asked her what makes her lover special among men and have received their answer: there is none more handsome, none more splendid. It is clear too that she, the beloved is the "most beautiful of women." Why then are they not together? Where has he gone? As is typical in the Song, the daughters are questioners, speaking for you, the Song's hearer. They ask what you would like to ask, and the question here is about apparently inexplicable separation. The words used—"departed," "turned aside"—echo those used in the Song's earlier depictions of separation (→1:7; →3:1–6; →5:3–7; also →6:2). Here, as there, puzzlement and sadness are woven together: he is, as she has just told the daughters, surpassingly handsome and desirable; they are lovers; but they are separated and she does not know where he is. Furthermore, he is the one who has gone away. Their separation is depicted as not accidental but deliberate: he has left her. The new note added here is the daughters' suggestion that they might look for him with her.

The theological question here is difficult and pressing: if the Lord loves his people, why does he go away? Why is he not always there, kissing and caressing them? Why must the beloved wander the streets of the city looking for her lover (3:2–4)? Why, if the Lord loves you with a passion, does it so often seem that he is nowhere to be found, distinguished by absence rather than presence? Why was Mary abandoned by Jesus, first when as a boy he stayed behind in Jerusalem to debate the things of the Lord with the learned, and then by dying on the cross? There are two trajectories for thought here. Along one, we develop the idea that the Lord really does leave us, that there are times when he is simply absent. Along the other, we think that he is always identically present and that his absence is apparent only, an instance of the world's damage.

The rhetoric of the Song, as of much in scripture, resonates closely with the first of these trajectories. But the truth is approached more closely by following the second. The Lord does not leave those he loves, even though it seems that he does. His distance from his beloved Israel-church, like his distance from you, has two causes only: the first is the blindness of the beloved, and the second is the damaged diminishment of the world. Apparent absence caused by the beloved's blindness is perfectly compatible with full presence: Augustine makes this point elegantly by writing: "Your eyes participate in the light and so you see. Do they close? You have not diminished the light. Do they open? You have not increased the light."[134] The lover's departure in the Song is on this reading to be understood as the beloved's inability to see that he is there. In addition to blindness as an explanation for apparent absence, there is also the fact of the world's damage. Since the fall and the disorder produced by it—a disorder of the material cosmos as well as of human appetite and knowledge—the Lord must sometimes be economically or dispensationally absent, absent as a means of making later closer union possible. Jesus, after Pentecost, is present in the flesh to the church for only a few days: he ascends in order that the Spirit may come and in order, finally, that we may be fully and finally reunited with him. That absence carries with it no note of rejection or anger; it is required, regretfully and regrettably, by the state of things and accompanied always by prevenient and continuing love for us. Whether seeming or genuine, then, the Lord's absence from his beloved is never sought by him and never brought about by him as anything other than an act of love. The beloved's anguish at her lover's absence, together with the daughters' puzzled questions about it, should be read in this way: anything else is incompatible with the Lord's character. This view does not make our sense—the beloved's sense—of the Lord's absence any less agonizing.

He for Her, She for Him #2 (6:2–3)

> My delightful man has gone down into his garden
> to a seedbed of spices
> to graze in the gardens
> to gather lilies.
> I am for my delightful man and my delightful man is for me—
> the one who grazes among lilies.

The beloved replies to the daughters' question about where her lover has gone: "into his garden," she says, which means, in accord with the Song's standard usage, both to herself, for she is the garden, the place in which he disports himself and upon which he grazes, and to the place of lovemaking. She does not answer their question about whether they should or might accompany her in her search for

134. Author's translation of Augustine, *Tractatus in Iohannis evangelium* (Homilies on the Gospel of John) 39.8 (Latin and French in M.-F. Berrouard, ed. and trans., *Homélies sur l'Évangile de Saint Jean*, Oeuvres de Saint Augustine 71 [Paris: Études Augustiniennes, 1988], 294).

him. The implied answer to this is negative: she knows quite well where he is, and so she does not need their help in finding him.

The beloved has already (5:13) described her lover's cheeks as being like "seed-beds of spices" (*areola aromatum*), and now the same phrase is used to describe the "garden" into which he has gone. It is an image of sensory delight in the olfactory register: "spices," more than anything else, give intense pleasure to the nose, and the vocabulary of smell is threaded through the Song almost from its beginning. The lover's acts of love are "fragrant" (1:3); her "spikenard" perfume "gave off its scent" (1:12) as she lay on her lover's couch; the one "ascending through the desert / like a wisp of smoke" is "spiced with frankincense and myrrh / and all the perfumer's powders" (3:6); the "scent" of the beloved's "ointments is above all spices" (4:10); and in the garden scene of 4:12–5:1 there is a bouquet of smell and spice words, all in the service of depicting olfactory sensual delight as synecdoche for lovemaking. And the "seedbed" is a place, scripturally speaking, of special fertility appointed by the Lord: it is the place where good things grow (→5:13).

The repetition of "seedbed of spices" is significant in another way. In its first occurrence it was used by her of him—more specifically of his cheeks. Now it is again used by her to describe the garden to which he has gone. But the garden, as is evident in the pivotal scene of 4:12–5:1, is a trope for her. She, the "sister-bride," is the "closed garden," and it is in her as garden that he finds his pleasure. When she says of him that he has gone "into his garden" where there is "a seedbed of spices," the hearer who has the pattern and grammar of the Song in mind will see another instance of exchange: what has been said of him is also said of her, and what has been said of her is also said of him. The couple's boundaries blur and blend, just as their bodies merge in lovemaking. The exchange of epithets represents and participates in the intimacy of their union.

Much the same is true of the mention of grazing. This, in the Song, is usually his activity, and even when it is not—as when he encourages her to "graze [her] young goats" (1:8) and when he likens her breasts to "doe-born twins / grazing among lilies" (4:5)—the grazing of others is responsive to and participatory in his. He is the one who grazes and the one who causes or helps others to graze, as their "pastor." The lover does not merely graze, she tells the daughters. He does so in "his garden" and "among lilies." She is his garden, and she is the lilies he gathers. She tells the daughters in this way that he is where she is: what he is doing is exactly, as always, making love to her, seeking her out, caressing her, grazing upon her body (→1:7; →4:16–5:1).

There is in this verse a double paradox: he is absent from her (she is answering a question about where he has gone), and yet in saying where he is she describes him as being just where she is. The Lord's apparent absence, deeply and agonizingly felt, is signaled by the Song's grammar and rhetoric as precisely his presence. Second, what is said of the Lord's loverly beauties can also be said of his beloved's: each is a seedbed of spices, a bouquet of fertile beauty. For you, if you hear the Song as the Lord's lover, your imagination can be conformed to these paradoxes: his felt absence is his presence; your beauty is his, by epithet exchange.

The theme of separation that is really an intensification of intimacy, so strong in the Song, begs a christological and therefore also a mariological gloss.

The felt absence of Jesus between his deposition from the cross on Friday and his appearance to his followers on Sunday is, for Christians, the paradigmatic case of separation. The Lord is dead; he is not with us; his body lies, in fact, anointed with myrrh and aloes, in a garden tomb, "a seedbed of spice," to which, on Sunday morning, the women bring the *aromata*, the spices that they have prepared (Luke 24:1; John 19:38–42). But that absence, the absence of the crucified one, is both a preparation for the resurrection, a full presence, and also itself a presence to those separated from his presence in hell, a place to which he descended during the three days. That is the first christological separation-as-intensification-of-intimacy. The second is evident in the ascension: Jesus leaves in order that the Spirit, the comforter and advocate, might come and in order that he might be present to the church in its liturgy and especially in its eucharistic liturgy. We, as worshipers of the triune Lord, do not see any of the persons of the Trinity as they are, and that fact is a source of grief and lack: we do not yet know as we are known. But we do see and touch and taste the body and blood of the risen Lord in the Eucharist and are comforted and inspired thereby.

The suffering of separation as an intensification of intimacy has also a Marian form. Mary, figured by the Song's beloved, laments the absence of the Lord, who is her son, now dead and no longer with her; that lament has been depicted by the church endlessly both visually and musically, in the figure of the pietà and in the settings of the *stabat mater*. It is a genuine lament for a genuine absence. But even that absence, given interrogative form in the daughters' question, "O most beautiful of women— / where has your delightful man departed? / Where has he turned aside?" (6:1), is in fact the activity of love. As Mary holds the dead body of Jesus on her lap (not a scene depicted in scripture, but one consonant with what is said there and one whose frequent depiction in the church's art is the result of the Spirit's guidance of the church), he is, in descending into hell, doing what is necessary to prepare heaven for the queenship into which she will enter when she is assumed.

The trope of absence—he "has gone down into his garden"—is at once overwritten or reinterpreted. Yes, he seems to her to have left her, and yes, she languishes with love (2:5; 5:8); but in fact the only place he ever goes, and therefore the place always to find him, is just where he seems absent. Her body and soul yearn for him; but in that yearning is to be found his presence. The refrain with which the beloved ends her reply to the daughters underscores the point: "I am for him and he is for me" (→2:16). Here, as in both of its other occurrences in the Song (2:16; 7:11), this expression of confidence in ineradicable and unavoidable closeness to the lover is tightly linked with images of physical intimacy—of the lover grazing upon the beloved's lilies (2:16; 6:3), that is, making love to her or being encouraged to lick, suck, and chew upon her throat (7:10–11).

The Song's pendulumlike movement between separation's pain and meeting's pleasure is evident most deeply here, even if seeing it requires some hard looking. For a beloved to wail to her friends her pain at the lover's absence—and then to answer their question about where he has gone by saying that he is caressing me right now—is dramatically counterintuitive. But it is a central theme of the Song and of the life of the church with the Lord: the Lord is never absent from his Israel-church, even though he might seem to be.

To find the absent Lord is easy: he is always with her (and you), seeking her lips, filling you with apples (2:5), his left hand under your head and his right embracing you (2:6; 8:3). The drama of the position provides, too, a template for the proper interpretation of our loves for one another. We are, especially when we love most truly, at the same time present to and absent from one another. Understanding this dialectic as figured by the Song's dialectic of presence and absence intensifies and transfigures our personal loves. You are for him and he is for you; so much is true, as well, and by participation, for you and your human lover.[135]

Praising the Beloved's Body #2 (6:4–7)

> O my beloved—you are beautiful like Tirzah
> splendid like Jerusalem
> terrible like an ordered rank from the camps.
> Turn your eyes away from me
> for they disturb me.
> Your hair like a flock of nanny goats
> coming down from Gilead;
> your teeth like a flock of sheep
> ascending from the bath
> each pregnant with twins
> not a sterile one among them;
> your cheeks like a fragment of pomegranate
> through your veil.

She has just (6:2) acknowledged his absent presence, grazing in her garden, the garden that she is, and reaffirmed her confidence in the uniqueness and indissolubility of their union (6:3). Now, at once, he speaks directly to her in a voice of fear and delight, opening with these words his second hymn of praise to her body. Most of what he says in these verses is said directly to her in the vocative, a voice speaking to her in the second person: "O my beloved ... you ... your ... your ...

---

135. On the theme of separation as intensification, see Christopher W. Mitchell, *The Song of Songs* (St. Louis: Concordia, 2003), 977–84.

your." He praises the features of her face ("eyes," "hair," "teeth," "cheeks") in words substantially identical to those used elsewhere in the Song (4:1–6; 7:2–6). And in his concluding simile ("terrible like an ordered rank from the camps") he uses words repeated verbatim almost at once (6:10) by the "queens and concubines" (6:9).

In this rapturous direct address, he begins, as usual, by calling her his *amica*, his "beloved," and then likens her beauty to that of "Tirzah" and her splendor to that of "Jerusalem." These similes compare her to the capitals of both the northern and southern kingdoms, cities than which there are, scripturally speaking, none more beautiful because they have been chosen by the Lord as the preferred places for his beloved Israel (1 Kgs. 15:33; 16:6–23; 2 Kgs. 15:14–16; cf. Josh. 12:24; 1 Kgs. 14:17; 15:21).[136] Tirzah, and the northern kingdom of which it is a part, is shadowed, scripturally, by destruction and the loss of the ten tribes. Tirzah's beauty (→1:10), therefore, is transient, while Jerusalem's is not and is better called "splendor," a term that belongs especially to the Lord and to others to the extent that the Lord grants it to them (→1:16). Likening her to these cities emphasizes both her beauty and her radiance in the eyes of others, a splendor granted her by the Lord as a signal of her special intimacy with him.

Not only is she splendid and beautiful: she is also "terrible," an epithet used of her only here and at 6:10, where the formulation "terrible like an ordered rank from the camps" recurs verbatim. "Terrible" is used most often in scripture for the Lord himself, or for his deeds, or for a place closely associated with the Lord and his deeds (Joel 2:11; 2 Macc. 1:24; Gen. 28:17; Deut. 28:58 [the Lord's name]; Judg. 13:6; Heb. 10:27 [judgment day]; cf. Wis. 18:17 [dreams]; Sir. 9:18 [loquacious people]; Dan. 2:31 [the vision statue]). Calling her "terrible" associates her closely with the Lord, just as does calling her "splendid." But the connotations of the former word are different. Terrible things strike fear or at least apprehension into those faced with them, as the Lord's presence typically does to those who encounter him in scripture. Splendor may do this too: you may be dazzled by it, forced to look away, eager to be somewhere else; but it may also delight and impress. The three epithets for her in 6:4 ("beautiful … splendid … terrible") show her to be in his eyes at the same time delightful, awe-inspiringly impressive, and downright frightening. He desires her, is awed by her, and fears her all at once, a gamut of responses not rarely predicated of those in scripture who are faced by the Lord or, by extension, by Israel, his chosen one. Elihu's speech to Job, just before the Lord's speech from the whirlwind, brings together these ideas and this vocabulary, in speaking of the Lord's majestic presence: "From the north comes golden splendor [*splendor auri*], / surrounding the Lord in terrible majesty [*terribilis maiestas*]" (Job 37:22; cf. Isa. 18:2–7 [Israel as she appears/will appear to the nations]). The description of the beloved in Song 6:4 makes her an

---

136. Tirzah is also the name of Zelophahad's daughter (Num. 26:33; 27:1; 36:11), but she does not appear to be remembered for her beauty, and so the scriptural resonance with the city is what counts for the Song. But see Kingsmill 2009: 268–69 for a different view.

intimate participant in the Lord: his predicates are exchangeable with hers, and it is his mouth that says so.

The simile at the end of 6:4, to which "terrible" is applied, contains a string of words—"ordered," "rank," "camp"—found only here in the Song and in the repetition of this verse at 6:10. The trope is military (→8:9–10): the terror of her appearance, her beauty and splendor, is like that of a troop of soldiers, standing to attention and caparisoned for war. The terms "rank" and "camp" occur fairly frequently elsewhere in scripture, and usually with this clear military reference.[137] "Ordered" (*ordinata*) is a little more suggestive. The verb connotes orderly arrangement, which certainly fits the military simile in play here: the troops are ordered, standing in ranks, drawn up for display of battle-readiness. But it is never used elsewhere in scripture in a military connection. Instead, wisdom is said to be ordered—set up, established in orderly fashion, given as ordered—by the Lord from the beginning (Prov. 8:23); the law is ordered (Gal. 3:19); the priests of the Solomonic temple stand in order (2 Chr. 30:16); the days required for the keeping of feasts are ordered (Neh. 8:18); and so on.[138] These echoes may illuminate from afar the figure in play in Song 6:4. That the beloved's terribleness is "ordered" likens her distantly to the figures of wisdom and the law, both gifts of the Lord.

From hymning her beauty, splendor, and terror, the lover passes to the praise of her face. Here, unlike the other hymns of praise to her body (4:1–6; 7:2–6), only those parts of the body above the neck are mentioned: "eyes," "hair," "teeth," "cheeks." The last three of these are treated in terms identical to those used elsewhere in the Song (→4:1–6); and in the lover's mention of the beloved's eyes as disturbing—"turn your eyes away from me / for they disturb me"—he returns to the theme of the eyes' danger and the wound of love they can inflict.[139] This theme, earlier adumbrated (→4:9), is here deepened by its close connection to the beloved's terribleness. Love wounds: and the Lord too is wounded in love, figurally here and really on the cross.

The Only One (6:8–9)

> Sixty queens
> eighty concubines
> young girls beyond number—

137. *Acies* ("rank") can mean "battle/military engagement" (1 Sam. 4:16; Deut. 20:2) or "troops ready for battle" (1 Sam. 17:2; 2 Sam. 10:17). *Castrum* ("camp") is either a military camp (Exod. 14:20; 32:26) or a label for the temporary residence of a people on the move (Exod. 19:16–17; Heb. 13:11–13).

138. Luke too writes to Theophilus that his account will be given *diligenter ex ordine* (1:3), which is to say diligently and in ordered sequence.

139. The verb translated "disturb" (*conturbare*) is found only here in the Song. Elsewhere in scripture it can connote fear *simpliciter* (the boy's response to the demon in Mark 9:20) or the disturbances of desire (Sir. 51:29 [= 51:21 RSV]). Both meanings are no doubt intended here.

> but the dove—my perfect one—is the only one
> her mother's only one
> set apart by her genetrix.
> The daughters saw her and proclaimed her supremely blessed
> the queens and concubines also praised her.

A dramatic shift in tone and topic produces uncertainty as to whose voice to attribute these words to. Probably the lover continues to speak. He has just been addressing the beloved directly in the second person, and if these words are read as his then he now speaks about her in the third person ("the dove—my perfect one ... / her ... her"), providing facts about her ("her mother's only one / set apart by her genetrix") and specifying what the "daughters" and "queens and concubines" think of her. He speaks once in the first person ("my perfect one"), which supports the reading of these words as his: only he would say this of her. The lyric shifts position and forces your attention away from a scene of his direct address to her and toward one of his thought about her and what others have said of her. It is as though he, the lover, the Lord, moves from stage right, where he was gazing at her brightly and beautifully lit face, to stage center, where he soliloquizes to the audience about her. The stage lighting alters too: her face ("eyes ... hair ... teeth ... cheeks") has just been illuminated; but now that part of the stage goes dark, and the light shifts to him, ablaze with thought about her.

The "sixty queens" and "eighty concubines" are called up before you in a phalanx of magnificence to contrast with the singularity of "the dove ... the only one," who is still more magnificent: she is the lover's "perfect one." Magnificent and numerous though the queens and concubines are, their function is only to praise her and in doing so to show how much she exceeds them. The number of queens—"sixty"—is the same as the number of "strong men" surrounding "Solomon's bed" in 3:7, and the number has a certain resonance elsewhere in scripture as good and auspicious.[140] The "queens" and "concubines" are not mentioned anywhere

---

140. Isaac is sixty when Jacob and Esau are born (Gen. 25:26); there are sixty captured cities in Bashan (Deut. 3:4; Josh. 13:30; 1 Kgs. 4:13); Solomon's Temple is sixty cubits long (2 Chr. 3:3); the Second Temple is sixty cubits in height and width (Ezra 6:3). But against these, Nebuchadnezzar makes a golden statue sixty cubits high (Dan. 3:1). There is, so far as I can see, no similar scriptural resonance for the number "eighty." Theodoret of Cyrus, *Explanatio in canticum canticorum* on 6:8 (Hill 2001: 98–99; *Patrologia Graecae* 81.172–73), gives an elaborate numerological analysis to explain "sixty" and "eighty," explaining the former as a multiple of the six days of the creation account in Genesis, and therefore as referring to the souls who have been made perfect in virtue—by analogy to the formation of the world as good. And "eighty" is explained as denoting those souls who obey the law only out of fear of the Lord's anger, not (like the "sixty") out of love of his goodness. Cf. also Rupert of Deutz, *Commentaria in Canticum Canticorum* (Commentary on the Song) on Song 6:8 (Deutz and Deutz 2005: 502–8), for a substantially similar analysis. Both Theodoret and Rupert are dependent, whether directly or indirectly, on Augustine's analysis of the number six (and hence sixty) in *De civitate dei* 11.30 (Latin at www.augustinus.it/latino/cdd/index.htm; English in Henry Bettenson, trans., *St. Augustine: Concerning the City of God against the Pagans* [London: Penguin, 1984], 465).

else in the Song, while the "young girls" and "daughters" are (see introduction: "Naming the Song's Voices").

The "queens" and the rest are many, while she, the beloved, his "dove" (→1:15), is one: "my perfect one ... the only one / her mother's only one." She is said to be "perfect" only here in the Song. In calling her this, the Song aligns her with Solomon's Temple (1 Kgs. 6:38), Israel's comeliness (Ezek. 16:14), the law (Jas. 1:25), and love (1 John 4:18; cf. Deut. 32:4; Matt. 5:48), all of which are called "perfect" elsewhere in scripture. Her good qualities, unspecified in these verses but with the praise of the particular good qualities of her face echoing still in your ears (Song 6:4–7), are maximal and unique ("only one ... only one"). Her uniqueness is given by election: she has been "set apart" (*electa*) by her "mother ... genetrix," and it is because of this that she is "her mother's only one."

The Song considered by itself is obscure in its several references to the beloved's mother/genetrix (1:6; 3:4, 11; 6:9; 8:1, 2, 5); but when read as a scriptural book, large interpretive vistas open, primarily that Eve is the beloved's mother, and secondarily that the beloved is the daughter of Israel personified (→3:4). The point of interest here is that the beloved has been "set apart" by her mother. The word *electa* is applied to the beloved only in these verses of the Song, first on his lips, and then on those of the daughters, queens, and concubines. She has been chosen, elected, set apart from all others, and in this she is like Jesus at the transfiguration, of whom the same word (in the masculine gender) is used, and like Jerusalem, the city among cities, set apart from all others.[141] In both these cases, the Lord is the one who has done the choosing and setting aside, and that grace note sounds loud and clear in the mind of the scripturally literate hearer of the Song.[142] She too, the Song's beloved, has been chosen by the Lord (with her mother as intermediate agent), and it is because of this that she has the unique character and status attributed to her in these verses of the Song.

When the massed female choir of "daughters," "queens," and "concubines" sees her, in the lover's mind's eye, they at once call her "supremely blessed" (*beatissima*). This word occurs only here in the Song and only once elsewhere in scripture, where it is applied to the good wife, whose "sons rise up and call her supremely blessed, / and her man also praises her" (Prov. 31:28). The nonsuperlative form of the word is more common in scripture, and especially important for the Song is the Marian echo: in Luke's Gospel, Elizabeth calls Mary "blessed" (*beata*), and Mary responds by taking the word to herself: "All generations will call me blessed" (*beatam me dicent omnes generationes*) (Luke 1:45–48). The Song's beloved is assimilated, by way of these echoes, to the perfect wife and mother and to Mary, whom all such wives and mothers figure.

141. The feminine form, *electa*, is used in scripture mostly for inanimate objects (vines, cypresses, cedars, and so on), to indicate that those so labeled are the best of their kind. It is used of Jerusalem in Tob. 13:11. The masculine form is used of Jesus at Luke 9:35 (cf. 1 Pet. 2:4).
142. The scriptural *locus classicus* for a discussion of election and the *electi* is Paul's in Rom. 11.

Second Question: Who Is She? (6:10)

> Who is she who comes out
> like the dawn rising
> beautiful like the moon
> set apart like the sun
> terrible like an ordered rank from the camps?

Although there is no explicit signal, I read these words as one more question spoken by the daughters of Jerusalem. The lover has just been describing the praise given to his "perfect" and "only one" by the "queens" and "concubines," and he now reports the question they ask him about who she is. This is the second of three such identity questions, each spoken by the daughters. The first question was: "What is this ascending through the desert / like a wisp of smoke / spiced with frankincense and myrrh / and all the perfumer's powders?" (→3:6; the third identity question is in →8:5a). Something unformed, wispy, not yet recognizable, comes through the desert toward the watchers; it smells of the spices used to prepare and beautify the ark and the temple and trails with it, therefore, clouds of glory. That question was asked about something given no sex, something in the grammatical neuter ("this"). That first question was immediately followed by the description of Solomon's approaching litter/bed (3:7–11), and as a result hearers are disposed to consider that description the question's answer.

But the Song's question sequence makes that reading seem inadequate, even though not wrong. There is a progression of specificity within the Song, and by the time we reach this second question, it is clear that the one whose identity is being asked about is female ("who is she?") and that she is beautiful, like the "dawn," the "moon," and the "sun." The last line of the question ("terrible like an ordered rank from the camps") repeats verbatim the last line of 6:4, and the repetition brackets the intervening praise-hymn (6:5–9) to the beloved's body. These cues are clear enough: the Song's hearers almost inevitably identify the one whose bodily beauties are praised in 6:5–9 with the one whose identity is asked about in 6:10. And the connection with 3:6 is clear and strong too: the "wisp of smoke," beautifully scented but far away, is now at hand, and she is a woman "like the dawn rising." What the daughters do not know is her name: we, those who benefit from a long tradition of hearing and interpreting the Song, do know that name: it is Mary, and by extension the Lord's Israel-church.

In likening the unnamed woman who approaches to "the dawn rising," the daughters use words that occur only here in the Song.[143] "Sun" and "moon" occur often in scripture, most often as instances of the radiantly impressive beauty of the ordered cosmos that are, in spite of their magnificence, creatures of the Lord

---

143. The "dawn" (*aurora*) is an ambiguous trope in scripture. It can be used positively, as when the just king, in this case David, is likened to it (2 Sam. 23:4). But it can also be used negatively, as when it is used of Babylon's king, called "son of the dawn" and "light-bearer" (*lucifer*) (Isa. 14:12).

and subject to his providence (Ps. 72:5; 121:6; Sir. 43:1–8; Isa. 60:19). She, the beloved, in being likened to them, is being likened to the most beautiful and awe-inspiring among creatures, but shown also to be a creature, subject to the Lord. That the beloved exceeds even the splendor of the heavenly bodies is suggested by the resonances with Rev. 12:1: "A great sign appeared in heaven: a woman crowned with the sun, with the moon under her feet, and with a crown of stars above her head." This verse has been applied to Mary, and especially to her status as *virgo assumpta* and *regina caeli*, by the church since early times, and has been the basis for visual representations of Mary as Queen of Heaven at least since the reforms of the Council of Trent in the seventeenth century. The Song's beloved is, if this interpretive line is followed, not only "beautiful like the moon / set apart like the sun," but also with the moon as her footstool and the sun as her crown.[144]

If the answer to the question "who is she?" has often been "Mary," it has also often been "the church." If Mary is understood to figure the church then the two answers do not stand in contradiction; and it is often the case that premodern commentators on the Song who have little or nothing to say about Mary read as though they are speaking of her when they speak of the church. Here is Giles of Rome (late thirteenth/early fourteenth century):

> *Who is she appearing like the dawn?* For the early church rose through the desert like a column of smoke, because of the persecution of the tyrants. But the church of today *appears like the dawn*; for persecution has ceased and day is approaching, and the church is *beautiful as the moon* through faith. For what we know by faith we see as it were in the light of the moon, because we do not apprehend it clearly. It is *bright as the sun* by reason of hope, according to which it is uplifted to the desire for the heavenly Jerusalem, which by reason of its brightness can be called the sun.[145]

Nut Garden and Chariots (6:11–12)

> I went down into the nut garden
> to see the fruit trees in the valleys
> to look closely at whether the vineyards had flowered
> whether the pomegranates had budded.
> My mind did not notice

144. "A striking example of this process [the adaptation of the Song of Songs for Marian feasts] can be seen in a composite version of the Song of Songs 6:10 [6:9 RSV] and 6:4 [6:3 RSV] which in the Antiphoner of Compiègne appears as an antiphon for the Vespers of the Feast of the Assumption of Mary"; E. Ann Matter, *The Voice of My Beloved: The Song of Songs in Western Medieval Christianity* (Philadelphia: University of Pennsylvania Press, 1990), 153.

145. Giles of Rome, *Super Cantica Canticorum* (On the Song) on Song 6:10 (English in *Giles of Rome: Commentary on the Song of Songs and Other Writings*, ed. John E. Rotelle [Villanova, PA: Augustinian Press, 1998], 142–43).

when it placed me in the four-horse chariots of the prince of my
people.

The daughters' question of 6:10 is not answered: whatever else the words under
discussion here might be, they cannot be seen as an answer to that question. There
is here another of the Song's sharp and jarring shifts, discomfiting to the hearer.
There is no overt indication in these verses of who speaks or to whom: everything is in the first person, meditative and cool: someone reports that (s)he has
gone into a "nut garden" to see whether the signs of spring—flowering vineyards
(→1:6b), budding pomegranates (→4:3b)—are visible. Then someone, presumably the same person (the first-person voice continues, without notice of change),
does not notice that he (if it is he) has been put in one of his prince's "four-horse
chariots." The subject of the verb "place" (*ponere*) in the last line of 6:12 is entirely
unclear: perhaps it is the "mind" of the preceding line; perhaps it is someone or
something else altogether. The translation I give is as literal as I can make it so
that your puzzlement might be as great as mine.[146]

The movement from the preceding verses to these is from a lyric about the
beloved's face and beauty and splendor to one focused upon the coming of
spring, a theme prominent elsewhere (2:11–13; 7:12–14) in the Song. The place
where the lovers are or would like to be is the cultivated garden in the spring,
a place of fertility and beauty. He has earlier (2:10) encouraged her to get up
and accompany him out into that pastoral world, and she will later (7:12) do
the same to him. Here, there is a report on someone's (his?) own wandering
there, and some of the tropes used for this are present elsewhere in the Song,
notably the flowering "vineyards" and the budding "pomegranates," the "valleys"
and "fruit trees." Some of the vocabulary of these verses is found only here in
the Song. This is true, most notably, of "nut garden." The atmosphere is one of
fertility and growth: that atmosphere is the correlate and frame of the couple's
love and desire. The growth of the signs of spring is matched by the growth of
their love and desire. It was in the garden that they made love (5:1), and the
recurrence of pastoral images throughout the Song, usually in close proximity
to the delighted depiction of her body or to an ardent expression of desire,
assimilates their lovemaking and delight to the carefully cultivated growth of
the orchards and vineyards.

The pastoral imagery of 6:11 has some resonance in scripture, much of it already
discussed. "Valleys" in scripture are often, as here, places of fertility and beauty,
contrasted with mountains and deserts (Bar. 5:7; Ezek. 7:16; 31:12). And "fruit
trees" (the word *pomum* can mean both the fruit of the tree and the tree on which

146. Renderings given in English versions made from the Hebrew or the Greek vary quite widely
among themselves, and none is of much help in understanding the Latin of the New Vulgate. For an
eloquent expression of not only the difficulty of 6:12 but its utter impenetrability, see Robert W.
Jenson, *Song of Songs* (Louisville: Westminster John Knox, 2005), 68–69. He goes too far, but I
can see why he does.

it grows)[147] are often mentioned in scripture, with all the predictable connotations of beauty and deliciousness and fertility; they are appropriate offerings to the Lord (Lev. 19:23; 26:20; 27:30). Sometimes, by ordinary scriptural extension, Israel is likened to such fruit: "Like grapes in the desert / I found Israel; / like the firstfruits [*quasi prima poma*] of the fig tree in its prime / I considered your fathers" (Hos. 9:10). And this resonance is helpful for interpreting the Song, for it deepens the identification of the beloved with the Lord's Israel-church: when the lover, the Lord, goes down into his "nut garden" (which is not mentioned anywhere else in scripture) looking for the fruiting signs of spring, he is wandering in his beloved's garden—the garden that she is—and seeking from her the fruits of love (→4:12–5:1). Those fruits, together with the tree that bears them—the double meaning of *pomum* as fruit and fruit tree is helpful here—are together appropriate offerings to the Lord who seeks them.

The difficulties of 6:12 are not, however, much illuminated by placing them into the broader context of scripture. Some of the language and imagery of this verse is found in scripture only here in the Song. This is true of the phrase "my mind did not notice" (the verb *advertere* is unique to this place in the Song). Some small help can be had with "four-horse chariots" (*quadriga*). These conveyances are mentioned often in scripture, sometimes in tandem with another word for "chariot" (*currus*), which also occurs in the Song (1:9). In contexts like this, *quadriga* is used descriptively for a machine of war and symbolically to represent military power (1 Kgs. 10:29; 1 Chr. 18:4 [David has twenty thousand]; Jdt. 7:20; "chariot cities" [*civitates quadrigarum*] in 1 Kgs. 10:26; 2 Chr. 1:14; 8:6; 9:25); the Lord too is sometimes said to have "four-horse chariots" or to be expected to come with them on the day of judgment (Isa. 66:15). *Quadriga* is also used once to describe, by simile, what the ark of the covenant looks like when covered by the cherubim (1 Chr. 28:18; cf. 1 Sam. 6; 2 Sam. 6); the idea is that the cherubim make a canopylike covering over the ark, and in that way make the whole thing seem like a four-horse chariot, which also comes with a canopy to protect its occupants from the sun.[148]

With all this in mind, some further things can be said about Song 6:12. First, it is clear that someone, gender unclear, finds himself or herself in a lordly chariot, and does so unawares. There is also the point, tenuous but not nonexistent, that temple and ark imagery occurs elsewhere in the Song (1:5, 13–14, 17; 3:6–11; 8:2) and that some of it suggests a likening of the beloved's body to both temple and ark (→1:13–14). Suppose, then, we read "the four-horse chariots" as a trope for the ark and the beloved's body; a possible construal—a very loose paraphrase—of the

147. *Pomum* is often indistinguishable in meaning from *fructus* (Song 2:3; 4:13; 5:1; 7:9; 8:11, 12). The forbidden fruit of Gen. 3 is *fructus* rather than *pomum*.

148. This description is among the roots of the development of the baldacchino or pillared altar canopy. See André Lacoque and Paul Ricoeur, *Thinking Biblically: Exegetical and Hermeneutical Studies* (Chicago: University of Chicago Press, 1998), 258–63 (though I do not endorse Lacoque's conclusions).

verse then might be: "While I was unaware / she put me / in the ark of her body."[149] And this would be an obscure but suggestive reference to the incarnation: the Lord enters the body of Mary. This is an instance of the necessary obscurity of scripture, an obscurity that cannot be exhausted and that is among the explanations for the church's inability to exhaust scripture by coming to understand everything it means.

The Sulamite (7:1 [= 6:13 RSV])

> Return—return—O Sulamite
> return—return—so that we might contemplate you.
>
> What will you look at in the Sulamite
> when she dances between two choruses?

Another shift, this time to the imperative: someone, unnamed, calls to someone else, named as the "Sulamite," the woman from Shulam, and asks/demands that she come back "so that we might contemplate you." The speaker could be the lover: the imperative mood suggests this because the other occurrences of address in the imperative (2:11; 5:2) are on his lips, which provides some expectation on the part of the hearer that it is the lover who speaks here too. But the speaker could also be the daughters, the female chorus: the first-person plural "we" might suggest this. You might reasonably think of the speaker(s) of these words and the subjects of the verb "contemplate" as both the lover and the daughters. Both verbs, "return" and "contemplate," occur only here in the Song.

The lover (if it is he) has been in his garden (6:11–12), suspended in the Song's presence-absence dialectic. Now, in another example of the Song's frequent shifts from absence to the desire for presence, he wants her back, wants her in his presence, repeating the demand four times: "return ... return ... return ... return." And he wants her back for a specific purpose, so that he, together with the daughters, might examine her closely, might contemplate her body and its beauties. He has earlier (4:1–6; 6:4–7) praised these particular charms, and is about (7:2–10) to do so again. Here he expresses his urgent desire to see her face again.

The verb the lover uses to implore his beloved to "return" (*convertere*) has both a general and a specifically theological meaning in the canon of scripture. Generally, it means to turn attention from one thing or person to another (2 Chr. 18:33; Neh. 3:36 [= 4:4 RSV]; Matt. 26:52 [Peter asked by Jesus to turn his sword]); this general meaning is derived from and participatory in a more exactly theological meaning, in which the verb is used to denote the Lord's (re)turning—coming

---

149. Ariel Bloch and Chana Bloch give a lovely rendering of the verse (from the Hebrew) along these lines: "And oh! before I was aware / she sat me in the most lavish of chariots"; *The Song of Songs: A New Translation with an Introduction and Commentary* (Berkeley: University of California Press, 1998), 97. They of course do not have incarnational or Marian meanings in mind.

back—to us, something he is often implored to do in the Psalms, and, correspondingly, our (re)turn to the Lord, most often from the worship of idols (Tob. 14:5–6;
Ps. 6:5 [= 6:4 RSV]; 9:18 [= 9:17 RSV]; 21:8 [= 21:7 RSV]; 79:4; Lam. 5:21;
Luke 1:16; Acts 26:20). When the lover implores his beloved to return to him,
therefore, the verb he chooses suggests a return to him as her Lord, something
he desperately wants her to do; it suggests, as well, his return to her, a renewed
focus of his gaze upon her.

The verb "contemplate" (*intuere*) also has deep theological resonance in scripture. Most fundamentally, contemplation, close looking that sees deeply into
the truth of things, is something the Lord does. He does this to David's heart
in instructing Samuel to choose him as king and to the hearts of human beings
generally (1 Sam. 16:7; 2 Macc. 7:35); Jesus does it to the rich young ruler when
he contemplates him with love before asking him to give away everything he owns;
and Jesus also does it to Peter and to the twelve (Mark 6:41; 10:27; John 1:42).
The suggestion is always of a close and loving (which may also be judging) look.
There is a question as to whether we can contemplate the Lord in this way, sometimes answered negatively and sometimes positively (Job 26:14; Num. 24:4; Acts
1:10). And there is also a derived sense of the verb to indicate human beings' close
examination of particular things or people (Lev. 13:32–39; Judg. 13:19; 1 Kgs.
3:21; Prov. 23:31; Isa. 21:7; Matt. 16:6; Luke 22:56 [the serving maid examines
Peter closely]). The lover-Lord calls the beloved back so that he can examine every
inch of her (Song 7:2–10 describes this close physical examination), and in asking
this of her he asks also that she return to him to offer him her unreserved love.

"What will you look at in the Sulamite?" The speaker(s) of these words are
not signaled explicitly, though the context requires, almost beyond question,
that their second-person addressee ("you") be the lover who has just spoken. The
interrogative form of these words suggests that they are spoken by the daughters
of Jerusalem, the female chorus. Almost every rhetorically marked question of
this sort (3:6; 5:9; 6:1, 10; 8:5) is on the lips of the chorus, and what they say is
almost always in interrogative form. But there is another possibility. The words
could be spoken by the beloved to the lover. He has just addressed her (perhaps
along with the daughters) with a plea for her return; if she is speaking to him here,
she responds with a coquettish question, referring to herself in the third person as
"the Sulamite": Why do you want me back? What is it that you want to look at if I
do come back? Either reading is possible, which also means that both are possible.

If it is the beloved who speaks, her question is first about what her lover will
"look at" when she returns. The verb *aspicere* echoes the one (*intuere*) he has just
used in his plea: he has said that he wants to "contemplate" her, to look closely
at her in such a way as to discern the truth of her, body and soul. She throws the
verb back at him: just what does he need to examine closely, to contemplate, to
"look at" in order to arrive at an understanding of what she is? And not only
that: what will he look at "when she dances"? Dancing is mentioned only here in
the Song; elsewhere in scripture the verb (*saltare* and cognates) has two ranges

of meaning. First it is an expression of self-abandoned praise to the Lord, praise that forgets the self and the self's dignity and thrums responsively to the Lord's gifts. It is in this sense that David dances before the Lord (2 Sam. 6; 1 Chr. 15), an abandoned and undignified dance for which Michal, the urbane one, despises him, judging the performance unworthy of a king.[150] Second, and rarely, dancing may be seductive, a means used by a woman to inflame a man's desire for her. It is in this sense that Herodias's unnamed daughter dances before Herod (Matt. 14 || Mark 6). The two ranges of meaning are here combined. "The Sulamite"—if it is she who speaks, she takes the name to herself—will dance before her Lord, her lover, and in so doing will abandon herself to praising him, responding to his presence by the movements of her body, giving herself ecstatically to him. She will also, in so doing, seduce him, engage and inflame his passions, responsively make him want her, as lovers do.

The intertwining of the text's surface with its deeper meanings is here evident and dramatic. The Jewish girl from Shulam, "the Sulamite," dances seductively for her lover in preparation for lovemaking with him; the Lord's Israel-church, his delight, shows her beauty to him as her gift of praise; and Mary, in her act of assent, shows the dance's culmination in the complete reception of the Lord into herself. None of these layers of meaning should be lost: the girl from Shulam does not vanish into the church, and neither is absorbed into Mary. She, Mary, is what they both figure and participate in; their reality and beauty is not diminished but enhanced by that fact. The reality and beauty of your dances, metaphorical and real, for your lover, are also enhanced by seeing, as the Song permits you to do, those dances as participatory in and anticipatory of those you will one day, soon, be giving to the Lord.

The Lord's passion for his beloved should not be forgotten either. He has begged her to return (7:1) and is about to detail, again, the delights of her body (7:2–10). His passion for her is as real as hers for him, and infinitely deeper. The Lord is no simple spectator here: he asks her to return so that he "might contemplate" her. He is as involved with, as desirous of, you as you are of him.

There is an alliterative resonance, in English and Latin (and in Hebrew, for that matter) between the epithet "Sulamite" and the name "Solomon." The two words contain the same three root consonants and require the same movement of the tongue from teeth to palate and the same opening and closing of the lips in simulacrum of a kiss. If it is she who speaks here, in response to him, then their mouths, as they exchange and repeat the epithet, mirror one another's movements. Your mouth, as you speak the words of 7:1 aloud, reforms itself in the shape of the word "Solomon," a word that occurs at the very beginning of the Song (1:1) and then again almost at its end (8:11–12). In speaking of the Sulamite you

150. Compare the references in Ps. 29:6 and 114:4–6 to one or another creature—valleys, mountains—dancing before the Lord. Compare also Eccl. 3:4, in which dancing is the antonym of mourning.

recall Solomon, and in speaking of Solomon you recall the Sulamite: the act of naming required of you by the Song's text signals the participatory intimacy of the Song's couple.[151]

Praising the Beloved's Body #3 (7:2–7 [= 7:1–6 RSV])

> O prince's daughter—
> how beautiful your sandaled feet;
> the curves of your thighs like necklaces
> formed by craftsmen's hands;
> your vulva like a lathe-turned bowl
> never needing to be mixed with wine;
> your belly like a heap of wheat
> fortified by lilies;
> your two breasts like two fawns
> doe-born twins;
> your neck like an ivory tower;
> your eyes like fishpools in Heshbon
> in the gate of Bathrabbim;
> your nose like the tower of Lebanon
> facing Damascus;
> your head like Carmel
> its tresses like purple
> the king captured by your ringlets.
> How beautiful you are
> and how splendid
> O my dearest
> in your pleasures!

He responds to her question about what he will look at when she dances for him by listing, with passion and in detail, exactly what he will look at. He begins by addressing her as "prince's daughter," and then for twenty-two lines (7:2–7) he praises her and her body, addressing her in the second person ("your . . . you") with the occasional interjected epithet ("O my dearest"). He begins with her "sandaled feet," moves up to her "thighs like necklaces," to her "vulva like a lathe-turned bowl," to her "belly like a heap of wheat," her "breasts like two fawns," her "neck like an ivory tower," her "eyes like fishpools," her "nose like the tower of Lebanon," and her "head like Carmel." The direction, from feet to head, is cued, perhaps, by

151. On the meaning of the epithet "Sulamite," see J. Cheryl Exum, *Song of Songs: A Commentary* (Louisville: Westminster John Knox, 2005), 225–28. She writes about the Hebrew version, in which the root consonant resonance embraces not only "Solomon" and "Sulamite," but also *shalom* ("peace"), as in 8:10.

the mention of her dancing in 7:1, which directs attention to the feet: that cue is among the reasons why the lover begins here with her feet and moves up to her head, reversing the direction of his first (4:1–6) praise-hymn to her body. The list that begins in 7:2 and ends in 7:7 is couched in the language of delight rather than desire (although desire is behind it and shines through it); and it is, in form, a list of similes, almost all of which occur elsewhere in the Song.

The hymn of praise to her body begins with her "sandaled feet." Feet are mentioned only here and in →5:3, where the beloved wonders whether she can, or should, get out of bed and walk across the room to let her importunate lover in, thus dirtying her feet. There the beloved's feet were hesitant; here they are eager, not only to walk to him but to dance for him,[152] in response to his invitation. The beloved's "sandaled feet" are characterized as "beautiful" because they are doing what our feet should do when commanded or entreated by the Lord to "return" (7:1): that is, to do what he says, joyfully to approach him. It is remarkable that her feet are "sandaled" (*calceamentum*—a word found only here in the Song), whereas in the earlier (5:3) mention of her feet they were bare. The contrast between shod and unshod feet (the sandal being the ordinary scriptural protection for the foot, almost the only one mentioned there) is a complex one in scripture. On the one hand removing the sandals is a proper gesture of reverence before the Lord: the Lord tells Moses to remove his sandals when he approaches the burning bush because he is walking on holy ground (Exod. 3:5, quoted in Acts 7:33; cf. Isa. 20:2). On the other, the sandaled foot is the one ready to do the Lord's work, to go where the Lord commands (Exod. 12:11 [the people of Israel eat the Passover meal wearing sandals, ready to go]; cf. Deut. 29:4 [= 29:5 RSV] [the sandaled feet of the people wandering in the desert]). That the beloved dances for her lover not barefoot but sandaled can be read therefore to mean that she is sufficiently intimate with the Lord not to need to be unshod in his presence and that she is doing his work, responding to him as he wishes and hopes. You, hearing of her sandals, might ask yourself where yours are. When the Lord wants to "contemplate" (Song 7:1) you, will he find your "sandaled feet" as beautiful as Mary's, as quick to dance as those of the church?

From her feet to her "thighs," their "curves" "like necklaces." The "thigh" (*femur*) is mentioned also in the description of Solomon's bed, where the soldiers guarding it are said to have swords strapped to their thighs (3:8). That is a standard scriptural image for military readiness, and consideration of it does not add much to our understanding of the grammar of the body in the Song. The instance under discussion here is more interesting. It provides another instance of the comparison of the body to things made with human hands. The beloved's "neck" and "nose" are both likened to a tower made with hands (4:4; 7:5); the lover's "hands are lathe-turned gold" (5:14), and his "legs are marble pillars" (5:15); and the beloved's "vulva" is

---

152. See Claudel 1948: 315–16 for a lyrical treatment of the foot and its movement as synecdoche for the person in motion, in this case toward and in response to the Lord.

"like a lathe-turned bowl" (7:3). In the case of her thighs, the likeness to "necklaces" emphasizes the graceful beauty of adornment (→1:10): her thighs have been made as ornaments to her body, attractive both to the eye and to the caressing hand. This series of similes and metaphors of making and craft for the parts of the body should be taken together with the similes and metaphors that liken the body to things not made with hands (animals, plants, and so forth). Those latter predominate, but they do not suffice. It is not enough to say that the body is one among the beauties of nature and the natural world, exceeding those beauties, perhaps, but still of their kind. It must also be said that the body is like the best things made with human hands, exceeding the beauty of those as well. The body, as a whole and in its parts, belongs at once to both spheres, and delighting in it is therefore to delight both in the created order and in the world of human making.

The lover, moving upward from the thighs, speaks next to the beloved's *gremium*. It is not clear how to translate this word. It occurs only here in the Song and elsewhere in scripture only at Gen. 48:12, where Joseph is said to remove his sons from Jacob's *gremium*. In that place, "lap" seems the most natural rendering. The aged Jacob is meeting Joseph's young sons for the first time, and holding them, it seems, on his lap or his knees. But "lap" will not quite do as a rendering of this verse of the Song. Some body part between the thighs (7:2) and belly (7:3) is needed, and one that can appropriately be likened to a "lathe-turned bowl" (*crater tornatilis*), a phrase that also occurs only here. "Vulva"—the external opening of the vagina, the entry to and exit from the womb through which babies come into the world and into which the penis is inserted—seems a better rendering given these constraints, and there is some evidence in non-Christian Latin for this meaning of the word.[153] If this is the correct rendering, then the first meaning of the text is that her "vulva" is, like her thighs, as beautiful as the most beautiful things made with hands ("like a lathe-turned bowl"), and always moistly ready—intoxicatingly so—for sexual intercourse, "never needing to be mixed with wine," which is to say always giving, effortlessly and spontaneously, what is needed for fruitful entry into her. The entry is a double one: as Mary-church she is open to the Lord so that she might become pregnant; and she is open to us, as a fruitful reservoir of intoxication. In entering her in this second sense the primary gift is hers to us. We do not give her children as the Lord did. Rather, we become her children, begotten and raised by her for intimacy with the Lord.[154]

153. See *Oxford Latin Dictionary*, s.v. *gremium*, third meaning—with citations to Virgil, Catullus, Lactantius, and others. In the Vulgate, the word is *umbilicus*; it is interesting that the editors of the New Vulgate chose to change this to *gremium*, since there is no apparent warrant in the Septuagint or the Masoretic Hebrew text for the rendering. One thought may have been that talk of the female navel may serve, scripturally, as polite periphrasis for the vulva, rather as reference to a male's feet may for the penis (Isa. 6:2). Contemporary English versions of Song 7:3 made from Hebrew typically use "navel"—so, for instance, the Revised Standard Version and the New Revised Standard Version.

154. On the "source de vie au milieu de l'Eglise, ce réservoir d'un liquide pur et puissant où nous trouvons le salut et l'apaisement à notre soif," see Claudel 1948: 318–24. He comments on the Vulgate

Her "belly" (→5:4) he says, is "like a heap of wheat / fortified by lilies" (→1:7). These are images of fertility, purity, and delight. From the "belly" the lover grazes upward, verbally and visually, moving to her "breasts," of which he says that they are "like two fawns / doe-born twins." These words occur verbatim at →4:5. He likens her "neck" (→1:10) to "an ivory tower" (→4:4), which is an image that here finds its first occurrence in the Song: "ivory" because smoothly beautiful, and a "tower" because impregnable to foes, accessible to be licked and sucked (7:10) only by him.

He praises her "eyes" again, this time as like "fishpools," full of clear and life-supporting water in which beautiful things can be seen, and mentions two places— "Heshbon" and "Bathrabbim" in which those fishpools might be found. "Bathrabbim" is mentioned only here in the entire canon of scripture; "Heshbon" is also mentioned only here in the Song, but is found elsewhere in scripture (1 Chr. 6:66 [= 6:81 RSV]; Josh. 21:39), where it is said once to have been the capital city of the Amorites, incorporated now into Israel. A symbolic resonance that suggests itself is that of a place once alien, now domesticated and fruitful for the Lord and his people. This adds a new grace note to the meanings of the eyes in →1:15.

Still praising her face, the lover turns now to the beloved's "nose" (*nasus*), which here finds its only mention in the Song. It is, he says, "like the tower of Lebanon / facing Damascus." The tower trope suggests strength and indomitability, especially defensive strength, a meaning intensified by its connection with "Damascus," mentioned only here in the Song. Damascus is, scripturally, a foreign place on the northern edge of the territory of the tribe of Dan; it belongs to the Arameans and is from time to time a military threat to Israel. It is also a place of wealth and luxury. To speak of a Damascus-facing tower (→4:4), then, is to conjure a place of strong defense against the rich and threatening enemy. Locating that tower in "Lebanon" adds to this an accent of beauty: Lebanon is exactly that, a place from which aromatic woods and spices come (→3:7–11). Solomon's litter is made "from Lebanese trees" (3:9), for example.[155] The beloved's nose, then, is strong, straight, beautiful, and not easily overcome by strangers. The tropes suggesting these things belong to the same sphere of meaning as these words, on the lips of the beloved: "I am a rampart / and my breasts are like a tower" (8:10), and to the mentions of the beloved's neck as towerlike.

The beloved's nose appears in the Song as something to admire and perhaps be awed by (because it is so strong) and to gaze at with delight (because it is so beautiful). But it is not depicted in the Song as having to do with smelling and smells, which is its dominant use elsewhere in scripture (where it appears rather

text rather than the New Vulgate, and hence takes the body part in question to be the navel rather than the vulva. But in every other respect my comments here resonate with and are indebted to his.

155. Damascus is a place of riches (2 Kgs. 8:9; Isa. 8:4), of danger for the people of Israel (1 Kgs. 11:24; 2 Kgs. 14:28), of the Arameans (1 Chr. 18:5–6; 2 Chr. 24:23), and on the northern boundary of the territory of Dan (Ezek. 48:1). The road to Damascus is also the place of Paul's vision (Acts 9).

rarely).[156] The word used in 7:5, *nasus*, appears only twice elsewhere in the canon of scripture, and both times in contexts where disfigurement is the topic (Lev. 21:18 [in the list of body parts that, if disfigured, prevent someone from functioning as a priest]; Ezek. 23:25 [in the oracle against Jerusalem the harlot, who will, among other things, be punished for her harlotry by having her nose cut off]). The beloved's *nasus*, by contrast, is as far from being disfigured as it is possible to get. Much more common in scripture is the (plural) word *nares*, best rendered "nostrils." These almost always are connected with the sense of smell, or with the breath: the smoke of the sacrifices rises to them (Deut. 33:10), or the Lord blows the breath of life into them (Gen. 2:7). But this is not the sphere of discourse to which the Song's single mention of the beloved's nose belongs.

The lover concludes his third hymn to the beloved's body with a mention of her "head" and "hair" (→4:1b), the former "like Carmel," and the latter with "ringlets" sufficiently beautiful to have "captured" the king. Carmel is a holy and beautiful place, the place of Elijah and Elisha: to liken her head to it is to give it these properties, as well as to suggest that her lover might like to find refuge in it, as did the prophets on Carmel. To say that her "tresses" are "like purple" (→3:10) is to give them a royal color, to make them royally attractive.

The simile catalog for the beloved's body parts ends at 7:6, and in the concluding verse of his third hymn of praise to her body, the lover sums up with an ecstatic expostulation: "How beautiful you are / and how splendid," again drawing upon vocabulary already much used in the Song (→1:10; →1:15; →1:16). But then he adds a new word, "pleasures" (*deliciae*), which occurs only here in the Song: he delights in her pleasure at giving him pleasure, a recursive and intensifying cycle of delight familiar to all lovers: the delight of each is intensified by knowing that the other is likewise delighting, and this is another aspect of the gift of love: just as the principal gift a lover gives to the beloved is to make her a beloved and thus capable of being a lover, so the gift of being delighted in is among the necessary conditions for taking delight in the one delighting in you. The lover's pleasure in her "pleasures" signals this.

Elsewhere in scripture, "pleasures" are both negative and positive. They are negative when depicted as delights separated from the Lord, delights that one can attempt to live by as though they are self-sufficient and can by themselves bring satisfaction. "Those who live in pleasures," in this negative sense, "are dead" (1 Tim. 5:6; cf. Sir. 31; Rev. 18:3–9 [the pleasures of Babylon]). But "pleasures" are splendidly and infinitely positive when it is understood that the Lord is the first and last giver of pleasure. Consider the following passage:

> I was then with him as a craftsman,
> constantly delicious [*delectatio*] to him,
> at play before him always throughout the world,
> taking pleasure [*deliciae*] in the sons of men.

156. Scents and smelling are important in the Song: in →1:3a the lover's loves are "fragrant with [his] best ointments," and →1:12–13 mentions the scent of the beloved's spikenard and myrrh.

> And now, sons, listen to me:
> those who guard my ways are blessed.
> Attend to my discipline and be wise:
> do not neglect it.
> The man who attends to me
> and who is daily vigilant at my gates
> and observant at my doors—
> he is blessed.
> The one who finds me finds life,
> and gains pleasures [*delicias*] from the Lord.
>
> —Prov. 8:30–35
> (cf. Isa. 11:3; Job 22:26; 36:11; Ezek. 28:13)

The speaker here is Wisdom (*sapientia*). She was, she says, with the Lord at the beginning as one who makes, an *artifex* or "craftsman," and was delicious to the Lord. The deliciousness the Lord took and takes in her is mirrored by the pleasures she takes in us, a pleasure-taking we are meant to reciprocate. The cycle of delight initially connects the Lord to his Wisdom, which is to say the first to the second person of the Trinity. It is a deliciousness internal to the divine economy: the Lord, being internally self-related, is delicious to himself. But that is only the first movement in the cycle of delectability: Wisdom takes her ("her" because she is grammatically feminine) pleasures in us, in each of us severally and in all of us collectively; and we, to the extent that we attend to the delight that Wisdom— and, hence, the Lord—takes in us, and are responsive to it, find pleasure in and from the Lord. When, therefore, the Song's lover-Lord says to his beloved, "How beautiful you are / and how splendid / O my dearest / in your pleasures," he is noting and delighting in her pleasure in him, reminding us of his pleasure in each of us and encouraging you, especially, the hearer of the Song, to remember and seek again the delight of being loved by the Lord.

Seizing Her (7:8–10a [= 7:7–9a RSV])

> Your height like a palm tree's
> your breasts its clusters.
> I said—I will ascend the palm tree
> and seize its fruit
> and your breasts will be like clusters on the vine
> and the scent of your mouth like apples.
> Your throat is like the best wine—

Following the apostrophe of 7:7 to the beloved's pleasures, the lover expatiates upon her "height," which is likened to that of a "palm tree," and her "breasts" to the fruit "clusters" on that tree. He is impelled, he says, to climb that tree and to "seize its fruit," by which he means both her breasts and her lips, caressing the former "like clusters on the vine," shifting the image from the fruit of a palm tree to that of grapes on a vine, and kissing the latter ("the scent of your mouth like apples"). The language shifts here from delight to desire: he has been admiring her and communicating his desire to her, but now he wants to embrace her, to extend his appreciation of her from the visual to the tactile and the olfactory. The texture of her breasts and lips and the scent of her breath call him now, and he concludes with a mention of her "throat," which is "like the best wine."

The tropes of these verses are scattered broadside through the Song. Her "breasts" (→1:13), "mouth" (→1:2), and "throat" (→2:3b) have all been praised before; and the mixed language of palm trees and vines is also everywhere in the Song (→1:6b; →5:11; cf. "cluster" in →1:14 and "apple" in →2:3a and →8:5b). His delight in her "scent," here of her "mouth," echoes his pleasure in the scent of her spikenard (1:12), of her ointments (4:10), and of her clothes (4:11). She is delightful to all his senses, and what he says to her here about her "throat"—that it is "like the best wine"—brings in the gustatory: he wants to taste her as well as to look at her and smell her and touch her. But 7:10 breaks off suddenly.

Sipping and Ruminating (7:10b [= 7:9b RSV])

> worthy to be sipped by my delightful man
> ruminated by his lips and teeth.

The speaker shifts at this point, suddenly, as is indicated by mention of the addressee: "my delightful man." She is now talking, responding to his desire talk with some of her own. He has just said that her "throat is like the best wine"; she responds by saying that she wants it to be "sipped" by him and "ruminated by his lips and teeth." She wants not just to be drunk by him but to be consumed: to be ingested, that is, in every possible way. The verbs "sip" (*potare*) and "ruminate" (*ruminare*) occur only here in the Song, and they are direct and uncompromising in their physicality. The image is one of good wine being taken into the mouth and then held there and swirled around so that all its flavors are savored and delighted in. That is what the beloved wants the lover to do with her throat and, by extension, with herself. Elsewhere in scripture, the verb *ruminare* is used only to denote what cud-chewing animals do in repeatedly masticating their food before swallowing and digesting (Lev. 11:3–7; Deut. 14:6–8). This might suggest that "chew" would be a better translation; here, however, because the image has to do with wine, a translation that focuses upon keeping the liquid in the mouth is preferable, and "ruminate" effectively does that.

The Lord's Israel-church here declares her worthiness to be savored and ingested by the Lord. This is a strong claim, and one easy to misread as a declaration of intrinsic merit, a demand that the Lord should savor her because of what she, independently and of herself, is like. Rather, her claim to worthiness is responsive. She has just been addressed by the Lord, offered her status as beloved as gift, and it is in response to that offer that she calls herself, or rather her throat, "worthy." The dynamic of love, whether human or divine, is always responsive in this way. No one, not you and not me and not the church, is a beloved or has a beloved's beauty and desirability until loved. Once loved, once the status of beloved has been given and received (it can always be refused), everything else follows: then you can say, "I am beautiful, worth savoring," but only then. The Lord's Israel-church is beautiful because she is beloved and aware of her beauty and desirability in response to the gift of love. Mary too, whose savor gives the Lord special delight, is to be understood as aware of her delightfulness in this way. She receives the greatest gift of the Lord's love, which is the Lord himself in her body, exactly as unexpected and unanticipated gift. Having become the beloved, she can then say that she is "worthy to be sipped" by the Lord, and in a sense not open to anyone else, the sense given by his physically drinking from her, sucking her breasts.

He for Her, She for Him #3 (7:11 [= 7:10 RSV])

> I am for my delightful man
> and his appetite is for me.

Following immediately upon her eager encouragement of her man to consume her, to drink and ruminate her, she uses a refrain that occurs, with small variations, twice elsewhere (→2:16; 6:3) in the Song. The keynote here is confidence in ineradicable intimacy: her, the beloved's, purpose (end, goal) is intimacy with the lover, just as his is for intimacy with her. They want one another, exclusively, finally, and without remainder, and she is confident that this indissoluble intimacy will be the actual outcome as well as the desired one. The refrain as it occurs here contains the word "appetite" (*appetitus*), which is found only here in the Song. The word makes sense in this context: the verses immediately preceding have been his words of desire for her, and to say that the lover's "appetite" is for her is consonant with this context. "Appetite" elsewhere in scripture is ambiguous. Its object can be good (1 Tim. 3:1 [the office of bishop]; Heb. 11:16 [heaven, a better homeland]); but it is also connected with mastery or domination, in the sense that what you have an appetite for has power over you and typically will, or easily may, master you. In Genesis, when the Lord curses Eve after the fall, he promises her that her appetite will be for her husband, and that her husband will (therefore) have mastery over her (Gen. 3:16); and when the Lord speaks to Cain after his offering has been refused, but before Cain murders Abel, he says, "Sin lies in wait outside for you: its appetite [*appetites*] is for you, but you should master it" (Gen. 4:7; cf. 1 Tim. 6:10 [on money and appetite]). Resonating with these passages, the Song here suggests that the lover's appetite for his beloved gives her, or may give her, mastery over him. It is her he wants, her in particular he chooses, and this provides her power. She may reject him, turn her lips from his, refuse to permit her throat to be licked, sucked, and savored like wine. This dynamic connection of appetite and mastery gains special force when it is recalled that the lover is the Lord and his beloved his Israel-church. To be Lord is, in Latin, to be *Dominus*, to have *dominatio*; but to be a Lord who loves and has chosen, who has appetite for the beloved, is to relinquish some portion of that *dominatio*, to give it over to the beloved by becoming her lover.

The dialectic of love and desire among humans is in considerable part a play of submission and dominance. It is not (usually) that the roles are distributed in such a way that one partner is consistently dominant and the other submissive. Neither is it that the male part is to dominate and the female to submit: that you, whether you are male or female, can come to see yourself in the position of the beloved in this verse, noting your lover's "appetite" for you, shows that. It is rather that submitting yourself sometimes to an act of dominance and sometimes performing one—all within the economy of the gift—is a constitutive part of the rhythm of love, both physical and emotional. This is as true of male lovers as of female beloveds. But the play of dominance and submission can occur only in a context of love's certainty, wherein the beloved knows that she is for her delightful man, and he, without doubt or hesitation or exception, is for her. Then love can act. Here is an especially direct instance of the depth of transformative possibility to be found in reading the Song as if it were about you and your loves—of the Lord, certainly, but also of your human lover.

Into the Country (7:12–13 [= 7:11–12 RSV])

> Come, my delightful man—
> let us go out into the meadow
> let us linger in the villages
> let us hasten early to the vines
> to see whether they have flowered
> whether the flowers have opened
> whether the pomegranates have flowered—
> there I will give you my loves.

Here the beloved shifts from the declarative ("I am"; 7:11) to the imperative: she now urges him, her "delightful man," outside, into the delights of the spring-gravid cultivated world. Her words are laden with the pastoral imagery that echoes through the Song (→2:10–13a and →6:11–12; vineyards and vines in →1:6b; pomegranates in →4:3b and →4:13; and fruit trees in →6:11). She wants him to accompany her to "the meadow," the vineyards, "the villages," and there to look for the flowering signs of spring. They must do this with urgency, "early," first thing in the morning, an echo of the frequent repetition in the Song of the imperative "get up!" (→2:10; →2:13b; →3:2; →4:16; →5:5). The world in which she wants them to wander is that of the rural garden (→4:12–16), not that of the city (→3:1–4; →5:6–7) or the wilderness (→2:14). What she promises him there is her "loves" (*amores*), which means her acts of love, her kisses and caresses and intercourse (→1:2; →5:1). The garden is the Song's paradigmatic place for love-making, rivaled in that only by the beloved's mother's house (→3:4) and bedroom (→8:1–2). There she will "give" him what she has "saved" (7:14) for him: herself, fully and completely.

Most of the vocabulary and imagery of these verses occurs elsewhere in the Song: the "pomegranates," especially, occur frequently (4:3, 13; 6:7, 11; 8:2), and they are figures for beauty and fertility—think of the juice that runs down your chin as you eat one—as well as for a beautiful thing that can serve as a decoration for the temple, the Lord's dwelling. When she encourages him out, to look at the flowering pomegranates, she is directing his gaze to the promise of beauty and sensual delight. She is also assimilating that place to herself: its beauty and fertility become a figure for hers, and so the imagery of flowering vines and pomegranates is heard by the attentive reader as a trope for herself, as Israel-church and as Mary-church: the fertile vineyard that she earlier (1:6) acknowledged she had failed to care for is now assimilated to herself, and this transformation is given sense by her being, by now, the Lord's lover. Her juices—and yours and mine—will run down her lover's chin as he bites into her.[157]

Mandrakes (7:14 [= 7:13 RSV])

> The mandrakes give off their scent—
> all the best of the fruit trees in our gates
> new and old
> I have saved for you, O my delightful man.

The pastoral world in which the lovers move is, she tells him, saturated with the scent of "mandrakes." *Mandragorae* are mentioned only here in the Song, and outside the Song in scripture only in a narrative episode about Jacob and Leah and Rachel (Gen. 30:14–18). Jacob is married to both women, daughters of Laban. Reuben, one of Leah's sons by Jacob, gathers mandrakes in the fields one day and brings them to his mother. Rachel asks Leah if she may have some of the mandrakes he has gathered; Leah, voicing her envy of Rachel as the favored wife, refuses. Rachel offers Leah Jacob's sexual services for that night in exchange for the mandrakes, and when the bargain is kept and Jacob has sex with Leah, she conceives

---

157. Claudel 1948: 420–26 provides a lovely discussion of the assimilation of the grape and the pomegranate to the Lord's lovers, whether in the person of the church, of Mary, or of himself, as participatory lover.

and bears her fifth son to Jacob, Issachar by name. This story is in large part about fertility. The *mandragorae* play a symbolic part in it: Rachel's bargain with Leah makes them represent the capacity to become pregnant and bear a child, and that is part of the resonance they bear in this part of the Song, as well. For the scripturally attuned hearer of the Song, this is the only overtone audible in the mention of "mandrakes": when the beloved mentions them in the context of urging him to the garden's delights—their mention is immediately preceded by her promise, "there I will give you my loves"—these verses of the Song are further saturated with the anticipation of lovemaking and conception. She will, she promises, be fruitful for him. The thought that "mandrakes" are eaten by those who would like to conceive is often referred to by premodern commentators on the Song[158] and buttressed by appeal to the humanlike shape of the root: to eat such a thing is to encourage a human to take root and grow. Applied to the Lord's Israel-church and to Mary, its figure and essence, several meanings suggest themselves: Mary offers her fertile body to the Lord as a proper vehicle for himself; Israel-church, disporting herself with the Lord in a mandrake-saturated garden, permits herself to be impregnated by the Lord with gifts for the world—gifts of word and action and sign; and you, breathing in the mandrake scent with the Lord at hand, swell with the breath of his spirit and bloom with the blossom of his word.

Her Mother's House #2 (8:1–2)

> Who can give you to me as my brother
> sucking my mother's breasts
> so that I might find you outside and kiss you
> and no one would despise me?
> I will seize you and lead you into my mother's house—
> there you will teach me
> and I will give you a cup of flavored wine
> with the pressed juice of my pomegranates.

Following the beloved's promise and offer of herself, body and soul, to her lover in the immediately preceding verses—the two have been exchanging the compliments of desire in 7:7–14, and she has urged him out into the pastoral paradise of fertility where she has said she will make love to him—there is a halt and a change, an expression of frustrated desire. She wants to be free to kiss her lover outside, in public, without shame, so that "no one would despise" her. She imagines that she could do this if, counterfactually, her lover were her brother, someone who had, together with her, sucked their "mother's breasts." Then, their public kisses would be those of siblings, and without erotic meaning. But the question of this verse

158. For example, in Rupert of Deutz, *Commentaria in Canticum Canticorum* (Commentary on the Song) on Song 7:14 (Deutz and Deutz 2005: 560–62).

("who can give you?") expects a negative answer: no one can; the lover is not her brother; her love for him is scandalous; and if she does kiss him "outside," where "the mandrakes give off their scent" (7:14), then she will be despised.

But still she imagines, speaking perhaps in soliloquy or directly to him, that she might "seize" him (using *apprehendere*, a verb of coercion; also at 7:9; cf. *trahere* in 1:4) and take him into her mother's house, where they might make love. He will "teach" her there, and she will respond by giving him "a cup of flavored wine" with "the pressed juice of [her] pomegranates." The sexual imagery is quite direct: he will instruct her in lovemaking, and she will respond juicily, offering him her wet sweetness.

Much of the imagery here is frequent in the Song: the work opens (1:2) with a request for a kiss, a desire repeated here; the beloved's mother and her house and bedroom are mentioned elsewhere, as a place of safety where lovemaking might occur (→3:4; 6:9; 8:5); and tropes connected with "wine" (→1:2–4) and "pomegranates" (→4:3b; cf. →4:13) are frequent. The "pomegranates" are especially important here: they represent juicy fertility, clearly, but also, because of their use as temple decorations, a response to the presence of the Lord. In offering him, the lover-Lord, the juice of her pomegranates she acknowledges him exactly as the Lord.

But some of the vocabulary in these verses is new: they contain the only mentions of "flavored wine" and of "pressed juice." The participle "flavored" (*conditum*) occurs a few times elsewhere in scripture, always in a positive sense: the incense for use in the Tent of Meeting (Exod. 30:35) is to be *sale conditum* ("seasoned or flavored with salt"); graceful speech ought always to be so flavored (Col. 4:6); and it is a mark of honor to embalm a dead body in such a way that it is seasoned with aromatic spices (Gen. 50:26). To call the wine she offers him "flavored," therefore, is to say that it is delicious and, by way of resonance with the temple's incense, also holy, set apart, consecrated. What she offers is something close to, intimate with, the Lord. "Pressed juice" (*mustum*) is also, when it occurs in scripture, generally a good and delightful thing. It most often means unfermented wine or grape juice (Job 32:19; Isa. 65:8); but it may also by extension mean the juice of any fruit—in this case, of pomegranates.

If the beloved's mother figures Eve, the mother of all the living and the mother in a special way of both Israel and Mary, who in responding (sometimes) rightly to the Lord's caress recapitulate and reverse their mother's rejection of that caress, then that the beloved's lovemaking with her lover is planned to take place in Eve's house takes on particular significance, as also does the Lord "teaching" her there as she responds with the gift of herself. What does he teach her? Exactly so to respond. How does she receive the teaching? Exactly by so responding. The caress is offered and the "pressed juice" of the "pomegranates" flows responsively.

But there remains a barrier. All that these verses say is in subjunctive mood ("who can?") and future tense ("you will"). Here below, the perfect act of intercourse with the Lord, as well as the final reversal of Eve's work, is a matter of hope and anticipation, not of realization. Just as your lovemakings with your lover are never quite what they might be, never the untrammeled, violence-free gift exchange they ought to be, so is the intercourse of the Song's beloved with her lover. She wants him; she wants to give herself to him and thereby himself to him as her lover; but she is not in her mother's house and in the pastoral paradise she cannot kiss him. Even the kisses offered to the Lord by his Israel-church are preliminary and anticipatory in this sense: they foreshadow the embraces to come, but they are not yet what those embraces will be.

Fourth Adjuration (8:3–4)

> His left hand is under my head
> his right embraces me.
>
> O daughters of Jerusalem—I adjure you
> not to enliven or awaken this delightful woman
> until she wishes.

In another sudden and jarring shift, she describes again the posture of lovemaking in a formula found verbatim elsewhere in the Song (→2:6), where it also occurs in a description, remembered or anticipated, of lovemaking. There the refrain concludes a scene in the lover's wine cellars; here it comes at the end of one in the beloved's mother's house. The adjuration formula ("I adjure you") here is the third near-verbatim occurrence of words spoken to the daughters of Jerusalem by the lover (the others are at 2:7 and 3:5; cf. 5:8–9). Here, as in the earlier occurrences, the connection between the adjuration—he asks the daughters not to awaken the beloved until she wishes—and what precedes and follows it is unclear. You are jarred by it. She has just (8:1–3) been imagining making love to him in her mother's house, promising him her body in its sweetness and fertility; and now he asks the daughters not to awaken her. As with the earlier occurrences of this formula, there is a suggestion that she is asleep and that the words the beloved has just spoken (7:10–8:3) might belong to dream or reverie. This instance of the adjuration formula is also, like the earlier ones, a structural marker (→2:7). One lyric—the pastoral idyll with its fertile promises—has come to an end, and another is about to open (→6:10).

Third Question: Who Is This Woman? (8:5a)

> Who is this woman ascending from the desert
> leaning on her delightful man?

A question follows the adjuration, as it has once before (3:6). There, the question was about something neither masculine nor feminine ("what is this ascending through the desert?") and was at once followed by the hymn of praise to Solomon's bed, which was presented as coming toward the daughters through the desert. In the second case (6:10), the question was about someone feminine ("who is she who comes out?"). Here too the question is about something explicitly feminine (*ista*), which means, again, the beloved.[159] In 3:6 she was indistinct, "a wisp of smoke"; in 6:10 she was clearer, and you, the Song's hearer, were faced with her as radiantly beautiful "like the dawn"; here, at last, the emphasis is on the relation she bears to her lover, her "delightful man" upon whom she leans, coming up "from the desert." There is no indication of the speaker here, and the Song's hearers are unlikely to worry very much about this. With the earlier identity questions echoing in mind (→3:6; →6:10), you are likely to assume that the question is yours as much as the daughters' or the lover's.

The desert theme of 3:6 is recapitulated here. She is coming up "from the desert" with the Lord, her lover; the motif of ascent calls to mind the wanderings of the people of Israel toward, eventually, Zion; the beloved's ascent, already with the Lord, is toward a place he has prepared for her, a place of greater intimacy than the barren purities of the desert permit. That place is the marriage bed, the place for intercourse; it is also the place for the intimate caresses that the Lord exchanges with his Israel-church in worship; and, finally, it is the New Jerusalem, a place of final intimacy in which the Lord's beloved will see his face and know his body fully.

The question asked here, "who is this woman?" is about to be given an obscure and shadowy answer in the Song itself. A clearer answer is known to the church: she is Mary, the one among women who leans most intimately on the Lord.

Birth under the Tree (8:5b)

> Under an apple tree I enlivened you
> there your mother gave you birth
> there your genetrix gave you birth.

Someone speaks in the first person, directly addressing someone in the second. The gender and identity of neither is marked, but the mention of the addressee's "mother" and "genetrix" in the second and third lines makes the identification of the addressee as the beloved very likely. Every other mention of the "mother" and "genetrix" together in the Song (3:4; 6:9) has made it clear that they are the beloved's; and so the clear surface reading is that here the lover addresses the beloved. The connection with the immediately preceding question asked by the daughters of Jerusalem ("who is she?") remains, however, quite unclear. He

---

159. For a fascinating analysis of medieval Jewish treatments of this verse as being about the soul of a martyred Jew ascending into heaven, see Michael Fishbane, *The Kiss of God: Spiritual and Mystical Death in Judaism* (Seattle: University of Washington Press, 1994), chap. 2.

addresses her, not them; and what he says is, on the surface, not at all an answer to their question.

There is, however, a suggestive verbal echo. The verb "enliven" (*suscitare*) occurs thrice elsewhere in the Song (→2:7; 3:5; 8:4), and on each occurrence it is in the adjuration formula spoken by him to the daughters, the last of which has come just a few lines earlier than the words under discussion here. The lover commanded the daughters there not "to enliven or awaken this delightful woman / until she wishes" and in so commanding them implied that he was reserving the action of "enlivening" to himself. It is for him, then, to bring her into being, to awaken her, to give her life, to excite her sexually—for all these connotations are present in the scriptural uses of the verb. He is her lover and her Lord, and he has chosen her, his Israel-church with his virgin, Mary, at its center, for his own, as his exclusive partner.

In 2:3 the beloved likens her lover to "an apple among forest trees" in response to his likening of her to "a lily among thorns"; and a few lines later she demands of him that he "fill [her] with apples" (2:5). These echoes, internal to the Song, provide one dimension of depth to his mention of the apple tree here: he has "enlivened" her in his own shade, the shade he himself provides and that she has earlier (2:3) mentioned with delight.[160] There is another depth to these words, indicated by the mention in them of the beloved's "mother"/"genetrix" (→3:4) and by her connection with another tree. The beloved, as Israel-church and Mary-church, has been birthed by Eve, the mother of all the living, in order that Eve's work under the shade of a tree might be recapitulated and reversed. Eve's fault was to reject the Lord's embraces in favor of a self-possession that moves toward death; Mary's perfection is to accept those embraces in such a way as to permit herself to be "enlivened" by them. Eve's pregnancies and births after her eating of the fruit are painful and bloody: she produces murderers and victims; Mary's pregnancy and birth after she has been "enlivened" produce Jesus, the Lord himself.

The nineteen (English) words under discussion here are enigmatic; any comment on them will therefore be speculative,[161] and they invite infinitely more commentary.

Delight and Death (8:6–7)

> Place me like a seal on your heart
> like a seal on your arm
> because delight is as strong as death

160. For the connection between the apple trees of 2:3 and 8:5, see Theodoret of Cyrus, *Explanatio in canticum canticorum* on 8:5 (Hill 2001: 114–15; *Patrologia Graecae* 81.203; compare Hill 2001: 55–56; *Patrologia Graecae* 81.88). Theodoret interprets the father as Jesus, and the mother/genetrix in 8:5 as the Holy Spirit: the latter gives birth to the church.

161. I play here with Paul's words in 1 Cor. 13:12: *Videmus enim nunc per speculum in aenigmate.*

and zealous desire as hard as hell
whose lights are lights of fire and divine flames.
Many waters have not been able to extinguish loving-kindness
neither have floods been able to overwhelm it
if someone should give all the substance of his house for delight
they would despise him as if he were nothing.

She, the beloved, responds to the enigmas just discussed. So you are likely to think, even though there is no surface sign of the gender or the identity of the speaker of these verses. He has just told her of his exclusive love for her, and now she asks to be placed "like a seal" on his "heart" and his "arm," and this because "delight is as strong as death" and "zealous desire as hard as hell." About this hell we are told further that it has fiery "lights" (*lampades*—also "torches"), lit by "divine flames." The imagery then shifts from the fiery to the watery. Just as "delight" and "zealous desire" cannot be overcome by fire, so also "loving-kindness" cannot be extinguished or overwhelmed by "waters" and "floods." "Delight" (*dilectio*) provides the through-line in these verses: it is "strong as death," and that is why someone might "give all the substance of his house" for it. If he were to do so, some unnamed ones—the inhabitants of the world who think little of love and, therefore, less of the Lord—would "despise" him.

Most of the vocabulary of these verses is found only here in the Song. This is true of "arm," "death," "strong," "hell," "zealous desire," "lights," "fire," "divine," "flames," "extinguish," "overwhelm," "floods," "substance," and "nothing." This contributes to the hearer's sense that a rhetoric and stance not previously audible in the Song is in play here. These are no longer words of delight or desire; neither do they express the agony of separation or the passion for reunion. Instead, a different interlocutor is in mind: the skeptical worldling who thinks that *dilectio* and *amores* and all that go with them are transient and will dissolve with death. Why then, on such a view, follow them with such passion? It is in response to a view of this sort, belonging to those who "despise" abandonment to delight, that she (if it is her) asks to be sealed upon his arm and his heart. The elect, John writes, are marked with the seal of the living Lord (Rev. 7:1–9); and Paul writes of the Corinthians as the "seal," the ineradicable identifying mark, of his status as an apostle (1 Cor. 9:2; cf. Ezek. 28:12; Hag. 2:23; Rom. 4:11).[162] Those seals are ineradicable, metaphorically visible marks of a relationship that cannot be dissolved. That is what the beloved asks for when she asks to be sealed on her lover's arm and heart: she wishes to be marked as his own forever by being written upon the flesh of his body.

"Delight" here goes with "zealous desire" (*aemulatio*): they are sides of the same coin, and together they overcome death and hell. *Aemulatio* is a difficult

---

162. In →4:12 the beloved is spoken of as a "sealed spring," there with an overlapping but significantly different sense of the word.

word to translate into English. If you are an *aemulator*—one who has or performs *aemulatio*—you may be one who zealously or eagerly desires something, one who will brook no rivals for what is desired, one who is envious of some other who has what is desired, one who jealously does what is necessary to continue to possess what is desired, and one who eagerly imitates others who have what is desired. The Lord is often said in scripture to be an *aemulator* or to have *aemulatio*, and most often when his Israel-church is rebellious (Exod. 34:14; Deut. 4:24; 5:9; 6:15; Josh. 24:19; Nah. 1:2). Some English versions of this way of talking about the Lord call him "jealous." One human being's rivalry for another may be labeled by the same word; and our own zealous desire for the Lord or for the good may also be so called.[163] Here, because of its pairing with "delight," "zealous desire" seems the best rendering. The two go together because taking delight in a beloved is intimate with zealously desiring to maintain that connection with her (or him); and it is often, in human cases, a very short step from such delight to the twin horrors of envy and jealousy.

The principal point of the Song here is to emphasize that not even "death" and "hell" can overcome or bring to an end the Lord's delight in his Israel-church. "Hell" (*infernus*), paired here with "death," is common in scripture as a descriptor of the place where dead people go. It is not always depicted as a place of punishment or fire; but it is consistently represented as a place to which one would rather not go, a place in which the praise of the Lord is difficult or impossible and in which the ordinary pleasures of life are absent (Num. 16:30–33; Ps. 16:10 [quoted at Acts 2:27–31]; 18:6 [= 18:5 RSV]; Prov. 15:24; 27:20; Luke 16:23). Hell's depiction as a place of "divine flames" and "lights of fire" is not paralleled elsewhere in scripture.[164]

If hell's "divine flames" cannot overcome "delight" and "zealous desire," then, equally, "waters" and "floods" are incapable of overcoming "loving-kindness" (*caritas*). The word appears to be used here as a gloss on "delight," and it is, for the scripturally attuned Christian hearer of the Song, a close-to-explicit signal that the "delight" being discussed here is that taken in his beloveds by the Lord. In its only other occurrence in the Song, the beloved is led by her lover into his wine cellar, where, she says, "loving-kindness was his banner above me" (→2:4). The banner in question is the Lord's, and those gathered under it are his beloved Israel-church. This banner and what it represents cannot be overcome by floods of chaos water any more than they can by burning fire. Augustine comments:

163. 1 Pet. 3:13 exhorts us to be *boni aemulatores*; Peninah is Hannah's *aemula* in 1 Sam. 1:6; Paul tells the Corinthians that he has *aemulatio* for them like that of the Lord (2 Cor. 11:2); and Luke describes Paul as having *aemulatio* for the law (Acts 21:20; 22:3).

164. *Flammae* are frequent in scripture, and the closest resonance with these verses of the Song is to be found in the apocalyptic literature (Dan. 3:88 [= Song of the Three Children 66 RSV]; 7:9; 2 Thess. 1:8 [= 1:7 RSV]). But the flames are not elsewhere qualified as *divinae*.

"Delight is as strong as death." When death comes it is impossible to resist, no matter what arts and medicines are used. No mortal can avoid death's violence. In the same way, the world can do nothing against the violence of loving-kindness. "Death" is here used as a contrastive comparison: just as it is supremely violent [*violentissima*] in carrying us off, so loving-kindness is supremely violent [*violentissima*] in bringing us to salvation. By means of loving-kindness, many have died to the world so that they might live to the Lord; by this loving-kindness the martyrs were set aflame.[165]

Augustine is characteristically rhetorically excessive, but beautifully so: as "death" is the world's final and irresistible power, its characteristic violence, so is *caritas* for the Lord's Israel-church. Those bound by delight in the Lord are irresistibly carried off by it toward love's final embrace, which is the Lord's kiss; those bound to the world's embrace are death lovers, carried off irresistibly toward the embrace of an absence, a lack. Necrophilia and the love of the Lord are the two end points on this gamut.[166]

The last line of 8:7 is among the most theologically suggestive in the whole of the Song, and it is multilayered: "If someone should give all the substance of his house for delight / they would despise him as if he were nothing." The first meaning is clear enough: the skeptical world would despise such a man, but would be wrong to do so. If the gift of "delight" and "loving-kindness" really is what the Song claims it to be—that is, stronger than death or hell, incapable of being overcome by the water of chaos—then of course someone who gave up all his "substance," his worldly goods and possessions, for it would be doing the only good thing and would be worthy of praise for doing it.

But there is a deeper reading prompted by the verbal echo in Luke's parable of the two sons. There, the younger son asks his father for his share of the family estate (*substantia*, the same word as in the Song) due him; he consumes it all *vivendo luxuriose*, by extravagant and luxurious living (15:13); and he descends to living with the pigs. He has, it seems, done exactly what the Song appears to commend: he has given "all the substance of his house for delight." But it was not for delight or loving-kindness; it was, rather, for a simulacrum of those things. When the younger son realizes his error he returns to his father and asks for forgiveness, whereupon he has his inheritance—"the substance of his house"—returned to him. This is a good gloss on Song 8:7: not only would the world "despise" someone who consumed his substance for delight and loving-kindness; in doing that, the world would show that it cannot see the impossibility of doing this. The gift of substance, of all that we are and may be, is prevenient and inexhaustible, and seeking the delight of loving-kindness can do nothing other than assure its continued

165. Author's translation from Augustine, *Enarrationes in Psalmos* (Explanations of the Psalms) 121.12 (Latin at www.augustinus.it/latino/esposizioni_salmi/index2.htm; compare Maria Boulding, trans., *Expositions of the Psalms*, Works of St. Augustine: A Translation for the Twenty-First Century [Hyde Park, NY: New City Press, 2000–2004], 3.20.27).

166. See David Bentley Hart, "Christ and Nothing," *First Things* 136 (2003): 47–57.

gift to us, pressed down, shaken together, and running over. Substance capable of being consumed is no substance; and delight capable of consuming it is no real delight; the Song's attentive hearers have their understanding of that fundamental matter developed and nuanced when they hear the Song in the resonant echo chamber of scripture.[167]

The final rhetorical elegance of the Song here is its use of *nihil*: "They would despise him as if he were nothing." Indeed they would: he would so seem to them, and on their assumptions, they would be right to do so because once your substance has been consumed, devoured, eaten up, you are indeed nothing, for your substance is what makes you what you are. But here too the thought of the cultured despisers is a distorted, reverse image of the truth. To become as nothing before love's delights is the only way to become something: it is to respond to the Lord's gift by accepting it, to his kiss by kissing him back, and to his caress by returning it. There is no other substance than that given and taken in love's economy.

The Little Sister (8:8–10)

> Our sister is little
> and without breasts—
> what shall we do for our sister
> on the day she is spoken for?
> If she is a rampart
> we should build silver battlements upon it;
> if she is a door
> we should buttress it with planks of cedar.
> I am a rampart
> and my breasts are like a tower;
> and so I have become before him
> like one who arrives at peace.

Who speaks these words, and to whom? Again, there is no surface indication. There is a mention of "our sister"; but the only echo of this elsewhere in the Song is in the cluster of bridal and nuptial imagery in 4:9–5:2, where the lover frequently addresses his beloved as his "sister-bride." Given this cue, perhaps the lover speaks in the first-person plural (8:8–9) and the beloved responds in the first-person singular (8:10). Another interpretation, equally possible, is to attribute the first-person plural speech to the daughters of Jerusalem, on the twin ground that only they have spoken in the first-person plural elsewhere in the Song and that the Song's other questions (3:6; 5:9; 6:1, 10; 7:1; 8:5) belong mostly to them.

167. On the theme of love and death in the Song, see David Ford, *Christian Wisdom: Desiring God and Learning in Love*, Cambridge Studies in Christian Doctrine (Cambridge: Cambridge University Press, 2007), 380–91.

On that interpretation, 8:8 is spoken by the daughters, 8:9 by the lover, and 8:10 by the beloved. On both interpretations, the beloved's voice speaks in 8:10, and she is the one spoken about in 8:8–9; the difference between the two lies only in who speaks the two opening verses. The two possible positions on that matter are, so far as I can see, equally likely, which is the same as to say that the text, on its surface, provides no reason to choose one over the other. You, the Song's hearer, should embrace this indecision, this puzzlement, as the Song's gift. Obscurity is as much a feature of scripture as clarity, and it is to be welcomed as a stimulus to repeated reading and to the multiplication of interpretations.

The semantics of these verses are clearer than the question of their speaker. Someone, "our sister," is sexually immature, unready for marriage and sex: she is "little / and without breasts." "The day she is spoken for" is the day when she is asked for and given in marriage; what, the unnamed speaker(s) ask(s), should be done when that day comes? At that point, the tropes, drawn from the world of combat and siege ("rampart," "battlements," "tower"), indicate the strength and fortified beauty of the sister-beloved. These same tropes are used elsewhere in the Song for her neck, which is "like an ivory tower" (7:5) and "like David's tower" (→4:4) and, in the case of "rampart" (→5:7), for the walls around the city that are under the care of the watchmen who beat her. The sister's strength and magnificence are, the speaker(s) say(s), to be made at once stronger and more beautiful with "silver battlements" and "planks of cedar,"[168] and her beauty in that way made simultaneously more forbidding, more defensible, and more attractive. The beloved has already been described as "terrible like an ordered rank from the camps" (6:4, 10); the imagery in 8:9–10 is in the same register.

The voice of the beloved then breaks in and takes the images of fortification and terrible beauty to herself ("I am a rampart"). In doing so, she denies that she is "without breasts": her "breasts," she says, "are like a tower," gorgeous and well developed. She is ready for lovemaking, that is, and has as a result "become before him / like one who arrives at peace." These words too are enigmatic. I have rendered them literally, and the verb *reperire* ("arrive at") and noun *pax* ("peace") occur only here in the Song, and not elsewhere in scripture in this combination. She declares her readiness to be loved, sexually and otherwise by "him," the lover-Lord, and in so declaring finds "peace," the place, we might say, of her fulfillment. In accepting the metaphors of forbidding inaccessibility, the beloved does not emphasize her sexual unavailability to her lover; rather, she shows that she is exclusively his, unavailable to all but him, fortified against and protected from all but him.[169] She is his "only one" (6:9), his dove, hidden and

---

168. Recall "our cedar-beamed house" in 1:17: "cedar" there and here as an image of something beautiful to look at and to smell, as well as something strong and enduring.

169. On the theme of exclusivity in these verses, I have profited from Ariel Bloch and Chana Bloch, *The Song of Songs: A New Translation with an Introduction and Commentary* (Berkeley: University of California Press, 1998), 215–18, even though they expound a version of the Hebrew text that differs in several particulars from the Latin I work with here.

inaccessible to all but him "in the chinks of the rock / in the precipitous cave" (2:14). In being hidden from the world, protected from the world, her availability to him alone is emphasized.

Suppose we take the first interpretation of the speaker in 8:8–9, seeing him as the lover. Then, the words about her sexual immaturity ("without breasts"), together with the question about what to do when she is spoken for, serve as preface to his assertion that he will decorate and ornament her for himself by making her more inaccessible to others: that is what the cedrine planks and silver battlements are for. Her response in 8:10 is one of acceptance. If, however, it is the daughters who speak, then it is they who plan to prepare their sister for lovemaking by means of the same ornamentation and protection. The upshot is in both cases the same: she, the beloved, finds peace as one who is exclusively and without remainder for him, fortified against the world so that she can be his alone. Reading 8:8–9 as spoken by the lover allows, however, a more elegant figural reading than does reading those verses as spoken by the daughters. Suppose, then, we consider the Lord, the lover, as the one who acknowledges the beloved's unreadiness and then fortifies and ornaments her so that she can declare her readiness.

Then it becomes easy to see that the Song's beloved's fortification in the service of exclusive love of the Lord figures and finds its fulfillment in Mary's. Mary, like the Song's beloved in these verses, was virginal, fortified against the world of sex and men precisely as a virgin (Luke 1:34). She too found her peace in assenting to the Lord's claim upon her. And it is in Mary's ornamented fortification and exclusive love that the love of the Lord's Israel-church for him also finds its most perfect fulfillment. The figure of the Song's beloved's "silver battlements" and door buttressed "with planks of cedar" is translucent to Mary as *mater ecclesiae*. The Lord's beloveds, Mary and Israel-church, are, when considered by themselves, independent of the Lord's election and caress, "without breasts," unready to return his love. Only when he ornaments them and fortifies them can they say, as they have said and continue to say, "My breasts are like a tower / and so I have become before him / like one who arrives at peace." You too can say this, and in saying it can find your impulse to fortify your human beloved, whoever he or she may be, against the world so that he or she can be exclusively for you deepened and vivified by contemplating what the Lord has done for you in the figure of what he does for the Song's beloved.

Solomon's Vineyard (8:11–12)

> Solomon had a vineyard
> in Baalhamon;
> he handed it over to guards.
> A man brings for its fruit
> one thousand pieces of silver.

> My vineyard is before me—
> one thousand for you—O Solomon—
> and two hundred for those who guard its fruit.

Someone speaks about "Solomon," thinking about his "vineyard" "in Baalhamon," a place-name that occurs nowhere else either in the Song or in scripture. That vineyard is large, requiring guards and, apparently, subcontractors: someone pays "one thousand pieces of silver" for what it yields. The speaker, now in the first person, contrasts Solomon's vineyard with "my vineyard," and the words that follow can be construed in at least two different ways. According to one, the person meditating on his or her own vineyard contrasts its size with Solomon's: whereas the yield of Solomon's is worth "one thousand," the yield of this smaller one is worth only "two hundred." On the other reading, the one meditating upon these two vineyards is himself a payer of rent to Solomon and employs guards for his (or her) own vineyard. There is no explicit indication as to who is speaking or to whom. This is one of the deeply puzzling segments of the Song, almost as much so as 6:12 and 8:13. But there are some suggestive verbal resonances with places elsewhere in the Song.

The cluster of vineyard talk here finds an echo in the almost equally enigmatic 1:6: "My mother's sons were angry with me / they placed me as guard of the vineyards / but I did not guard mine." One phrase, *vinea mea* ("my vineyard" = "mine"), occurs verbatim in both verses; and it is worth noting that the words of 8:11–12 occur almost as close to the end of the Song as the words of 1:6 did to the beginning, another small piece of evidence in favor of an approximately chiastic view of the Song's structure. The common thread here is the idea that the beloved has a vineyard, and this provides some help with the interpretation of the words under discussion. It suggests at least that the first-person speaker in 8:12 is the beloved and that whereas at the beginning of the Song she lamented that she had not cared well for her vineyard, here at its end she is reclaiming it, acknowledging it as her own, even though in some complex relation of dependence upon Solomon's vineyard (→1:6b).

Another link with 1:6 is the verb "guard" (*custodire*) and the related noun "guard" (*custos*), both of which occur in 8:11–12 and in 1:6. The noun occurs also in 5:7: "The guards found me, / those who walk around the city / those who care for the ramparts." In that setting (compare the "watchmen" of 3:3), the "guards" are threatening and violent, those who control the barren world of the city in which she wanders in desolation, separated from her lover. One of the deep interpretive puzzles belonging to this part of the Song, and to a lesser extent also to its early verses, is its bringing together of pastoral and urban imagery ("vineyard" and "guards"). Attending only to the text of the Song, it is difficult to do more than say that a lament given at the beginning, about the beloved's failure to guard what was hers, is here in some fashion resolved—though in just what fashion remains enigmatic.

One scriptural text outside the Song provides some help: the parable of the wicked tenants, in which a landowner plants a vineyard and leaves it in the care of tenants when he travels. When he sends his servants, and eventually his son, to ask them for its fruits, they refuse to give them, beating and wounding the servants and killing the son (Matt. 21:33–41 || Mark 12:1–12 || Luke 20:9–19; cf. Isa. 5:1–7, the *locus classicus* for the Lord and his vineyard-Israel). There are verbal resonances with these verses of the Song: the "vineyard" and its "fruit"; there is also an echo of what the "guards" do to the beloved when she wanders around the city ("they ... wounded me"; Song 5:7), which is just what they do to the landowner's servants. The story of the wicked tenants, on the lips of the Lord himself, is about what can happen when a vineyard's true owner is not properly acknowledged. The same themes are present, if obscurely, in Song 8:11–12. Where the tenants do not acknowledge that the vineyard is the Lord's, the beloved, who failed to do so in 1:6, here acknowledges Solomon (a figure for the Lord) as the vineyard's rightful owner. What was wrong is set right: Mary offers the Lord's Israel-church and herself to him.

The Woman in the Garden (8:13–14)

> The woman who inhabits the gardens—
> lovers are listening—
> make me hear your voice.
> Escape, O my delightful man—
> be like the does
> and like the fawns among the harts
> upon the spice mountains.

The Song's concluding words are almost incapable of paraphrase or summary. A "woman" (rendering the feminine pronoun *quae*) dwells in "the gardens": it is, presumably, the beloved. That she both lives in and is a garden is by now a familiar theme. Then "lovers are listening" (*amici auscultant*): presumably, they listen to her, the beloved in the garden ("overhear" would be an equally possible translation). And then, in the imperative ("make me hear"), someone in the first person demands that (s)he be made to hear what the lovers listen for or to: that is, again presumably, the woman who inhabits the gardens. Perhaps it is the lover who speaks: he wants to hear her voice, responding to his. But perhaps instead—or as well—the Song speaks now for and as you, its hearer: it is you who needs to ask—to demand—to hear the voice of the beloved, the Lord's beloved Israel-church who has Mary at her heart. The closest echoes within the Song (and they are not very close) are found in the Song's crux (5:1), which contains the only other occurrence of "lovers" (*amici* plural), there addressed to the pair as, or just after, they make love in the garden. That verse is at the center of a complex of garden terms, also echoed here in 8:13 (→4:9–5:1).

There is a relative dearth of hearing and listening words in the Song. The "voice" (his) is mentioned (→2:8), but the act of attending to what is said by it is not separated out for treatment. In the Song, the lips and mouth are for kissing and eating, not for speaking; and the ears are one part of the body never mentioned. This makes the occurrence of two verbs of listening or hearing at the end of the Song all the more striking. The Song can be heard here as commending attention to its own words: those words are about a beloved in a garden. "Lovers"—you and me and all of us—are now encouraged to listen to what is said of her. It is not unusual for scriptural texts to show awareness of themselves as texts;[170] this is a peculiarly subtle instance.

The Song's very last sentence is a little clearer. He, the "delightful man" who is the Lord, is addressed for the last time, and presumably by her, since every instance of such address is most easily read as coming from her lips. He is urged to "escape," a term found only here in the Song, and to behave like deer (→2:7) upon "the spice mountains." This resonates with her injunction to him to "turn back" and "be like a doe or fawn among harts / on Bether's mountains" (2:17) and his declared intention to "go to the mountain of myrrh / and to the hill of frankincense" (→4:6). "The spice mountains" are places of high, rarefied, and intense beauty where the Lord disports himself and encourages others to approach him for love. In Song 4 the lover's mention of them came at the end of one of his hymns of praise to her body; and it was clear in that context that he meant to indicate her body with the phrases about "the mountain of myrrh" and "the hill of frankincense." The same is true here. When she orders him to "escape," she is ordering him to leave others and come to her, to enjoy her body. That body, the body of Mary and of the Lord's Israel-church, precisely is "the spice mountains": he, the Lord, will take his pleasure there because that body is the one he has chosen and "set apart" (*electa*) (6:9) for himself. It is the body in which he himself, in the person of the Son, takes flesh.

---

170. Luke-Acts does so at the beginning of each of the books that constitute that corpus, and the Gospel of John does so close to its end (20:30).

BIBLIOGRAPHY

Frequently cited works are listed here. Other works are documented in the footnotes.

Chrétien, Jean-Louis. 2005. *Symbolique du corps: La tradition chrétienne du Cantique des Cantiques*. Paris: Presses Universitaires de France.

Claudel, Paul. 1948. *Le Cantique des Cantiques*. Paris: Gallimard.

Deutz, Helmut, and Ilse Deutz, ed. and trans. 2005. *Rupert von Deutz: Commentaria in Canticum Canticorum*. 2 vols. Fontes Christiani 70/1–2. Turnhout: Brepols.

Hill, Robert C., trans. 2001. *Theodoret of Cyrus: Commentary on the Song of Songs*. Early Christian Studies 2. Brisbane: Centre for Early Christian Studies.

Kingsmill, Edmée. 2009. *The Song of Songs and the Eros of God: A Study in Biblical Intertextuality*. Oxford: Oxford University Press.

Lawson, R. P., trans. 1956. *Origen: The Song of Songs Commentary and Homilies*. Ancient Christian Writers 26. New York: Newman.

Tanner, Norman P., ed. 1990. *Decrees of the Ecumenical Councils*. London: Sheed & Ward.

SUBJECT INDEX

Aaron, 88
Abraham, and Sara, 105
absence, 73, 123–24,
  131–32. *See also*
  presence-absence
  dialectic
Adam and Eve, eyes
  of, 45
adjuration formula,
  58–63, 82, 91, 126,
  159, 161
adultery, 74
aemulatio, 162–63
agility, 62, 65
Alan of Lille, xli
allegorical reading, lvii,
  23, 32, 40, 86
  removes eroticism,
  xxxviii–xxxix
aloe, 113–14
Amana, 106–7
Anna, 5
anointing, 11–13, 36
anthological meaning,
  of title, 3–4
anticipation, 24
appetite, 154–55
apple tree, 50, 79, 161
approach and
  withdrawal, 92
ark of the covenant, 38,
  87–88, 99
arm, 162–63

arousal, 90
ascent, 83–84
Augustine, xxviin11,
  xxxixn27, 66, 77,
  111n21, 116n126,
  132, 163–64
authorial intention, 11
authority, critical and
  juridical, xxx
autographs, xxiii–xxix
awakening, 59

Baalhamon, 168
Babylon, 77, 84
banner, 53–54
baptism, 16, 37, 103
Barak, 2
Bathrabbim, 150
Bathsheba, 6, 89
beauty, 28, 43, 47, 62–
  63, 111, 113, 156
bed, 47–49, 75, 85–86
belly, 120–23, 129, 150
beloved, xxxvi, xliv, 9,
  29, 136
Bether's mountains, 73
Bezalel, 11–12
black, 17–20, 22
black Madonna, 23
blessed, 139
blessings, 79
Bloch, Ariel, 144n149
Bloch, Chana, 144n149

body, 330–32
  christological-ecclesial
    understanding of, 32
  desire for, 41
  ensoulment of, 40
body-hymn, 91, 127,
  147–51
breasts, 33, 39–42,
  62, 100–101, 150,
  152–53, 165–66
bride, 91, 104
brothers, 20

Cain, 154
calling, 66
canticum, 3
Canticum Canticorum,
  xxv
caress, 10, 16, 43
Carmel, 95–96, 151
Catholic Church, xxx,
  xxviii
  on Eucharist, 32
cave, 70
cedar, 48, 130, 166, 167
cellars, 16
certainty, of election,
  73–74
chaos, 163
chariots, 143
cheeks, 32–33, 34,
  98–99, 128–29, 137
chewing, 97

chink, 69
chrism, 37
Christian doctrine, lv
Church, xxxviii,
  xxxix–xl. *See also*
  Israel-church
  as body of Christ,
    16, 32
  as bride of Christ, 16
  election of, 35
  intimacy with the
    Lord, 16
  as Israel, 23n25
  and Mary, xl–xlii,
    22–23
  as mixed body, 19
cinnamon, 113–14
circumincession, 243
city, 75–76, 77
classics, xxxviii
clothes, 45, 109, 114,
  128, 153
Columba, 44
comeliness, 35, 69, 127,
  130
concubines, 138–39
confection, Song of
  Songs as, xxiii,
  xxvi–xxvii, xxxi
confession, song as, 3, 5
confirmation, 16, 37
consummation, 17, 113
contemplation, 145

SCRIPTURE INDEX